Tolley's
Managing Email
and Internet Use

Second Edition

by
Lynda A C Macdonald MA FCIPD LCM

Routledge
Taylor & Francis Group

LONDON AND NEW YORK

First published by LexisNexis

First published 2001

This edition published 2011 by Routledge
2 Park Square, Milton Park, Abingdon, Oxon OX14 4RN
711 Third Avenue, New York, NY 10017, USA

Routledge is an imprint of the Taylor & Francis Group, an informa busitness

© Taylor & Francis Ltd 2004

A CIP Catalogue record for this book is available from the British Library.

ISBN - 978 0 7545 2443 4

Typeset in Great Britain by Columns Design Ltd, Reading

Note About the Author

Lynda A C Macdonald is a self-employed, freelance employment law advisor, management trainer, and writer. For fifteen years, prior to setting up her own consultancy business, she gained substantial practical experience of employee relations, recruitment and selection, dismissal procedures, employment law and other aspects of human resource management through working in industry. With this solid background in human resource management, she successfully established, and currently runs, her own business in employment law and management training/consultancy. She is also appointed as a panel member of the Employment Tribunal service in Aberdeen, where she lives.

Lynda is a university graduate in language and a Fellow of the Chartered Institute of Personnel and Development. Additionally, she has an LLM degree in employment law.

Contents

Contents

Table of Cases

Table of Statutes

Table of Statutory Instruments

1 Uses and Abuses of Communication Systems in the Workplace

Introduction [1.1]

Employees in today's workplaces have the facility to communicate quickly and easily with colleagues and outsiders as a result of the advent of modern communications systems such as email and the internet. Although such modern means of communication have brought many benefits, they have also created new problems for employers. Apart from the potential legal liability that employees' use of email and the internet may create for employers (see **CHAPTER 2**), there may be a rightful concern about the amount of time employees spend surfing the net, playing computer games, or sending emails to their friends.

Although email, when it was first introduced, was a revolutionary method of communication that vastly increased the opportunities for companies to advertise their products or services, keep in touch with clients and customers, conduct research and inform their employees about a wide range of company-related activities and policies, there are many types of communication for which it is not suitable.

Use of the internet has of course given employees in many organisations almost unlimited access to information on unlimited subject matter. Businesses have gained substantial advantages through the use of web-based communications, such as the opportunity to win new customers, set up closer ties with business partners, keep in touch with employees who are mobile and gain access to a vast source of information. All this has brought many benefits, but along with these, a multitude of problems.

Business Email and Internet Use – What is Beneficial for the Business [1.2]

The advent of email and internet access has brought immense benefits to businesses and the employees who work for them. The most obvious of these benefits are described below:

Cost Savings [1.3]

Communication by email is a cost-effective way of sending and receiving information. Because messages and attached documents can be sent to any number of people at the same time, this eliminates the need to print out and send individual packages with the associated postage and packing costs. Messages sent by email to another country can thus save substantial postage costs. In most cases, sending an email costs less than a local telephone call.

There is also a potential cost saving if email messages are retained in electronic format only rather than being printed out in order to form a hard-copy file. This has further advantages for the environmentally-conscious organisation in terms of reducing the amount of paper consumed by the business.

For marketing purposes, advertising a product or service on a website is considerably less expensive than producing a glossy brochure and distributing it to large numbers of potential customers.

Speed [1.4]

Information and documentation can be sent across the world within seconds, whilst a package sent by post or by courier can take many hours (or days) to reach its destination. Even a long fax can take up to an hour to print out at the recipient's office location.

Preparing an email is also quicker than writing a letter in that no time is needed to print the document out – the document is sent following the simple click of a mouse.

Time and place [1.5]

Long and short documents can be sent by email over long and short distances quickly and easily. Time differences between different countries become irrelevant as the email message can be sent during the sender's working day irrespective of time zones and then read by the recipient during their own office hours. Businesses can reach their customers all over the world, increasing trade links and expanding markets whereas budgets may not extend to world-wide marketing by any other means. Internet access too can be achieved 24 hours a day from any location with a computer and a modem.

Convenience [1.6]

Employees can choose when to access their incoming emails and it is open to them to organise their work so that they deal with incoming messages at set times each day, rather than being subjected to continual interruptions by telephone. Email messages can also be accessed remotely, allowing employees opportunities to communicate with their colleagues irrespective of whether they are working in the office, at home or travelling away from home on company business. Similarly, internet access can be made from any computer with a modem, including portable laptop computers, irrespective of the person's physical location.

Permanent record [1.7]

An email message can, if necessary, be printed out to form a permanent record, and even if it is held only on the computer's hard-disk, this provides a more credible and usable record that someone's vague recollection of a telephone conversation.

Research [1.8]

The internet provides unlimited opportunities for companies to conduct research into the business activities of their potential customers and suppliers, to analyse what the competition is doing and to accumulate information on an infinitely wide range of subjects relevant to the business. Much of the information available on the internet is free, or else accessible on payment of a modest fee.

Abuse of Email and the Internet – Problem Areas [1.9]

Despite the irrefutable advantages and benefits to businesses of email and internet access, there are many problems and disadvantages associated with the granting of access to these means of communication to employees. Sending an email has often been compared to sending a postcard – the message is not confidential and may be intercepted or read by someone other than the intended recipient. One of the other major problem areas is potential time wasting and the consequent loss of productivity. These, together with other problem areas, are analysed below:

Time wasting [1.10]

The internet can be likened to an endless library containing unlimited information on every imaginable topic, providing an indispensable source of knowledge to employees in every sector of business. Although this can greatly enhance employees' effectiveness, it can also, because of the sheer volume of available information, be very damaging to productivity. Locating information relevant to a specific query can be a very time-consuming exercise. Surfing the net in particular can involve a lengthy process of entering words and phrases in the search facility which may then produce literally thousands of possible results. Even once these potential web-sites are scanned through and a suitable selection made, the next level of search may still not produce anything useful or relevant.

Loss of productive time [1.11]

The distractions of the internet are many, and there is a growing problem for employers of loss of productive time due to employees surfing the net for both legitimate business purposes and personal entertainment purposes. It can be argued that providing internet access is akin to placing a television on an employee's desk, such is the likely level of distraction. In the case of *Franxhi v Focus Management Consultants Ltd [1998] Case No 2101862/98*, for example, there was evidence that an employee had visited 150 web-sites during working hours whilst trying to book a holiday. The employee's dismissal was fair because she had received previous warnings and knew that this type of conduct was considered unacceptable to her employer.

One survey conducted in 1999 (by Infosec, Netpartners and Secure Computing Magazine) estimated that 76% of workers were using company time to search the internet for a new job. The results of the survey (which covered 200 international companies) also suggested that in a company of 1,000 employees, there was likely to be a loss of some £2.5 million a year as a direct result of employees using the internet for non-business purposes. The same survey reported that 50 per cent of workers were using the internet to visit 'adult sites'. In another survey, conducted the same year by Integralis Network Systems, a company specialising in network security, it was estimated that up to two hours a day were being wasted by employees who used email or surfed the internet for personal purposes. This was estimated to be costing a business with 1,000 employees about £3.9 million. There are thus major practical and cost implications for employers in terms of loss of productive working time.

Downloading material can also be a time-consuming activity, occupying valuable computer access time and running up large telephone bills in the process. Employers should rightfully be concerned about the amount of time employees spend using the internet, and should introduce policies governing such use in order to avoid excessive time-wasting.

Employee distractions [1.12]

Email, because of its speed and convenience, has presented employees in all types of organisations with tempting opportunities to send and receive personal and private messages indiscriminately. The world-wide web is crowded with lists of jokes being distributed widely from person to person and from company to company. The total amount of lost working time has been estimated variously as anything from half an hour a day per person up to three hours a day per employee on average.

Computer access can also tempt bored employees into wasting time playing games on screen. Unless the employer has a policy in place governing employees' use of computer facilities and setting out the parameters, these and other time-wasting activities could cost businesses a great deal of money in terms of lost productivity.

Other problem areas

Availability of inappropriate material [1.13]

There is no public body with control over the quality of material that is posted on the internet and there is thus no guarantee that information accessed on a particular site is accurate, reliable, complete or up-to-date. Although the speed with which information can be updated makes the distribution of information via the internet an attractive prospect, it is not uncommon for sites to be abandoned by their creator, thus leaving out-of-date or incorrect information open to anyone who chances upon the site. Employers should be aware of this and take steps to advise their employees to scrutinise all accessed information with a critical mind. Relying on information obtained from unknown and unregulated sources could obviously lead to poor business practices.

It is well known that the internet provides an easy source of pornographic material. Because there are virtually no restrictions on what can be placed on the world-wide web, the transmission of adult and child pornography is widespread.

Individual attitudes [1.14]

Although email communication tends to be treated with the same degree of informality as a telephone conversation, it produces a permanent record of any dialogue. Even after an employee has deleted a message from their computer files, it can usually be retrieved because of the way in which computer systems are backed up. An email may also be replicated on several different servers, and its various elements, for example the time and date when it was sent and the subject header, may be retained and pieced together at a later date.

An employer who does not impose minimum standards of professionalism on their employees in terms of how they use email risks damaging their business reputation in the eyes of the outside world. Emails that are sent quickly and without proper thought or care often contain errors of language, spelling or grammar and are frequently constructed without any regard to sentence structure. Additionally, many people have developed the habit of writing emails in a style that is more casual or flippant than the style they would use in a business letter. The result can be that messages become unclear, distorted or ambiguous leading to misinterpretation in terms of content or the conveyance of the wrong tone or attitude. As with all forms of communication, it is not only the clarity of the message that is important, but also the perceived professionalism and reputation of the sender and, by extension, the organisation for which they work.

Because of the speed with which it is feasible to reply to an incoming email, it is too easy for an over-worked or over-stressed employee to react in the heat of the moment to an incoming message by sending an inflammatory or vitriolic reply. Before the advent of email as a means of communication, the author of such an emotional reaction would have had enough time between printing out the letter and waiting for it to be uplifted from the out-tray to review its wording and create a toned-down and more rational re-draft.

It is advisable for all these reasons for employers to impose minimum standards of professionalism and a set of guidelines for email communication for all employees. Sample policy documents and clauses governing email use are contained in **CHAPTER 8**.

Information overload [1.15]

Because of the ease and speed with which email messages can be communicated to large numbers of people, many employees send messages without proper thought, and copy their messages to all and sundry 'just in case' the information may prove useful, or to 'cover their backs'. These practices can lead to severe information overload, which in turn can cause workplace stress for those who are regularly faced with an in-box containing dozens of incoming messages. The Institute of Management recently carried out a study of over 800 managers in Britain, from which it was reported that increasing volumes of email were causing an overload problem for many managers, resulting in stress. The study, titled '*Taking the Strain*', reported that keeping up with email correspondence was one of the top ten major workplace stresses.

The result of this type of overload and stress can be that the messages are not read at all, or are not dealt with promptly. Vital information may be overlooked in favour of volumes of trivia. Employees should be discouraged from forwarding messages to long circulation lists. Apart from information overload, such practices can seriously clog up the employer's communications network.

A recent trend has been for companies to designate Fridays as email-free days in an attempt to combat the overuse of internal email and the widespread stress this can cause. The aim is to reduce the amount of information that moves about from employee to employee, and encourage employees to meet face-to-face and talk about work issues instead of using email to communicate all the time. Arguably the objective behind such an incentive is commendable, although it is questionable whether just banning emails on one day of the week will achieve the desired outcome of encouraging employees to reduce the volume of emails they send to each other and use other more appropriate methods of communication instead.

Another method of reducing an overload of email communication would be to place a limit on the number of people to whom email messages can be sent. This could be coupled with a facility whereby an employee who believed it necessary to send a particular email to more than a defined number of people to obtain authority to do so from either their line manager or the organisation's IT manager.

System overload [1.16]

If employees are given unfettered access to email and the internet, and frequently use these facilities to transmit large files, the system could quickly become overloaded.

Security and loss of data [1.17]

It is surprisingly easy to send an email to the wrong address, or accidentally copy it to another party, and even if a message arrives only at its intended destination, there is no guarantee, unless the employer introduces measures to control the distribution of email messages, that the recipient will not forward the message on to others both within and outside the organisation in random fashion. Employers' policies should state whether there are any restrictions on the number of people to whom an email can be sent.

Unlike a telephone call, if an email link fails, the sender is not always aware that the message has not reached its destination. Assumptions should not, therefore, be made by users of email that once a message is sent, the issue to which it relates has been satisfactorily dealt with.

Damage to working relationships [1.18]

The availability of email as a means of convenient communication appeals to those whose verbal communication skills, or willingness to engage in face-to-face discussions, are lacking. It can, unfortunately be used as a means of avoiding face-to-face communication or avoiding addressing conflict, whilst at the same time giving the false impression that the person hiding behind their computer is a 'good communicator' because they disseminate lots of information to others.

The practice of sending an email to the person at the next desk or an adjacent office should be discouraged, unless there is a tangible and sensible reason for doing so. Similarly, managers should not use email as the main means of communicating with their staff as this method of communication, used in isolation, will not allow ideas, problems and other issues which may be important for both the business and for the employees to be properly identified, addressed and resolved.

Working relationships can be problematic enough for many individuals without the added detriment of reduced face-to-face communication. Furthermore, if there are differences of opinion, or a degree of conflict between individuals at work, these are unlikely to be capable of resolution through email communication. Realistically the only way to resolve difficulties of this nature is through open two-way face-to-face communication in which each party is willing to express their views clearly and listen fairly to the views of the other party. Curt, poorly thought out or carelessly written email messages are quite capable of creating animosity where none previously existed, and are highly likely to exacerbate any existing discord.

In summary, email should not be regarded as a replacement for other forms of communication between colleagues, but instead should be used only where it is the most appropriate method of communication for the message in question. Ultimately there is no substitute for two-way face-to-face communication between colleagues.

Company Intranets [1.19]

A company intranet is an internal system of computer communication, similar to the internet in its operation, but separate from the public telecommunications system and thus available only for employees to access through workplace computers and possibly laptops provided to employees who work remotely. Intranets are inexpensive and easy to use and can provide an excellent means for an organisation to keep its employees informed about a wide range of issues.

An intranet may, for example, be used to communicate:

- Up-to-date information about the company's products and services.

- Information about the company's customers, new contracts won and sales successes.

- Company policies and procedures.

- Details of terms and conditions that apply generally, such as holiday entitlement, pension scheme membership, private medical insurance scheme, etc.

- Job vacancies within the organisation.

- Training workshops offered on an open basis by the employer.

- Health and safety information and rules.

- The company's vision, goals and plans for the future.

- General company 'news'.

Using a company intranet to communicate this last item would remove the need for a company newsletter, thereby saving printing and production costs.

Another invaluable use to which an intranet could be put would be for online training, including induction training for new employees.

The efficient and imaginative use of a company intranet can help to foster a culture of openness, knowledge sharing and team spirit between departments and within the organisation as a whole.

Responsibility for the company intranet [1.20]

It will clearly be important for the organisation to appoint a senior manager as the person responsible for managing the intranet and ensuring that all the information posted on it is accurate and up-to-date. This person would also have responsibility for encouraging employees to use the intranet as an effective tool in day-to-day communication. One important decision to be made would be who should have the authority to post information – whether this facility should be offered to all employees, or whether only certain designated senior managers should have the authority to publish information. In either case it may be useful to include a statement within company policy that any employee who notices anything on the web-site that is wrong or out-of-date should bring this to the immediate attention of their line manager.

Security of the intranet [1.21]

One particularly important aspect of operating a company intranet is security. Since much of the information contained on the intranet will be confidential from the organisation's point of view, it will be essential to build in security systems, such as a corporate firewall. If employees are to be permitted to post information, there will also need to be a monitoring system set in place to make sure that no inappropriate information is published. A system of passwords that are changed regularly will help to protect the intranet from misuse.

A full discussion of how to set up, operate and control a company intranet is outside the scope of this book.

Use of Email and the Internet for Personal Purposes [1.22]

Employers should give careful consideration to the question of whether, and to what extent, their workforce should be permitted to use email and the internet for personal or private purposes. In a small company where the general manager knows every employee personally and has a close involvement in the day-to-day work of each person, formal rules or restrictions may seem inappropriate or unduly burdensome. In a larger organisation, however, where many employees have access to email and/or the internet for business purposes, only the most foolhardy or naïve employer would form the view that some form of restriction was unnecessary.

The problem of employees using their employer's communications systems for personal purposes is not a new phenomenon. Traditionally, most employees have had access to their employer's telephone system to one degree or another, and in many organisations reasonable use of the telephone by employees for personal and private purposes has been accepted as the norm. The difference with the advent of email and internet access is that the scope for undetected overuse and misuse is far greater than ever was the case with telephone communication. Whilst in the old days employees might have been criticised for spending too much time making and receiving personal telephone calls, or taking extended coffee breaks, today's problems tend to centre around issues such as employees surfing the net for their holidays and playing computer games during working time. It is therefore advisable for all employers, whatever their size or business sector, to decide whether:

- to introduce a strict 'no personal use' policy'; *or*

- to permit reasonable personal use of email and the internet, for example for essential purposes or occasional use only; or

- to permit personal use during employees' own time, for example during lunch breaks; or

- to allow employees unrestricted access and unlimited use of the company's email and internet facilities, and deal with any problems of misuse on an individual basis after they have arisen.

The subject of email and internet policies and procedures is dealt with fully in **CHAPTER 8**.

Guidelines and Network Etiquette [1.23]

Irrespective of whether or not an employer decides to introduce a formal policy governing employees' use of email and the internet, it is advisable to draft basic guidelines for employees who use these facilities covering the fundamental principles of how they should, and should not, be used. This section suggests some guidelines which employers may elect to adopt or adapt for their own use.

Housekeeping [1.24]

Guidelines on the use of email should be formulated and communicated to all employees along the following lines:
Employees should:

- Check their incoming email at least once a day, but no more often than three times a day to avoid continuous interruptions.

- Turn off the system that provides an alert to the arrival of a new message.

- Reply to all incoming email messages promptly – perhaps within one or two days – even if the reply consists only of an acknowledgement.

- Refrain from using the 'urgent' prefix or unless the message is genuinely urgent from the point of view of the business.

- Arrange for a colleague to deal with their incoming emails if they are to be away from the workplace for more than one or two days, or alternatively install an automatic reply system advising that they will be unable to reply until a defined date.

- Check all email addresses before an email is sent – bear in mind that once an email has been sent, it cannot be retrieved. If a mistake is made, send an apology.

- Always complete the 'subject' field in an outgoing email message in a way that is meaningful so that the recipient can identify what the email is about quickly and correctly.

- Take care when replying to incoming emails that the existing subject field is still appropriate.

- Use common sense and/or follow any company rules regarding when emails should be retained on the computer system and/or printed out and filed.

- Organise incoming and outgoing email messages that are to be retained on the computer in a properly labelled filing system.

- Refrain from printing out email messages unless there is a specific and tangible reason why a paper copy is needed over and above the electronic copy.

- Delete old or irrelevant email messages regularly so that the computer does not contain large quantities of out-of-date material, and in order to conserve disk space.

- Be told clearly if and when they need to obtain their line manager's approval before sending out an email.

There may also be guidelines on sending attachments, a limit on the size of attachments, or even a ban on opening incoming attachments (in case of virus infection). In particular, it may be prudent to advise employees not to retain incoming attachments on the email system, but instead to save them on the computer's hard disk. This will avoid burdening the company network with large files.

Content [1.25]

In terms of the content of an email message, employees should:

- Assess whether email is in fact the most appropriate means of communication for a particular message and consider whether (for example) it may be more appropriate to arrange a meeting to discuss the matter, or make a telephone call.

- Consider whether the content of a planned email is relevant to the intended recipient – think carefully about what information others need and want, rather than disseminating information randomly to large numbers of people.

- Refrain from automatically copying emails to others within the organisation – do so only if there is a specific valid reason justifying it.

- Take care, when replying to an email that has been circulated to other people, not to automatically copy them all in on the reply.

- Refrain from copying emails to management in order to play politics, score points or land a colleague in trouble – this is likely to cause untold damage to working relationships;

- Refrain from forwarding incoming emails on to other people unless the permission of the sender is first obtained;

- Think carefully whether it is appropriate to include the automatically generated copy of the original message in the response to an email – unless it is necessary, it is often better to delete the 'email trail';

- Limit the length of email messages and refrain from sending numerous or lengthy attachments (especially photographs or graphics) that could take hours for the recipient to download and possibly clog up the system. As a general guideline, anything that cannot fit on to a 1.44 megabyte disk should not be sent by email;

- Limit the content of each email to one subject – if more than one subject needs to be covered, send more than one email;

- Make it clear what action is expected as a result of the email, and within what timescale.

Suggested statements which could be incorporated into a policy document on email use are given in **CHAPTER 8**.

Style and language [1.26]

Employees should be encouraged to treat email communication with the same degree of care, attention and professionalism as they would treat a letter sent out on company-headed notepaper. They should:

- Think before writing and take care to express their message clearly;

- Aim to make a positive impression on behalf of the organisation;

- Aim to be courteous;

- Write as concisely as possible- remembering that the message will be read on screen;

- Start and end email messages in a business-like manner avoiding terms such as 'hi there' in messages that are to be sent outside the organisation;

- Pay proper attention to grammar, spelling and punctuation – mistakes look just as unprofessional on screen as they do on paper.

Research carried out by MSN Hotmail and Debrett's found that nearly half of 2,000 email users questioned did not bother about spelling, punctuation or style when writing emails. At the same time, more than half of email recipients stated that they found such carelessness annoying.

Things to avoid [1.27]

Employees should therefore be advised to refrain from:

- Careless style and poor spelling or punctuation.

- Careless or casual use of humour or sarcasm in email communication – because it may be misinterpreted.

- Sending emails in the heat of the moment.

- Using gimmicks excessively for example the written symbol [:-)] to convey a smile.

- Using capital letters in an email – this is often interpreted as shouting.

Defining Acceptable and Unacceptable Use of Communication Systems [1.28]

It is strongly recommended that every employer should formulate and introduce a policy and rules on email and internet use for all workers within the organisation. However, even if no formal policy or rules are put in place, there should at least be a written statement distributed to all workers that certain email and internet activities are prohibited. These would include:

● The use of unauthorised or pirated software.

● Downloading pornographic or sexually explicit material from the internet.

● Infringement of copyright through the copying or forwarding of material downloaded from the internet.

● Sending emails or email attachments containing statements or pictures that could be interpreted as sexual or racial harassment.

● Sending emails or attachments that contain derogatory or defamatory statements about any individual or organisation, or which would be likely to cause offence.

● The transmission by email of highly confidential or sensitive information outside the organisation.

● Sending or forwarding chain email messages.

● Excessive personal use.

The subject of policies, rules and procedures is dealt with fully in **CHAPTER 8**.

Conclusion [1.29]

The advent of email and the internet has brought many benefits and advantages for employers and employees alike, but at the same time has created a range of modern-day problems for employers. One of these problems is time-wasting by employees who may, unless regulated, choose to spend excessive amounts of working time using email and the internet for personal purposes.

Another important issue is the way in which employees treat email communication. Many people use it in a casual or slipshod manner without proper regard to correctness of style and language. This creates the risk that the outside world will gain a negative impression of the organisation. Employers should therefore take appropriate steps to ensure employees pay proper attention to matters of email housekeeping, content and style.

Questions and Answers [1.30]

Question

How can email as a means of communication save money within a business?

Answer

Communication by email is a cost-effective way of sending and receiving information. The costs associated with printing, packaging and postage can be saved and in most cases sending an equivalent email costs less than a local telephone call. There is also a potential cost saving if email messages are retained in electronic format only rather than being printed out. For marketing purposes, advertising a product or service on a website is considerably less expensive than producing a brochure and distributing it to large numbers of potential customers by conventional means.

Question

What other benefits are there to businesses as a result of email and internet access?

Answer

Email enables communications to be sent and received much more quickly than conventional means of communication. Long and short documents can be sent by email over long and short distances quickly and easily irrespective of time differences between different countries. Employees can choose when to access their incoming emails and the internet and can do so irrespective of whether they are working in the office, at home or travelling on company business. Additionally, the internet provides unlimited opportunities for companies to conduct research into an infinite variety of subjects.

Question

Is it right for an employer to be concerned about the amount of time employees spend using the internet?

Answer

There is a growing problem for employers of loss of productive time due to employees surfing the net for both legitimate business purposes and personal entertainment purposes. Because of the sheer volume of available information, it can be a time-consuming exercise to locate information relevant to a specific query, and even once the relevant information is located, downloading a file can also be a time-consuming activity, occupying valuable computer access time and running up large telephone bills in the process. Employers should rightfully be concerned about the amount of time employees spend using the internet, and should introduce policies governing such use.

Question

Should an employer insist that their employees treat email communication in the same business-like manner as they would approach a business letter, or is it acceptable for emails to be more casual in their style?

Answer

An employer who does not impose minimum standards of professionalism on their employees in terms of how they use email risks damaging their business reputation in the eyes of the outside world. Emails that are sent quickly and without proper thought or care often contain errors of language, spelling or grammar and are frequently constructed without any regard to sentence structure. Additionally, if an email is written in a style that is casual or flippant, the result can be that its message becomes unclear, distorted or ambiguous leading to misinterpretation in terms of content or the conveyance of the wrong tone or attitude. It is therefore advisable for employers to impose minimum standards of professionalism and a set of basic guidelines for email communication.

Question

To what extent is an email message secure?

Answer

Email is not a secure means of communication and has often been compared to sending a postcard. An email message should thus not be assumed to be confidential as it may be intercepted or read by someone other than the intended recipient. Furthermore, it is surprisingly easy to send an email to the wrong address, or accidentally copy it to another party, and even if a message arrives only at its intended destination, there is no guarantee that the recipient will not forward the message on to others both within and outside the organisation in random fashion.

Question

To what extent should a manager use email communication for the purpose of communicating with staff?

Answer

Managers should not use email as the main means of communicating with their staff as this method of communication, used in isolation, will not allow ideas, problems and other issues to be properly identified, addressed and resolved. Email should not be regarded as a replacement for other forms of communication between colleagues, but instead should be used only where it is the most appropriate method of communication for the message in question. Ultimately there is no substitute for two-way face-to-face communication between colleagues.

Question

Should an employer be concerned about the extent to which employees use the organisation's communications systems for personal or private purposes?

Answer

With the advent of email and internet access, the scope for undetected overuse and misuse of communications systems is far greater than ever was the case with telephone communication. It is therefore advisable for all employers, whatever their size or business sector, to decide whether to introduce a strict 'no personal use' policy', to permit reasonable personal use of email and the internet or to allow employees unrestricted access and unlimited use of the company's email and internet facilities, and deal with any problems of misuse on an individual basis after they have arisen.

Question

What sort of guidelines should employers devise for their employees as regards the ways in which they use email?

Answer

Guidelines on the use of email should be formulated and communicated to all employees to cover housekeeping matters (for example replying promptly to incoming emails, filing diligently and deleting out of date messages), content and style and language.

2 Legal Liabilities Arising From Misuse of Email and the Internet

Introduction [2.1]

Employees who are allowed unsupervised use of email and granted unlimited access to the internet at work may inadvertently (or deliberately!) cause legal problems for their employer. One problem is that emails are not secure and they can – and do – go astray and can easily fall into the wrong hands. Another cause for concern is that many employees view email as they would a casual telephone conversation. In a telephone conversation, remarks may be made that can be retracted, modified or subsequently denied. The nature of the communication is transitory. The same is not true of an email message which, once sent, provides concrete and lasting evidence that the remark was made and by whom it was made. Four copies of the email will immediately be created: one on the sender's computer, one on the sender's server, one on the recipient's computer and one on the recipient's server. If the recipient forwards the message on to others, multiple copies will then exist. Once a message has been sent therefore, it is almost impossible to eradicate all the copies.

Even after an email message has been deleted from the computer, including deletion from the 'trash', it will remain within the computer hard-disk for a considerable period of time and can be retrieved by means of software designed specifically for that purpose. Often the various elements of an email, for example the time and date when it was sent and the subject header, are capable of being pieced together long after the email was sent. Furthermore, email messages can be used in evidence in court proceedings and employers may be required by a court or tribunal to produce them in the course of such proceedings.

It follows that email messages should not be viewed in the same way as telephone conversations, but should instead be treated with respect, with serious consideration being given to their content, tone and to whom they should be sent. It is up to each employer to make sure that their employees understand these important principles.

Use of the internet has similarly led to attitudes that 'anything goes' and that individuals have the automatic right to free speech via this medium. Although largely unregulated, the internet is not a law-free zone and legal actions can be raised on account of inappropriate statements published on the internet, or inappropriate remarks written in an internet message.

Employer Liability [2.2]

Although the world of cyberspace, as it is known, is largely unregulated, this does not mean that employers and their employees can use electronic communication in any way they please without legal repercussions. The range of possible liabilities that can arise through misuse of email and the internet is surprisingly diverse, particularly when it is remembered that companies competing in the global marketplace inevitably use these facilities as mainstream tools. The world-wide web may have no geographical or cultural boundaries, but there are legal boundaries.

Employers may be liable in a number of ways as a result of employees' use of email and the internet. The laws of contract, defamation, copyright, harassment, obscenity and confidentiality apply to email and internet communications in the same way as they apply to traditional methods of communication. This is known popularly as 'cyberliability'.

Another worrying aspect of email and internet use is the risk of the transmission of a virus to the employer's computer system through email attachments being opened, or through software being brought in by employees to the workplace and loaded on to the employer's system without proper virus-checking.

The following is a summary of the main potential areas of liability:

Defamation [2.3]

There may be a liability for defamation if an email sent internally or externally contains material that is defamatory of an individual or of another company. The person who sent the message will be personally liable for any damage the libellous message causes to the reputation of the individual or company concerned, but the employer may also be vicariously liable. This is dealt with fully in **2.18** below.

Bullying and harassment [2.4]

If an employee sends an abusive or obscene email to a colleague, this may give rise to a claim for constructive dismissal, or, if the content of the message has sexual, racial, religious or homophobic connotations, may lead to a complaint of unlawful discrimination against the employer. The same outcome could occur following sexist, racist, religious or homophobic jokes sent by email from one employee to another or following the downloading or distribution of sexually explicit material from the internet. Harassment is discussed in **2.26** and bullying in **2.29** below.

Publication of obscene material [2.5]

If an employee downloads pornographic material from the internet, and/or circulates such material internally or externally by email (or by other means), this may constitute a criminal offence under the *Obscene Publications Act 1959*. Employees who find such material offensive may also bring claims for sexual harassment to tribunal. Further information is available in **2.34** below.

Disclosure of wrongdoing [2.6]

Employers should take very seriously any instance of an employee coming forward with a complaint that another employee is using the internet for illegal purposes. Depending on the circumstances, such an employee may be protected against detriment and dismissal under the provisions of the *Public Interest Disclosure Act*. This is further explained in **2.39** below.

The law of contract [2.7]

An email message is capable of forming or varying a binding contract and the employer will be liable in contract for any breach of an agreement so formed. Further details follow in **2.47** below.

Misrepresentation [2.8]

Any inaccurate or misleading statement (whether deliberate or accidental) about a company's products or services can lead to legal claims of misrepresentation. This principle extends to information provided by email. In particular, if the statements have had the effect of inducing an individual or an organisation to enter into a contractual agreement to purchase the company's products or services, legal claims could ensue. More information is provided in **2.52** below.

Copyright [2.9]

If employees are allowed unfettered access to the internet, and randomly download whatever they access, there could be an inadvertent breach of copyright law. Full details are provided in **2.54** below.

Confidentiality [2.10]

Where there are no restrictions on employees' use of email, a breach of confidentiality could occur through messages being sent outside the organisation which might contain confidential information about the company. This can easily happen as a result of a wrong email address being input, or a message being inadvertently copied to recipients on a distribution list. Additionally, employees may inadvertently or deliberately send internal emails containing confidential or inappropriate information about a colleague. The issues surrounding security and confidentiality are explored fully in **CHAPTER 4**.

The concept of vicarious liability [2.11]

Employers are responsible and will have legal liability for their employees' activities when they are using email or the internet in the course of their employment, irrespective of whether or not the employer is aware of each individual's specific activities. This is known as vicarious liability.

The concept of vicarious liability is not contained in any statute, but has developed as a result of case law. It means that an employer will be liable in law for the actions (or omissions) of an employee whenever those actions take place 'in the course of employment'. The notion of vicarious liability can be applied in many areas of the employment relationship, for example in connection with breach of safety standards, negligence in carrying out duties, fraudulent statements made by employees, acts of discrimination, etc. Thus an employer may be vicariously liable for the consequences of a defamatory message transmitted by one of its employees in an email in the same way as they could be vicariously liable for an accident caused by the careless driving of one of their van drivers.

In the course of employment [2.12]

In order for the employer to be liable, however, it must be shown that the employee whose misuse of email or the internet gave rise to legal action was acting in the course of employment when they committed the act in question. An employee can be acting in the course of their employment whether or not they are physically at their workplace, for example they may be working at home or away on company business. Equally, the time of day at which a misdemeanour takes place, and whether it is within or outside normal working hours, is irrelevant in determining whether a particular action occurred in the course of employment.

By contrast, if an employee goes off 'on a frolic of his own' (as one Court put it), and it can be shown that their actions had nothing to do with their job responsibilities or duties, then the employer is unlikely to be held liable for their actions or the consequences of those actions. For example, in the case of *Generale Bank Nederland NV v Export Credits Guarantee Department (Times Law Reports 04.08.97)*, the Court of Appeal judged that the employer could not be held liable for the acts of an employee who had assisted in the fraudulent scheme of a third party unless those actions were within the employee's actual or ostensible authority. Even though the fraud was committed during the employee's working time and even though the opportunity to commit the fraud had largely been brought about by dint of the employee's employment, these factors were not sufficient to render the employer vicariously liable. The rules relating to vicarious liability for the dishonest acts of an employee are less onerous than those relating to acts of negligence.

In *Lister & ors v Hesley Hall Ltd House of Lords 03.05.01*, a case involving a school where sexual assaults on boy pupils were carried out by a warden employed by the school, the House of Lords held that the employer was vicariously liable for the acts of the warden. The judgment stated that the employer would be vicariously liable whenever there was a close connection between the employee's act(s) and the nature of the job duties the employee was engaged to carry out. This case in effect broadens the scope of vicarious liability.

Case study   [2.13]

The following case study demonstrates the importance of the question of whether or not an employee is acting in the course of employment:

Case study

Joe is employed as buyer for a major engineering firm. In the course of his duties, Joe corresponds regularly by email with various suppliers both for the purpose of obtaining information about new products and for reviewing price lists and details of any available discounts. Joe has been particularly busy lately because one of his colleagues is off sick, and the pressure of work is mounting. He has received an email from a regular contact, Harry Harman of XYZ Office Supplies Ltd, detailing a special offer on printers, and another on desk-top photocopiers. If 20 or more printers are ordered within 7 days, a discount of 20 per cent will apply. The same discount will be applied to the photocopiers if ten or more are ordered. Joe, whose mind was not fully on his job that morning, has hit the 'reply button' on his computer and inadvertently sent an email to XYZ confirming the company's agreement to purchase 20 printers.

By coincidence, Joe's estranged wife, Josephine, works for the same firm as an evening office cleaner. Josephine is a devious character and is very bitter about her recent separation from Joe. She has, through illicit means, obtained a list of the suppliers with whom Joe regularly deals in his job. Since she is planning to leave the company anyway, and go and live with

---

her sister in Majorca, Josephine has decided to seek revenge on Joe and create trouble for him at work. She accesses Joe's computer one evening and sends an email to Harry at XYZ Office Supplies Ltd confirming that the company wishes to purchase thirty desk-top photocopiers at the discounted price, typing her own name at the bottom of the email.

Several weeks later, long after Josephine has absconded to Majorca, Joe uncovers both his own mistake and the devious activities of his ex-wife. In the meantime, XYZ Office Supplies has delivered both the printers and the desk-top photocopiers and is insisting that both deals should be honoured, threatening legal action if the company refuses to pay for them.

What would the company's liability be for the actions of Joe and Josephine?

The company would be vicariously liable for Joe's actions because, as company buyer, his job involves purchasing equipment from suppliers. He thus has actual and ostensible authority to commit the company to a contract to buy printers, and the email was sent in the course of his duties. The contract is a binding one which the company would have to honour unless they could persuade the supplier to agree voluntarily to take the printers back.

By contrast, however, the company would not be liable for Josephine's activities, since the job of office cleaner would not, by any stretch of the imagination, involve purchasing photocopiers from a supplier, nor using an office computer for work purposes. Josephine was not acting in the course of her employment when she accessed Joe's computer and placed the order for the photocopiers.

Supply of computer   **[2.14]**

Generally, an employer will be vicariously liable for the actions of an employee using email or the internet if the means are authorised, even if the specific act committed by the employee is not. Given that many employees are supplied with a computer by their employer for the performance of their duties, and similarly provided with access to email and the internet by the employer, misuse of these facilities by such employees, i.e. using the facilities in ways that are not authorised by the employer, will mean the employer will be liable in law for the outcome of the misuse. By contrast, an employee who is not supplied with a computer at work, nor with access to email and the internet, (like Josephine in the above case study), will not be acting in the course of employment for the purposes of vicarious liability if they illegitimately use the computer and create some mischief for the employer.

Checklist [2.15]

The following checklist is a guide to establishing whether or not an employee is acting in the course of employment when misusing email or internet facilities. If the answer to the first three questions is 'yes' and the answer to the following three questions is 'no', then it is likely that the employer would be vicariously liable for the actions of the employee.

- Has the employer provided the employee with a computer, and with access to email and the internet?

- Does the employee have authority to send emails, or to communicate via the internet, as part of their job?

- Was the employee's misdemeanour committed whilst they were using email or the internet for purposes associated with their normal job duties (for example was the employee sending a work-related email to a business contact?).

- Does the employer have a clear policy in place governing acceptable and unacceptable uses of email and internet facilities?

- Has this policy been properly communicated to the employee in question such that their misdemeanour is clearly a breach of the policy?

- Has the employee been given clear instructions and/or training in appropriate use of email and the internet?

Liability for acts of harassment [2.16]

Employers will also be liable in law for acts of harassment by their employees on grounds of sex, sexual orientation, race, religion or disability. Here the liability in law is wider than the strict limitations of vicarious liability. This is dealt with below under **2.28**.

Reducing liability by introducing a policy [2.17]

The likelihood of being held liable in law for employees' email or internet wrongdoings can be reduced if the employer introduces a rigorous policy defining acceptable and unacceptable uses of these facilities, and takes positive steps to communicate and apply the policy in practice. By taking such actions, the employer may be able to show that an employee who commits an act which is in clear breach of the policy was not acting 'in the course of employment'. Email and internet policies are addressed fully in **CHAPTER 8**.

Defamation [2.18]

Written material will be defamatory (i.e. libellous) if it involves the publication of an untrue statement which tends to lower a person in the estimation of right-thinking members of society generally. Such material is capable of defaming a company as well as an individual. Where a defamatory statement is made verbally, it is known as 'slander', whilst the term 'libel' means a statement that is committed to a permanent form. It is likely that a defamatory statement made in an email message would be regarded as libel rather than slander since email messages are capable of being printed and stored.

Substantial damages can be awarded following a successful claim for defamation, and in the case of defamation by email or on the internet, the sheer speed with which a defamatory statement can reach a large audience may mean that the damage to the reputation of the individual or business augments within a very short time-scale.

There is no distinction in the law of defamation between the content of an internal email and text contained in a printed letter or other written communication. Thus, there may be liability for defamation if an email sent internally or externally contains material that is defamatory of an individual or of another company. Similarly, if a defamatory message is posted on the internet, liability for defamation will accrue. If, however, a statement made is true, this will provide a defence to any claim for defamation.

Who is Liable? [2.19]

The person who sent the message will be personally liable for any damage the libellous message causes to the reputation of the individual or company concerned, but the employer may also be vicariously liable if the employee was acting in the course of their duties when they sent the email. This means that the employer will be regarded, for the purposes of a legal claim, as the author of the offending statement. The *Defamation Act 1996* expressly states that:

> 'Employees or agents of an author, editor or publisher are in the same position as their employer or principal to the extent that they are responsible for the content of the statement or the decision to publish it'.

In practice, it is much more likely that an employer will be sued for defamation than an individual employee since, from the point of view of the defamed party, the employer is far more likely to be in a position to pay out compensation.

The Norwich Union case [2.20]

In 1997, Norwich Union settled a major defamation action brought against them by their competitor, Western Provident Association, as a direct result of a widely circulated internal email message which was defamatory of Western Provident's financial position. The email circulating amongst Norwich Union employees had made untrue and damaging statements alleging there were financial problems at Western Provident and suggested that the firm was being investigated by the DTI. The outcome was that following a law suit by Western Provident for libel and slander, Norwich Union paid out £450,000 in damages and costs to Western Provident for defamation. Interestingly, the courts stepped in and ordered Norwich Union to preserve all the offending messages, and to hand over hard copies of these to Western Provident.

Liability as the publisher [2.21]

In addition to vicarious liability for defamatory statements made by their employees, the employer may be liable as the publisher of any offending statements made via electronic communication. Under the *Defamation Act 1996*, an employer can be held liable if they are the author, editor or publisher of a defamatory statement. A publisher is defined in the Act as someone 'whose business is issuing material to the public, or a section of the public, who issues material containing the statement in the course of that business'. Essentially an employer may be held to be the publisher of an offending statement if they are involved in any way in the dissemination of the defamatory statement. This means that if the employer controls, edits or vets what employees write, they may be held to be the publisher of the material. This does not, of course, mean that employers should give employees a free hand to write whatever they deem appropriate, or turn a blind eye to their employees' electronic communications, but rather that they should take concrete steps to make sure no defamatory messages are written or sent out.

Similarly, the fact that an employer provides their employees with computers and with email and internet access may be sufficient for the employer to be regarded as the publisher of all communications sent out by these media.

Defence against liability for defamation [2.22]

The *Defamation Act 1996, s 1(1)* provides a defence for organisations who use electronic communications against claims of defamation if they can show that:

- they were not the author, editor or publisher of the statement complained of;

- they took reasonable care in relation to its publication; *and*

- they did not know, and had no reason to believe, that what they did caused or contributed to the publication of a defamatory statement.

The Act goes on to say [*s 1(5)*] that:

'In determining ... whether a person took reasonable care, or had reason to believe that what he did caused or contributed to the publication of a defamatory statement, regard shall be had to –

(a) the extent of his responsibility for the content of the statement or the decision to publish it,

(b) the nature or circumstances of the publication, and

(c) the previous conduct or character of the author, editor or publisher.'

Example [2.23]

In the case of *Godfrey v Demon Internet Ltd* [*1999*], the High Court held that an internet service provider was liable for a defamatory email posted on a newsgroup site. This was because they had failed to remove the statement from the newsgroup as soon as they received notification that the statement was untrue. Although the internet service provider was neither the originator nor the publisher of the statement, they were still held liable in law for defamation, because, having been notified that the statement was untrue and been asked to remove it, they failed to do so promptly and continued to allow it to be posted. Thus the defence available under the *Defamation Act 1996, s 1(1)* that the publisher of a defamatory statement did not know, and had no reason to believe, that what they did caused or contributed to the publication of a defamatory statement could not be upheld.

Making employees aware [2.24]

Employers should take the responsibility of ensuring that their employees have sufficient awareness of the law on defamation to understand that any information they distribute by email or via the internet must not contain untrue or derogatory statements about, for example, a competitor. Text explaining the fundamental principles of the law on defamation could be included, for example, in an employee handbook. A model statement that could be incorporated into an employee handbook is given in the next paragraph. It is also recommended that employers make it clear to all their workers that the making of defamatory statements, whether in internal or external communications, will be regarded as a disciplinary offence. It may even be advisable to set up a vetting system for employees who regularly send emails to outside organisations so that a supervisor or other nominated person routinely screens the content of every message before it is sent.

Sample statement on the law of defamation [2.25]

The following is a sample statement designed to inform employees about defamation and prevent or reduce the likelihood of employees inadvertently making defamatory statements during the course of their email communications. Such a statement could be incorporated into an employee handbook, or could form part of an overall email or internet policy.

> Employees who, in the course of their duties, communicate internally and/or externally by email or the internet, must pay heed to the law of defamation. The same laws apply to email and internet communication as to any other document. Written material will be defamatory if it involves the publication of an untrue statement which tends to lower a person in the estimation of right-thinking members of society generally.
>
> It is important, therefore, to ensure that all statements made in emails or via internet communication are accurate and not misleading. Employees must not under any circumstances write any derogatory statements about an individual or another organisation. These rules apply equally to internal and external communications.
>
> If any member of staff is in doubt about the content of an email message or internet communication, they should seek advice, *before the communication is sent,* from their line manager.

Harassment [2.26]

Harassment by email is unfortunately a common modern-day phenomenon. If an employee sends an abusive or obscene email to a colleague which amounts to unfavourable treatment of that colleague (or another employee) on grounds of sex, sexual orientation, race, religion or disability, *the employer* will be liable for any discrimination complaint brought by the victim. The individual employee who wrote the email can also be held liable. The same outcome could occur following sexist, racist, religious or homophobic jokes sent by email from one employee to another. In addition, the downloading of sexually explicit material from the internet by male employees may create an atmosphere at work that is uncomfortable for female employees, thus constituting sexual harassment. This will be the case irrespective of whether there was an intention to cause offence to a particular employee.

There is no minimum length of service required for an employee to bring a complaint of unlawful discrimination to an employment tribunal, and compensation is unlimited. (**CHAPTER 3** provides full information on employers' liability for unlawful discrimination or harassment.)

Case study   **[2.27]**

Mandy has been asked by her line manager, Andy, to produce a detailed written report by the 15th of the month. In order to be able to complete the report, Mandy needs some key information from Sandy, a company accountant. Sandy is black, and has recently immigrated to the UK from Nigeria where he was born and educated. Anticipating the information that she would require from Sandy, Mandy had emailed him several weeks ago outlining precisely what details she needed. Sandy, however, has not yet supplied the information, and has not replied to her email. In the meantime Mandy has been updating her boss on her progress with the report, and has copied Sandy in on the emails she has been sending him.

When the 15th of the month arrives and the report has not arrived on Andy's desk, Andy is annoyed and emails Mandy to ask when he can expect to receive the completed document. This email is copied to Sandy. Mandy, in her frustration at Sandy's lack of cooperation (as she perceives it) replies angrily to Andy's email, saying the following: '*I asked Sandy for the financial information three weeks ago. I have not heard from him and he has made no effort to supply the information. Quite frankly I am thoroughly fed up with his lack of cooperation, laziness and general bad attitude. Maybe he should go back to the jungle and eat bananas rather than coming to England and taking up a job that could have gone to a local person. I am sorry the report is late, but it is not my fault.*'

In the heat of the moment, Mandy has overlooked the fact that this email, like the others, is copied to Sandy.

What legal claim, if any, could Sandy have against Mandy or the company on account of the text of this email?

Sandy would almost certainly be able to succeed in a claim for unlawful race discrimination against the company. The remark about going back to the jungle to eat bananas is derogatory, demeaning and would almost certainly be offensive to Sandy, thus constituting verbal racial harassment. In addition, the implication that Sandy has less right to work in the UK than a local person is potentially discriminatory. The tribunal, if it upheld the claim, would award Sandy compensation for injury to feelings in a sum that it considered just and equitable. There is no maximum to the amount of compensation that can be awarded for race (or sex) discrimination.

Furthermore, Sandy could cite Mandy as a second respondent in his claim for racial harassment, and the tribunal could, at its discretion, order Mandy personally to pay part of any compensation awarded.

Employers' liability for acts of harassment perpetrated by their employees [2.28]

All the laws governing discrimination in employment state that employers will be liable for an act of discrimination committed 'in the course of employment …whether or not it was done with the employer's knowledge or approval'. It is well established in law that sexual harassment can constitute an act of unlawful discrimination. The *Race Relations Act 1976* was amended in July 2003 to include an express definition of harassment as a distinct form of unlawful discrimination. In addition, the *Employment Equality (Religion or Belief) Regulations 2003 (SI 2003 No 1660)* and the *Employment Equality (Sexual Orientation) Regulations 2003 (SI 2003 No 1661)* expressly outlaw harassment. Harassment is defined as unwanted conduct (on grounds of race, religion etc) which as the purpose or effect of violating another person's dignity or of creating an intimidating, hostile, degrading, humiliating or offensive environment for that person.

Furthermore, in cases of alleged harassment, the test for liability is wider than the common law vicarious liability test. Under the vicarious liability test, an employer will be vicariously liable for an employee's actions carried out 'in the course of employment' only if there is a close connection between the employee's act(s) and the nature of the job duties the employee is engaged to carry out. In cases of harassment, however, a wider test is used, largely as a result of the case of *Tower Boot Co Ltd v Jones [1997] IRLR 168*. Full details of this case is provided in CHAPTER 3, paragraph 3.19. It is important to note also that an employer may be held liable for discriminatory acts against employees whether or not management was aware of what was going on.

In addition to the various anti-discrimination statutes, the *Protection from Harassment Act 1997* makes it a criminal offence to pursue a course of conduct (on at least two occasions) that amounts to harassment or which causes a person to fear that violence will be used against them. There is no need under this Act for the harassment to be linked to gender, race or any other particular motive or issue, nor does it matter (in a legal sense) whether or not the harassment was intentional. Paragraph 3.5 in CHAPTER 3 provides further information.

Bullying [2.29]

There is no employment law in the UK that specifically outlaws bullying at work. Furthermore, bullying behaviour that is not linked in any way to gender, marital status, race, disability, religion or sexual connotation cannot give rise to a claim under any of the anti-discrimination statutes.

However, there is an implied contractual duty of trust and confidence inherent in every contract of employment. Any type of conduct that has the effect of making working life intolerable for a particular employee would normally be regarded as a fundamental breach of the duty of trust and confidence. Clearly serious bullying, whether a single serious incident, or an ongoing series of incidents, would fall within this definition, as would a manager's failure, without good reason, to deal promptly and adequately with an employee's genuine complaint of bullying. Thus an employee who repeatedly receives inflammatory email messages from (for example) their supervisor could, depending on the degree of bullying involved, argue that the supervisor's conduct fundamentally breached the duty of trust and confidence and hence their contract of employment.

In the event of a fundamental breach of contract by the employer, an employee who has a minimum of one year's continuous service is entitled to resign (with or without notice) and bring a claim for constructive dismissal to tribunal. If such a case succeeds the individual may be awarded a basic award plus compensation for loss of earnings, both past and future.

The effects of bullying [2.30]

Quite apart from any legal implications, any form of bullying at work is clearly likely to have a detrimental impact on employee morale and productivity. An employee who is feeling upset, intimidated or degraded by the way they are being treated by (for example) their line manager will not be able to perform their duties to the best of their abilities. Bullying can, and often does, lead to severe stress, high levels of absence from work and high turnover of competent staff.

Bullying by email [2.31]

Managers should be vigilant to the possibility of bullying in the workplace and should not assume, just because no-one has complained, that a problem does not exist. In particular, the incidence of aggressive email messages, known as 'flamemails', appears now to be widespread in the UK. 'Flamemail' has been defined as an abusive, aggressive or deliberately anti-social email message. This can include emails that are viewed as rude, upsetting, unduly sarcastic or sexually or racially unacceptable.

Inevitably, one of the causes of flamemail is that many managers are over-worked, facing impossibly tight deadlines and suffering from stress. This may cause them to deal with issues such as employee feedback, job performance problems, criticism and discipline by firing off an angry email rather than arranging to discuss the matter with the employee face-to-face in a calm and constructive manner.

'Flaming' may of course simply be a new element in the traditional autocratic and aggressive style of management, which of course is regarded as wholly inappropriate in today's workplaces. Flamemails may be used as a shield for the manager who lacks the skills of face-to-face communication or for someone who would rather avoid any type of direct confrontation with others. The result can be that problems are created on account of hasty email messages causing misunderstandings, or on account of a sparsity of face-to-face communication. Equally, any problem areas that exist already are likely to escalate if email is the only form of communication used to deal with them, whilst a proper face-to-face discussion might be all that is needed to fully understand and resolve the problem.

At the other end of the spectrum, flamemails may be sent by the classic office bully who enjoys the feeling of power gained from abusing or harassing colleagues who may not be in a position to defend themselves, or who may be too embarrassed or intimidated to complain.

Flamemail is discussed further in **CHAPTER 8**, at **8.53**.

Whatever its cause and irrespective of the form it takes, aggressive behaviour towards colleagues is likely to be extremely destructive in any working environment, especially in a small workplace where teamwork and cooperation are vital for the success of the business. Bullying can lead to low motivation and morale, breakdowns in communication, difficult working relationships and workplace stress. These in turn will lead to poor performance on the part of individual employees and ultimately to low productivity and hence reduced profitability for the business.

Manager's use of email [2.32]

Given that research indicates that most cases of bullying at work involve bullying by an employee's immediate manager, managers should take great care in how they use email to communicate with their staff. Generally, email is not a suitable means of communication for matters such as staff appraisal, coaching, training, feedback, criticism of work, discussion of differences of opinion or disciplinary proceedings. These are matters that require open two-way face-to-face communication if any problems are to be resolved in a constructive manner, and if working relationships are to be maintained at a satisfactory level.

Model anti-bullying statement [2.33]

Given the level of bullying at work which research suggests exists, it may be useful for employers to devise and implement an anti-bullying policy statement. Such a statement could read as follows:

> The Company is committed to ensuring fair and equitable treatment for all its employees so that they may carry out their work in a comfortable working environment without fear of intimidation, embarrassment or upset. This policy on bullying aims to ensure that no employee or other worker is subjected to any form of bullying at work for any reason.
>
> Bullying is damaging and counter-productive in that it may make the victim feel intimated, embarrassed or distressed, leading to friction amongst colleagues and hence to lower levels of motivation and productivity.
>
> Bullying may take many forms, including (but not restricted to) shouting and swearing, insulting language, making excessive or unreasonable demands on someone, destructive or unfair criticism, or ostracising a colleague. Bullying may also take the form of 'flamemail' i.e. curt, abusive, aggressive or deliberately anti-social email messages. This can include emails that are viewed as rude, upsetting, unduly sarcastic or sexually or racially unacceptable. The Company will not tolerate this or any other form of bullying or harassment under any circumstances.
>
> Any employee who believes that they are the victim of bullying behaviour may raise a complaint either with their line manager or with … The complaint will be promptly investigated and appropriate steps taken to put a stop to any behaviour that constitutes bullying. Any employee who is found to have been bullying a colleague will be subject to disciplinary action up to summary dismissal. Complaints will of course be dealt with in a manner which respects the rights of both parties, and will also be dealt with in confidence.

Publication of Obscene Material [2.34]

There is evidence to suggest that more people in the UK use the internet to access pornography than for any other purpose. The possession or downloading of adult pornography is not illegal in the UK, but the transmission or distribution of such material is an offence under the *Obscene Publications Act 1959*. 'Transmission' is this context includes electronic transmission and so an employee who attaches an obscene picture to an email and transmits it to a colleague will be committing a criminal offence.

In order for material to be obscene for the purposes of the *Obscene Publications Act*, it has to be shown that publication of the material would tend to deprave or corrupt persons who are likely to read, see or hear the material. The scope of the Act is not limited to sexual material, but may also apply to the publication of material which depicts violent activities. Furthermore, under the *Protection of Children Act 1978* (as amended by the *Criminal Justice and Public Order Act 1994*), it is illegal to distribute, show or possess indecent child pornography. Thus an employee who is in possession of child pornography, or who downloads paedophiliac material from the internet will be committing a criminal offence irrespective of whether they transmit the material on to others.

Pornography in the workplace [2.35]

Irrespective of the legal status of pornography in criminal law, the downloading or distribution of pornographic material within a workplace is clearly inappropriate, and may give rise to claims of sexual harassment on the part of employees who find it offensive. For example, pictures of naked women downloaded from the internet, displayed on a colleague's computer as a screensaver, or sent to a colleague as an email attachment may cause serious offence to a female employee who may find the images demeaning and personally upsetting. This is over and above the inevitable distraction from work and time-wasting that such activities will entail.

Banning pornography and sexually explicit material [2.36]

It is in the employer's interests to make sure that there is a written policy and rules governing employees' use of email and the internet generally, and that the policy specifically bans the accessing, viewing, downloading, displaying or dissemination of pornographic or sexually explicit material. In addition, such activities should be clearly defined as gross misconduct in the company's disciplinary procedure, and employees informed unambiguously that any activities involving pornography will lead to their summary dismissal. Provided such a policy is clearly set in place and properly communicated to every employee, the employer will be in a position to deal firmly and fairly with employees who offend in this way. Further text on this aspect of company policy, and a suggested statement, are available at **8.60** below.

Without a clear policy and rules banning pornography in the workplace, it is possible that an employee dismissed for accessing or downloading pornography from the internet could succeed in a claim for unfair dismissal, as the following case demonstrates:

Key case **[2.37]**

Dunn v. IBM United Kingdom Ltd [1998] Case No 2305087/97

Facts

Mr Dunn had been challenged by his manager with regard to suspected misuse of the company's computer facilities in accessing pornography and other non-business-related material on the internet, and making printouts of downloaded pictures. He admitted these activities to his manager who decided that he was guilty of gross misconduct. A disciplinary interview was then convened which lasted only a few minutes. Mr Dunn was summarily dismissed, and he brought a complaint of unfair dismissal to a tribunal.

Findings

Despite the fact that Mr Dunn's activities involved the viewing and downloading of pornographic material, his dismissal was held by a tribunal to have been unfair. The tribunal took the view that there was no indisputable breach of company policy which automatically warranted the employee's summary dismissal. A further factor was that Mr Dunn had admitted the offences without being aware that this might lead to his dismissal. It followed therefore that the dismissal did not fall within the range of reasonable responses open to the employer. The tribunal did, however, reduce Mr Dunn's compensation by fifty per cent on account of his contributory conduct.

Implications

Irrespective of the potential seriousness of an employee's misconduct, and irrespective of whether it is or is not in breach of company policy, proper procedures must be followed otherwise a dismissal may be judged to be unfair by an employment tribunal.

The dismissal in the *Dunn* case (above) was unfair largely because the employer had not communicated in advance to the employee via a policy or written rules that downloading pornography would be regarded as an offence leading to dismissal. The material downloaded was not illegal and it could not therefore be argued that the employee's actions should automatically be regarded as gross misconduct.

Accidental access **[2.38]**

In the event that an employee is discovered to have accessed an internet site containing pornography, it should be borne in mind that it is genuinely very easy to access an internet site by accident. Managers should be open-minded to the possibility that an employee who alleges that they accessed pornographic material on an internet site accidentally may be telling the truth. A proper investigatory interview should be held with the employee and dismissal should not be instituted as an automatic response following such findings. If, on the other hand, the evidence proves that the employee has spent an excessive amount of time viewing the site in question, or that they have downloaded images from the site, the manager would be entitled to take appropriate disciplinary action up to summary dismissal in line with the company's procedure.

A manager investigating such an incident should also bear in mind that, if offensive material is found on an employee's computer, it may not be the employee who was responsible for putting it there. Depending on how carefully employees guard their passwords, and how common-place it is for employees to use their colleagues' computers for work-related purposes, it may be easy for one employee to use someone else's computer for illegitimate purposes, including downloading pornography from the internet. Unless there is some tangible evidence to suggest that the employee, and not one of their colleagues, has committed the offence in question, the employee should not be dismissed.

The subject of unfair dismissal is dealt with fully in CHAPTER 11.

Employees' Disclosure of Another Employee's Wrongdoing – Implications Under the Public Interest Disclosure Act **[2.39]**

As a result of the implementation of the *Public Interest Disclosure Act 1998* (known informally as the '*Whistleblowers Act*'), employees and other workers are widely protected in law against dismissal or detriment if they make a 'protected disclosure' concerning malpractice in the workplace. The broad aim of the Act is to encourage a culture of openness within businesses in an effort to prevent malpractice. The right to make a protected disclosure extends not only to employees of the organisation, but also to other workers who perform services personally for the organisation, for example agency workers. 'Worker' for the purposes of the Act will also include individuals who provide services via their own service company as is common in the IT industry.

There are, however, strict rules on the types of disclosure that are protected and strict criteria governing to whom the disclosure must be made if the worker is to gain the protection of the Act. The worker must also reasonably believe that the information being disclosed is true. This means that the worker does not require proof of malpractice to be protected by the Act, but rather that they must be acting in good faith and have reasonable grounds to believe that what they are disclosing is true.

If an employee makes a protected disclosure and is dismissed as a result, they will be eligible to bring a complaint of unfair dismissal to an employment tribunal irrespective of their age or length of service. Dismissal in this context includes being selected for redundancy if the fact that the employee has made a protected disclosure is a factor in the selection process. Such dismissals are automatically unfair and compensation for unfair dismissal in these circumstances is unlimited. In addition, it is possible for someone who has been dismissed as a direct result of making a protected disclosure to apply for an order for reinstatement until the case is heard by the tribunal.

Furthermore, any employee or other worker who suffers a detriment as a result of having made a protected disclosure may also bring a complaint to a tribunal. Detriment could be claimed if the worker was put at a disadvantage in any way or treated less favourably on account of having made a qualifying disclosure. This could take the form (for example) of unfair discipline, refusal to promote, removal of a perk or any type of victimisation or hostile treatment.

If an employee genuinely and in good faith raises a matter which would qualify as a protected disclosure under the Act, and if management ignores the matter, the employee could resign and claim constructive dismissal on the grounds of a breach of the duty of trust and confidence. In the case of *Broughton v National Tyres and Autocentre Limited [2000] Case No 1500080/00*, an employment tribunal held that an employee who had resigned following his disclosure to management that his boss had committed a criminal offence at work had been constructively dismissed because the employer had failed to investigate the matter and had ignored the employee's concerns. The tribunal stressed that it was very important for workers to be supported when making disclosures of malpractice to their employer and in this case the employer's failure to provide reasonable support was a breach of the mutual duty of trust and confidence.

The types of disclosure that are protected [2.40]

The types of disclosure that are protected under the Act are as follows:

- A criminal offence that has been committed, is being committed or is likely to be committed;

- The failure by a person to comply with a legal obligation (which was held by the EAT in *Parkins v Sodexho Ltd 1239/00*) to include an obligation arising out of an employee's contract of employment);

- Any miscarriage of justice that has occurred, is occurring or is likely to occur;

- Evidence that the health or safety of an individual has been, is being or is likely to be endangered;

- Damage to the environment;

- The likelihood of deliberate concealment of information relating to any of the above.

Since displaying child pornography or obscene material may constitute a criminal offence, the disclosure by one employee that another employee has been downloading such material from the internet, displaying it on a computer screen or sending it to colleagues as an email attachment could give rise to protection under the Act. Similarly a disclosure to management that a colleague has breached any other legislation in the course of their work, for example by committing a copyright infringement, could qualify as a protected disclosure under the Act.

If, however, the person making the disclosure commits a criminal offence by doing so, then they will not be able to benefit from the protection of the Act.

The person to whom the disclosure is made [2.41]

In order to gain protection under the Act, the worker must have made the disclosure in good faith either to the employer directly, or to one of the following authorised persons:

- A legal adviser;

- A Minister of the Crown;

- A 'prescribed person' – the list includes many public organisations such as the Health and Safety Executive, the Inland Revenue, etc;

- 'Other parties', but only where certain conditions are met, namely:

- The worker reasonably believes they will be dismissed or subjected to a detriment if they disclose the information to one of the other categories of authorised person;

- The worker reasonably believes that if they disclose the matter to the employer, the employer will proceed to conceal or destroy the evidence;

- The worker has previously made the same disclosure to the employer, or by means of one of the other prescribed routes;

- The matter is of such a serious nature that disclosing it by a different route is reasonable under all the circumstances.

Where a disclosure is made to the employer directly, the Act does not specify a level of management to whom it must be made in order for it to be protected. Thus, if an employee or other worker makes a disclosure of wrongdoing to their line manager, this will count as a protected disclosure under the Act. If, therefore, as a direct result of their having made such a disclosure, they are dismissed or victimised in any way, they would be able to bring a complaint to a tribunal.

Key case   [2.42]

The following tribunal case is interesting because it related to pornographic images stored on an employee's computer and the subsequent treatment of an employee who complained about it:

Chattenton v City of Sunderland City Council [2000] Case No 6402938/99

Facts

Mr Chattenton was a quality advisor working for the Council. In this role, he shared a room and a computer with a colleague. Following his discovery of pornographic images on the computer, Mr Chattenton reported the matter to a company director, as a result of which his colleague was suspended from work. Shortly afterwards, however, when Mr Chattenton returned from a holiday, he found he had been moved into an open-plan office and allocated different work. He considered that these changes were to his detriment and brought a complaint to an employment tribunal alleging that the reason for his treatment was that he had made a protected disclosure under the *Public Interest Disclosure Act*.

Findings

Under the Act, an employee is protected against detriment if they disclose activities to their line manager that constitute a criminal offence. The tribunal held that Mr Chattenton genuinely and reasonably believed that the pornography he discovered on the computer constituted a criminal offence. The tribunal also held that although the pornography in question

---

might not in fact have constituted a criminal offence, this was irrelevant. The important point was that Mr Chattenton reasonably believed that a criminal offence had been committed and had reported it to his employer. This meant that his disclosure of the pornography to the director was a protected disclosure under the Act.

The tribunal went on to find, however, that Mr Chattenton had not been subjected to a detriment in being moved to an open-plan office and allocated different work. It was reasonable for the Council, following the pornography incident, to decide to accommodate all staff except managers in an open-plan office, and equally reasonable for Mr Chattenton's manager to require him to perform the work which he had been allocated following the move.

Implications

An employee who complains to a manager that a colleague has been using a workplace computer to view pornography will in all probability be protected by the provisions of the *Public Interest Disclosure Act* irrespective of whether the pornography in question constitutes a criminal offence. If the employee who complains holds a reasonable belief that a colleague has committed, or is committing, a criminal offence and makes the disclosure in good faith to a manager, protection against dismissal and detriment will be available.

Taking complaints seriously [2.43]

Clearly it is important for managers to give very serious consideration to a complaint from an employee about pornography on a workplace computer, or any other type of abuse of email and internet facilities. It is equally important that the manager to whom a genuine complaint is brought should make sure that no employee is victimised or penalised in any way for having made such a disclosure.

The advantage of a procedure to allow disclosures [2.44]

For larger organisations, it may be advisable to devise and implement a procedure for abuse of email and internet facilities (and other types of computer abuse) to be reported to an appropriate senior manager. Essentially, If a problem exists, it is much better for management to know about it than to remain ignorant. If a responsible approach is taken towards employees who raise genuine complaints, this is likely to result in a more comfortable working environment for all workers. The alternative approach – for management to bury their heads in the sand or adopt a defensive attitude may well lead to legal problems, and of course, employee discontent and discomfort.

The employer's normal grievance procedure is not a suitable medium for employees to disclose wrongdoings on the part of their colleagues. This is because grievance procedures are designed to permit employees to raise work-related matters that are related to them personally and the onus is on the worker to prove their case at a grievance hearing convened for that specific purpose. A whistle-blowing policy on the other hand would be designed to allow workers to disclose wrongdoings or malpractice on the part of others which would represent a matter of interest to the business, rather than to the worker personally. The onus would then be on management to investigate the allegations and act upon them accordingly.

Introducing a whistle-blowing policy   [2.45]

It is in the interests of the employer either to introduce a general whistle-blowing policy, or at the very least to incorporate a whistle-blowing clause into the email/internet policy. This will:

- permit employees to raise genuine complaints internally without fear of retribution;

- alert management at an early stage to any illegal or other inappropriate activities on the part of employees who are using email and the internet;

- help to ensure that disclosures are made internally rather than to an outside party such as a regulatory body, thus keeping such maters confidential;

- provide some protection to employers against the likelihood of legal claims against them.

Some issues that management may wish to consider are:

- whether the making of such complaints could be incorporated into an overall company whistle-blowing policy or whether a stand-alone policy for the disclosure of email and internet pornography would be appropriate;

- who in the organisation should be responsible for the policy and to whom complaints should be brought, for example the IT manager;

- how complaints of email or internet abuse will be handled;

- a statement that all genuine complaints raised in a reasonable manner will be taken seriously, investigated properly and dealt with in confidence;

- measures to discourage and/or deal with unfounded or malicious complaints of email or internet abuse;

- measures to ensure that employees who raise genuine complaints are not penalised in any way for having done so;

- how the policy or procedure might deal with accidental access to offensive material.

Model procedure for complaints   **[2.46]**

The following is a suggested model procedure for the handling of complaints about misuse of email or internet facilities involving offensive material:

It is the company's aim to encourage responsible use of its communications systems, including email and access to the internet. If an employee reasonably believes that a colleague is misusing these systems, they should raise the matter. Misuse will include accessing, viewing and/or downloading pornographic or sexually explicit material from the internet and sending offensive jokes or material with a sexual, sexist, racist, religious or homophobic content to another employee (or outsider) by email or email attachment. Such activities are expressly forbidden. Use of email and the internet for other non work-related purposes may also give rise to grounds for complaint.

The Company recognises the sensitive and awkward nature of complaints of this type. An employee who believes that a colleague is misusing email or internet facilities may prefer to speak directly to their colleague and advise or request them to stop accessing, downloading or distributing the offensive or other non-work related material. Alternatively the employee may write a confidential note to their colleague instead of approaching them personally. Such a note should detail the behaviour which is deemed inappropriate and request that it should stop.

If such informal action fails, if the employee feels unable to take such action, or if the matter is of a very serious nature, employees are advised to raise a formal complaint in writing stating:

- the name of the colleague who is misusing email or internet facilities;

- the type of misuse that has occurred;

- dates and times (if possible) when the misuse occurred;

- the names of any witnesses;

- any action already taken by the employee to try to put a stop to the misuse.

Such a written complaint should be sent to the person nominated above who will also be available to provide advice and guidance on how the matter will be dealt with. Complaints of email and internet abuse will be taken seriously by the Company and treated in confidence insofar as confidentiality is practicable.

All genuine complaints of email or internet abuse will be investigated thoroughly and dealt with promptly and efficiently. If the investigation reveals that the complaint is valid, prompt remedial action will be taken to stop the misuse and prevent its recurrence. Disciplinary measures will be taken against any employee who misuses the company's email or internet facilities.

An employee who is found to have made a malicious claim of email or internet abuse will be subject to disciplinary action.

Employees who raise a genuine complaint under this procedure will not be subjected to any unfavourable treatment or victimisation as a result of making the complaint.

The Formation of Binding Contracts [2.47]

Many employees do not realise that it is possible, and indeed relatively easy, to form (or vary) a binding contract through an exchange of emails. Traditionally, formal written contracts are subject to strict management controls and procedures governing negotiation, agreement and signing off, whereas agreements reached by email rarely involve such formalities. Furthermore, in the UK many types of contract, including employment contracts, can be made irrespective of whether there is a signed document. Thus, certain contracts may be formed over the telephone, as a result of a face-to-face meeting, or by means of a verbal job offer at an interview. Email has the added certainty of providing a record of the transaction. Essentially, contracts formed electronically between UK companies are as binding as those formed by conventional means and are subject to the same employment laws and contract laws.

The laws in other countries are, of course, different from the laws in the UK and in many countries contracts can be formed only after complex procedures have been completed including, for example, the signature of witnesses on a formal document.

The law of contract [2.48]

The basic law of contract stipulates that for a contract to be binding, there must be:

- an offer;

- an unconditional acceptance of the offer; *and*

- consideration (which usually means payment).

It follows that, as soon as an organisation unconditionally accepts an offer made by a supplier to purchase goods or services, a contract is formed at that point.

Because it is quick, convenient and easy to communicate by email, employees dealing with suppliers can inadvertently create a contract without realising they are binding their employer. Provided an outside party reasonably believes that the employee sending the email to them has the proper authority to negotiate or enter into a contractual agreement, the business will be bound by the content of the emails exchanged. It will usually not be difficult for a supplier or potential supplier to claim that they reasonably believed that the person sending the email had the appropriate authority, since most email messages clearly state the organisation's name and the sender's name. Because email communication does not involve any face-to-face or verbal communication between the parties, there will be little opportunity for the recipient of an email to judge the position, level of authority, credibility or genuineness of the person sending it and hence draw a conclusion that the person was not properly authorised to complete the transaction.

Key case   **[2.49]**

The following case demonstrates how easy it is for a manager inadvertently to vary an employee's terms of employment:

Hall v. Cognos Ltd [1998] Case No 1803325/97

Facts

Mr Hall worked under a contract that contained detailed rules regarding the right to reimbursement of expenses. These rules included strict time deadlines for lodging claims. Having missed the deadline for making a claim on one occasion, Mr Hall sent an email requesting permission to lodge a late claim. His line manager replied to this email with the words, 'Yes, it is OK'. Subsequently, however, the employer refused to make payment for the expenses in question and Mr Hall brought a claim for breach of contract. The contract itself stated that 'any amendment or modification of this [contract] will be in writing and signed by the parties or it will have no effect'.

Findings

The two key issues for the employment tribunal to determine were whether email correspondence was capable of constituting a written document signed by the parties, and whether Mr Hall's line manager had ostensible authority to agree to a variation of the terms within his contract relating to payment of expenses. In relation to the first question, the tribunal held that an email that was printed out and that contained the name of the sender could be regarded as a written document signed by the parties. With regard to the second question, the tribunal took the view that the employee was entitled to rely on his manager's authority to vary the terms of his contract. The outcome was that the employer was bound by the variation to the terms of Mr Hall's contract that had been authorised by his line manager.

Implications

Managers should take care when communicating with their staff by email not to inadvertently make a statement that could be construed as a variation to the employee's contract of employment, or a variation of any of the company's rules or procedures.

It is clearly very important for employers to set systems in place that will minimise the likelihood of contracts being accidentally or deliberately formed or varied by those without the proper authority, and to conduct proper training of all employees who may use email or the internet for the purpose of purchasing goods or supplies.

Using email and the internet to order goods and supplies [2.50]

Clearly organisations may wish to make use of email to set up ordering systems with their suppliers and/or customers which will provide a speedy and convenient method of supplying or obtaining goods and services.

To obtain some protection from the accidental formation of contracts, or the formation of a contract on unacceptable terms, the organisation may wish to consider including within every email sent to existing or potential suppliers a statement that defines nominated persons from within the organisation with the authority to negotiate or enter into contracts. This will have the effect of putting the supplier on notice that any offer to form a contract emanating from any other person will not have the authority of the organisation to enter into a binding contractual agreement. Such a notice could state that:

'The persons within this Company who have authority to bind the organisation to contracts are Joe Jones, the Purchasing Manager and Jill Smith, the Contracts Manager. Any offer to enter into a contract on behalf of this Company from any other person will not have the authority of the Company and will therefore not be binding on the Company. If you negotiate with, or enter into an agreement with any other employee of this Company, or any other person purporting to have the authority of the Company to enter into contractual agreements, you do so at your own risk'.

Defining terms of trading [2.51]

It is also advisable for organisations who are in the business of supplying goods or services via email or the internet to clearly and accurately define their terms of trading. Such terms of trading should be produced in a written document, or as an email attachment, and sent to potential customers before any contract is entered into. Equally, the organisation's web-site should clearly state any terms and conditions of supply. If terms are sent out after an agreement to purchase has been reached by email, for example terms printed on the back of an invoice, then such terms will not be binding as part of the contract. A record should of course be kept of any email communications which may form part of a contractual agreement, preferably in electronic format. This will mean that if there is a dispute later on about the terms of the order, concrete evidence will be available to resolve the matter.

From the supplier's perspective, it is also very important to make sure that where orders are to be received and accepted on-line, the mechanism for ordering includes a 'tick-box' which the customer has to click on the computer screen to indicate their acceptance of the supplier's terms. This 'tick-box' should appear at an early stage of the internet transaction and should be designed so that it has to be completed before an order can be transmitted.

As another precaution, employees of the supplier company who are dealing with incoming orders should be trained not to accept any orders unless it is clear from the incoming message that the customer has accepted the company's terms. A statement might usefully be included in guidelines given to staff who deal with incoming orders along the lines of:

'All email enquiries must be replied to promptly and must include a statement of the Company's terms and conditions of sale'.

'In taking orders for the Company's goods or services via email, employees must check to make sure that the customer has accepted the Company's terms and conditions of sale that are posted on the Company's website'.

'If a potential customer does not accept the Company's terms of sale, or issues their own terms, the employee receiving the order must not agree to it or process it, and should instead refer the matter to the Department Manager. Normally it will be appropriate to send an email back to the customer stating that their offer will not be accepted unless they agree to the Company's terms. Unless this action is taken, the Company may be bound by a contract for the sale of goods or services on unattractive or unacceptable terms'.

Misrepresentation [2.52]

Any inaccurate or misleading statement about a company's products or services given via an email or on an organisation's website (or by other means) can lead to legal claims of misrepresentation, especially if the statements have had the effect of inducing an individual or an organisation to enter into a contractual agreement to purchase the products or services. For example, if an employee sends an email to a potential customer making a claim about one of their company's products that the company cannot meet, the claim might potentially be regarded as a term incorporated into the contract between the parties, thus leading to legal problems later on.

A further important legal issue is that any untrue descriptions of goods given on a website or by email (or by any other means) may constitute a breach of the *Trade Descriptions Act 1968*. This can lead to criminal liability.

Suppliers are also responsible for making sure that the prices they quote via email or the internet, for example on a website, are correct and up-to-date. Virgin, the airline company, was heavily fined for a breach of US law some years ago when the prices quoted on their website for flights had not been updated.

It is clearly advisable for businesses to include a general 'limit on liability statement' both on their website and within all email communication. Although such a statement will not act to exclude liability for fraudulent misrepresentation, it may give the business some protection against negligent or innocent misrepresentations. Legal advice should be sought in order to achieve maximum protection.

Copyright [2.53]

In the UK, copyright automatically comes into existence as soon as an original work is created. There is no formal system of registration of copyright unlike in the US where copyright has to be formally registered before a work is protected. Copyright can, however, be assigned to another person, for example the author of a book may assign copyright to a publishing company in exchange for an appropriate fee. In that case, the publisher becomes the owner of the work for the purposes of copyright law. In the UK copyright lasts for the lifetime of the owner plus 70 years without any requirement for it to be renewed.

The law of copyright applies to electronic communication in the same way as it does to printed material and other forms of communication. There is to date no Code of Practice governing the use of material published on the internet. This can create problems for employers whose employees may download documents or software from the internet during the course of their jobs and possibly copy such material or forward it on to others in breach of copyright. Equally, an employee may bring text they have downloaded from the internet at home into work, or load pirated software on to the employer's computer system for work-related (or personal) purposes.

The laws on copyright protect most materials on the internet, including computer software, screen-savers, documents, graphics, computer games and any literary, musical or artistic works. A web-page is classed as a 'literary work' within the meaning of the Act, and similarly any graphic image on a web-page will be classed as an 'artistic work'. Hypertext links from one website to another are normally permissible.

The fact that material is in the public domain does not prevent it from being copyrighted. Like the content of newspapers and books, the content of an internet site is open to the public to read (either free or on payment of a fee) but may not be copied or reproduced without permission.

The Copyright, Designs and Patents Act 1988 [2.54]

The *Copyright, Designs and Patents Act 1988* stipulates that only the owner of the copyright is allowed to copy the material. Thus any form of copying by anyone else for any purpose, including electronic copying, will be prohibited unless permission is first obtained from the copyright holder. Employees who randomly download material from the internet without express or implied permission to do so, or who use downloaded material in ways that are not permitted by the owner of the material, are therefore likely to be in breach of copyright law. If the material obtained is used in the course of the employee's work, their employer may then be vicariously liable for the infringement of the copyright.

Policy statement on copyright matters [2.55]

It is in the interests of every employer to incorporate a statement about copyright laws within their email/internet policy. Employees should be made aware of the types of restrictions imposed by copyright laws and informed about the types of activity that are prohibited.

A sample statement for employees in relation to their use of software could read as follows:

'Every employee must take reasonable precautions to ensure that they use software only within the terms of the relevant licence agreement. Some typical restrictions are:

- the software may be used only for the purposes set out in the agreement and only on computer systems covered by that agreement;

- the copyright statement must not be removed or altered;

- the software may not be transferred or loaned to another person.

It is important to note that only a personal, non-transferable and non-exclusive right to use the software or to the intellectual property in the software is transferred to the purchaser or user.'

Pirated software [2.56]

Employers are responsible for making sure that their employees do not use pirated software (i.e. software that is not properly licensed) at work. it is advisable for employers to have clear rules in place so that employees understand that it is against company rules to bring such material to work or load it on to a workplace computer.

It is important to note that it is not a defence to a legal claim for copyright infringement to argue that an employer did not know an employee had downloaded illegal or unlicensed software on to their computer system and used it for work-related purposes. However, if the pirated software is used by the employee only for personal purposes – for example to play computer games during a lunch hour – the employer will not normally be liable.

The Federation Against Software Theft (FAST) [2.57]

The Federation Against Software Theft (FAST) is a non-profit making organisation supported by the software industry and dedicated to counteracting the use of illegally copied software. They offer information, advice and training to businesses in this area and can provide software which will itself check for unlicensed software loaded on to a computer system. This may be helpful for employers as a measure to double-check that no employee has broken the rules and loaded illegal software on to the employer's system thereby creating potential legal liability for the employer.

Unfortunately it happens sometimes that an employee with a grudge against their employer deliberately loads unlicensed software on to the employer's system, and then reports the matter to an organisation such as FAST. This could occur, for example, if an employee who has been dismissed wishes to seek revenge on their employer for their treatment and has the opportunity to create mischief at work prior to their final departure.

Copyright notices [2.58]

If a business intends to place any copyrighted material on the internet, design a website, or communicate copyrighted material via email, the material should include an appropriately worded notice of copyright. This notice will define how the information may, and may not, be used by those who receive it or access it. For example, there may be a condition that the material can be downloaded or printed for personal use only, but cannot be copied, archived or stored.

Legal advice should be sought prior to ˙devising copyright notices. Nevertheless, a sample of the types of notice which may be used is given below.

Example

The material contained in this website is copyrighted. It may not be copied or reproduced in any way, nor forwarded on to others for any purpose whatsoever.

Example

The material contained on this website is copyrighted. The owner grants permission for recipients to reproduce it free of charge provided it is reproduced accurately and the source and copyright status of the material is made evident.

Example

Although the material contained on this site is copyrighted, the text may be freely downloaded to computer file or printer for private use, research or study purposes. Applications for permission for any other proposed use of this text should be made to ...

Example

This email and any attachment is intended for the addressee only. Its contents are confidential and may contain copyright material. If you receive this email in error, please notify us accordingly and then delete it from your computer system. Any copying, forwarding, disclosure or distribution of the email and any attachment to it is strictly prohibited.

Conclusion [2.59]

Use of email and the internet in business has created a range of legal liabilities for employers including potential liability for defamation, harassment, indecency and breach of copyright. There may also be inadvertent formation of contracts or misrepresentation as a result of careless, ambiguous or misleading statements transmitted across the internet. Employers can be held vicariously liable for the acts of their employees carried out in the course of their employment, and this will include a wide range of liabilities arising out of employees' use of email and the internet.

Emails are not secure and it follows that there may also be problems of breaches of confidentiality. Furthermore, email messages can be used in evidence in court proceedings and employers may be required by a court or tribunal to produce them in the course of such proceedings.

It is therefore very important for employers to take appropriate steps to inform their employees about their responsibilities in relation to use of email and the internet and the potential for legal liability and to provide clear guidelines for use, including a list of prohibited uses.

Questions and Answers [2.60]

Question

What kind of legal liabilities might an employer face on account of allowing employees unlimited access to email and internet facilities at work?

Answer

If employers and their employees use electronic communication in any way they please, there may be a range of potential legal repercussions for the employer. The laws of contract, defamation, copyright, harassment and obscenity apply to email and internet communications in the same way as they apply to traditional methods of communication. There may also be the risk of breaches of confidentiality occurring through messages being sent outside the organisation containing confidential information about the company.

Question

To what extent is an employer liable in law for their employees' misuse of email and the internet?

Answer

Employers are responsible and will have legal liability for their employees' activities when they are using email or the internet in the course of their employment, irrespective of whether or not the employer is aware of each individual's specific activities on a daily basis. This is known as vicarious liability. Thus an employee's misdeeds could bring legal liability on to the employer.

Question

Can an employer be liable in law for something an employee has done wrong at work even if the misdeed was not authorised by the employer?

Answer

In order for the employer to be liable for an employee's actions or omissions, it must be shown that the employee whose misdeeds gave rise to legal action was acting 'in the course of employment' when they committed the act in question. This means that there must have been a close connection between the employee's act(s) and the nature of the job duties they were engaged to carry out. By contrast, if an employee goes off 'on a frolic of his own' (as one Court put it), and it can be shown that their actions had nothing to do with their job responsibilities or duties, then the employer is unlikely to be held liable for their actions or the consequences of those actions. However, given that many employees are supplied with a computer by their employer for the performance of their duties, and similarly provided with access to email and the internet by the employer, it will be difficult for the employer to argue that the employee's activities carried out via the computer were not carried out in the course of employment. It follows that misuse of these facilities by an employee which takes the form of the employee using computer facilities provided by the employer in a way that is not authorised will in most cases mean that the employer will be liable in law for the outcome of the misuse.

Question

What can an employer do to reduce the likelihood of being liable for their employees' misdeeds involving misuse of email or the internet?

Answer

The likelihood of being held liable in law for employees' email or internet wrongdoings can be reduced if the employer introduces a rigorous policy defining acceptable and unacceptable uses of these facilities, and takes positive steps to communicate and apply the policy in practice. By taking such actions, the employer may be able to show that an employee who commits an act which is in clear breach of the policy was not acting 'in the course of employment' and that the employer is therefore not liable in law.

Question

What is defamation and can an employer be held liable for any defamatory statements made by employees in internal or external emails?

Answer

Written material will be defamatory if it involves the publication of an untrue statement which tends to lower a person (or organisation) in the estimation of right-thinking members of society generally. There is no distinction in the law of defamation between the content of an internal email and text contained in a printed letter or other written communication. Thus, there may be liability for defamation if an email sent internally or externally contains material that is defamatory of an individual or of another company. Both the employee and their employer may be held liable for any defamatory statements made by the employee during the course of email communication.

Question

What should employers do to reduce the chances of their employees making defamatory statements during the course of their email communications, and therefore reduce the likelihood of this type of legal action against the company?

Answer

Employers may wish to publish a statement designed to inform employees about defamation and thus prevent or reduce the likelihood of employees inadvertently making defamatory statements during the course of their email communications. Such a statement could be incorporated into an employee handbook, or could form part of an overall email or internet policy.

Question

What is the extent of employers' liability in law for material circulating in the workplace that could be construed as sexist or racist?

Answer

If sexist or racist material is circulating in the workplace, whether by email or by other means, the employer may be liable for any sex or race discrimination complaint brought by an employee who finds the material offensive on grounds of sex or race. Similar principles would apply to material that was offensive on grounds relating to religion or belief, or to homosexuality. In addition, the downloading of sexually explicit material from the internet may create an atmosphere at work that is uncomfortable for female employees, thus constituting sexual harassment. Complaints may be brought to an employment tribunal irrespective of length of service, and compensation is unlimited.

Question

If an employee is the victim of bullying by email, what remedy in law might they have against the employer?

Answer

There is no employment law in the UK that specifically outlaws bullying at work. However, there is an implied duty of trust and confidence inherent in every contract of employment and serious bullying would normally be regarded as a fundamental breach of this duty. Thus an employee who repeatedly receives inflammatory email messages from (for example) their supervisor could, depending on the degree of bullying involved, argue that the supervisor's conduct fundamentally breached the duty of trust and confidence and hence their contract of employment. Provided the employee had a minimum of one year's continuous service, they could resign (with or without notice) and bring a claim for constructive dismissal to an employment tribunal.

Question

What does the term 'flamemail' mean?

Answer

'Flamemail' has been defined as an abusive, aggressive or deliberately anti-social email message. This can include emails that are viewed as rude, upsetting, unduly sarcastic or unacceptable on grounds linked to sex, sexual orientation, race, religion or disability.

Question

If an employee downloads pornographic material from the internet, does that constitute a criminal offence?

Answer

Adult pornography is not illegal in the UK unless it can be classed as obscene, in which case it will constitute a criminal offence under the *Obscene Publications Act 1959*. In order for material to be obscene for the purposes of the Act, it has to be shown that its publication would tend to deprave or corrupt persons who are likely to read, see or hear the material. Child pornography, however, is illegal in the UK. Thus an employee who downloads obscene or paedophiliac material from the internet will be committing a criminal offence.

Question

If an employee is found to have deliberately accessed, downloaded or distributed pornography from the internet at work, would this give the employer a solid reason for dismissal?

Answer

Provided the employer had a policy statement and/or rules specifying that such activities were regarded by the company as gross misconduct, and provided employees had been unambiguously informed that any activities involving pornography would lead to their summary dismissal, the employer would have solid grounds to dismiss. However, if there is no clear policy and rules banning pornography in the workplace, it is possible that an employee dismissed for accessing or downloading pornography from the internet could succeed in a claim for unfair dismissal at tribunal.

Question

If an employee comes forward to management with a complaint that a colleague has been downloading obscene material from the internet, would the employee who raised the complaint be protected in any way by employment legislation?

Answer

Since displaying obscene material may constitute a criminal offence, the disclosure by one employee that another employee has been downloading such material from the internet could give rise to protection against dismissal or detriment under the *Public Interest Disclosure Act 1998*. In order to be protected under the Act, the employee must have made the disclosure in good faith either to the employer directly, or to one of a prescribed list of authorised persons. Provided the employee genuinely and reasonably believes that the material in question constitutes a criminal offence, they will in all probability be protected by the provisions of the Act irrespective of whether the downloading of the material was in fact a criminal offence. Genuine and reasonable belief on the part of the employee is enough.

Question

Is it possible to form or vary a contract by email?

Answer

It is possible, and indeed relatively easy, to form (or vary) a binding contract through an exchange of emails. In the UK, many types of contract, including employment contracts, can be made irrespective of whether there is a signed document. Thus, contracts formed electronically between UK companies are as binding as those formed by conventional means and are subject to the same employment laws and contract laws.

Question

How can a company minimise the chances of their employees inadvertently binding the business to a contract to purchase supplies through careless use of email?

Answer

To obtain some protection from the accidental formation of contracts, or the formation of a contract on unacceptable terms, the organisation may wish to consider including within every email sent to existing or potential suppliers a statement that defines nominated persons from within the organisation with the authority to negotiate or enter into contracts. This will have the effect of putting the supplier on notice that any offer to form a contract emanating from any other person will not have the authority of the organisation to enter into a binding contractual agreement

Question

How does copyright law impact on employers if, during the course of employees' work, they download material from the internet?

Answer

The *Copyright, Designs and Patents Act 1988* stipulates that only the owner of the copyright is allowed to copy the material. This law applies to electronic communication in the same way as it does to printed material and other forms of communication. Thus any form of copying by anyone else for any purpose, including electronic copying, will be prohibited unless permission is first obtained. Employees who randomly download material from the internet without express or implied permission to do so, or who use downloaded material in ways that are not permitted by the owner of the material, are therefore likely to be in breach of copyright law. If the material obtained is used in the course of the employee's work, their employer may then be vicariously liable for the copyright infringement.

3 Unlawful Harassment

Introduction [3.1]

Harassment can take many forms and can range from behaviour that is mildly objectionable to conduct that is seriously offensive. The effects of harassment on its victims can include, embarrassment, distress, loss of confidence, intimidation or feelings of having been demeaned or degraded.

Current Employment Law Covering Harassment in the Workplace [3.2]

The law governing harassment in employment has developed substantially in recent years, both as a result of court and tribunal decisions that have interpreted harassment as a detriment under discrimination law, and as a result of new legislation emanating from Europe which has provided a statutory definition of harassment. The *Race Relations Act 1976* was amended in July 2003 and now identifies harassment on grounds of race or ethnic or national origins as a distinct form of unlawful discrimination. The *Employment Equality (Religion or Belief) Regulations 2003 (SI 2003 No 1660)* and the *Employment Equality (Sexual Orientation) Regulations 2003 (SI 2003 No 1661)* each contain a parallel definition of harassment. Paragraph **3.28** below provides details.

The *Sex Discrimination Act 1975* and the *Disability Discrimination Act 1995* do not, as yet, contain a specific definition of harassment, but are said to be amended in the future to include similar statutory definitions. Both these Acts currently contain a provision that it is unlawful to subject an employee (or job applicant) to a detriment on the grounds of sex or on grounds related to a disability respectively *(section 6(2)(b)* of the *Sex Discrimination Act* and *section 4(2)(b)* of the *Disability Discrimination Act)*. As a result of court and tribunal interpretations of these detriment provisions, and of the detriment provisions in the *Race Relations Act 1976*, harassment has come to be viewed as a detriment, capable of amounting to unlawful discrimination. Detriment has been defined as:

- 'Putting under a disadvantage' (*Ministry of Defence v Jeremiah [1980] ICR 13*);

- 'Disadvantaged in the circumstances and conditions of work' *(De Souza v Automobile Association [1986] ICR 514).*

It follows that if, for example, an employee can show that they were placed at a disadvantage on grounds of sex as a result of the behaviour of one or more of their colleagues, a claim for sex discrimination may be made out. It is enough for the victim of harassment to show that the way they were treated was detrimental and was in some way associated with their sex.

Criminal laws on harassment [3.3]

Despite the absence of any specific employment law encompassing harassment, harassment may in certain circumstances be a criminal offence.

The Criminal Justice and Public Order Act 1994 [3.4]

The Criminal Justice and Public Order Act, in force in England and Wales (but not Scotland), was designed principally to make deliberate racial harassment a criminal offence. Nevertheless the Act covers all forms of harassment whether or not associated with a person's race, and the Act can apply irrespective of the motive behind the harassment.

Conduct under the Act will be an offence where one person intentionally causes another harassment, alarm or distress in either of the two ways described below:

1. by using threatening, abusive or insulting language or behaviour, or disorderly behaviour; *or*

2. by displaying any writing, sign or other visible representation which is threatening, abusive or insulting.

Clearly the term 'other visible representation' is capable of including material displayed on a computer screen. Thus employees deliberately exposed to highly offensive or insulting material via computer screens or hard-copy print-outs would have the option of complaining to the police, provided they could show that the harassment was intentional.

The Protection from Harassment Act 1997 [3.5]

The Protection from Harassment Act, which came into force in June 1997 throughout Britain, makes it a criminal offence to pursue a course of conduct on at least two occasions that amounts to harassment, or to cause a person to fear that violence will be used against them. Like the Criminal Justice and Public Order Act, this Act is not an employment law, but was introduced mainly to provide protection to people who are the victims of stalking. Unlike the Criminal Justice and Public Order Act, however, the Protection from Harassment Act allows harassment to be regarded as an offence even if it is unintentional. Even though the Act is not specifically designed for the employer-employee relationship, it could in practice be used by an employee who becomes the victim of email harassment at work, provided the content of the emails could reasonably be described as harassment. Apart from the possibility of a complaint to the police, the individual who was the victim of the harassment could pursue a civil action to claim damages against the harasser.

The Scope of the Sex Discrimination Act and the Race Relations Act

The Sex Discrimination Act [3.6]

The *Sex Discrimination Act 1975* makes it unlawful to treat a female employee less favourably than a male employee was or would have been treated in comparable circumstances. Protection under the Act applies equally to men, although in practice more women than men are the victims of sex discrimination in the workplace. Protection is also extended under the Act to discrimination on the grounds of marriage.

Discrimination on grounds of gender reassignment [3.6a]

A further aspect of sex discrimination legislation is that, following a major decision of the European Court of Justice in 1996 (*P v S and Cornwall County Council ECJ [1996] IRLR 347*), the *Sex Discrimination Act* was amended (via the *Gender Reassignment Regulations 1999 (SI 1999 No 1102)*) so as to incorporate gender reassignment within the meaning of 'sex' for the purposes of sex discrimination. Gender reassignment is defined as:

'a process which is undertaken under medical supervision for the purpose of reassigning a person's sex by changing physiological or other characteristics of sex, and includes any part of such a process'.

An individual is protected against discrimination if they plan to undergo a sex change, are currently undergoing treatment to achieve a sex change, or have in the past undergone a sex change. It follows that any kind of harassment on the grounds of gender reassignment will amount to unlawful sex discrimination.

Sexual orientation discrimination [3.7]

The term 'sex discrimination' in the *Sex Discrimination Act 1975* has consistently been interpreted strictly to mean discrimination on the grounds of gender, thereby not encompassing discrimination on grounds of sexual orientation or sexual preference.

However, the *Employment Equality (Sexual Orientation) Regulations 2003*, implemented in December 2003 as a result of an EC Directive, expressly render workplace discrimination and harassment on grounds of sexual orientation unlawful. The Regulations afford equal protection to heterosexuals (for example in the case of a mistaken view that the person is gay), gay and lesbian people, and bisexual people. Protection is available also against harassment motivated by a mistaken perception of someone's sexual orientation and on the grounds that an employee associates with someone of a particular sexual orientation.

Protection against discriminatory treatment on grounds of sexuality may also be available under human rights legislation. In *Macdonald v Advocate-General for Scotland* and *Pearce v Governing Body of Mayfield School, House of Lords [2003] UKHL 34*, the House of Lords upheld the principle that detrimental treatment on grounds of homosexuality breached an individual's right to a private life under Article 8 of the European Convention on Human Rights.

[The next paragraph is **3.10**.]

The Race Relations Act [3.10]

The *Race Relations Act 1976* makes it unlawful to discriminate against an employee or job applicant 'on racial grounds' (*section 1(1)(a)*). Like the *Sex Discrimination Act*, the *Race Relations Act* protects everyone equally whether black African or white Anglo-Saxon, whether Pakistani or English, etc.

The term 'race' under the *Race Relations Act 1976, s 3(1)* is further defined as encompassing:

- Colour;
- Race;
- Nationality (which includes citizenship);
- Ethnic origins;
- National origins.

Religious discrimination [3.10a]

The Employment Equality (Religion or Belief) Regulations 2003 (SI 2003 No 1660) outlaw religious discrimination and harassment. These Regulations came into force in December 2003. Protection is available to workers on grounds of 'any religion, religious belief or similar philosophical belief'. This definition excludes political opinion, but is wide enough to cover fringe religions.

Who is protected by discrimination legislation? [3.11]

All workers are protected against unlawful workplace discrimination and harassment, and not only those employed directly on a contract of employment, hence home-workers, casual staff, agency temps and contractors are able to rely on the various statutory provisions. This is because 'employment' is defined in the legislation as 'employment under a contract of service or of apprenticeship or a contract personally to execute any work or labour'. Job applicants are also covered by the statutes throughout the process of recruitment.

People posted to Great Britain [3.12]

Protection against discrimination applies not only to people working in Britain, but also to those who are posted to work in Britain for a temporary period.

People working outside Great Britain [3.12a]

If an employee's work is done wholly outside Great Britain, technically that employee will not be eligible to bring a complaint of unlawful discrimination in a British employment tribunal. If, however, the employee's work is for the purposes of their employer's establishment in Great Britain and if the employee is, or was, ordinarily resident in Great Britain either when they were recruited or at some time during their employment, then they will be eligible for protection against discrimination and harassment on grounds of race, ethnic or national origins, religion or belief and sexual orientation. In time the *Sex Discrimination Act 1975* and the *Disability Discrimination Act 1995* will include similar provisions. It follows that British employees temporarily assigned to work in other countries are protected in law against certain forms of harassment.

People working on ships and offshore installations [3.13]

People who work on ships registered in Britain or on aircraft are protected, as are those who work offshore on oil and gas installations. Unless the employment is wholly outside Britain, anti-discrimination legislation will apply.

Eligibility to complain of discrimination [3.14]

Employees and other workers are eligible to bring a complaint of discrimination to an employment tribunal irrespective of length of service or age, provided they do so within three calendar months of the discriminatory act complained of. In the case of a series of discriminatory acts, for example an ongoing course of conduct that amounts to sexual or racial harassment, then the tribunal claim must be lodged with the tribunal office no later than the end of the three month period following the latest in the series of incidents.

The comparative approach [3.15]

In general, the anti-discrimination laws in Britain are structured to facilitate claims based on a comparison between the treatment of one person and the treatment of another who is of the opposite sex, a different racial group, a different religion or a different sexual orientation. The *Disability Discrimination Act*, however, does not require a comparison to be made with a non-disabled worker. One commonly applied test is 'would the applicant have been treated in the way they were treated but for their sex (race, etc)' (a principle originating from the case of *James v Eastleigh Borough Council [1990] IRLR 288*).

Liability for Harassment [3.16]

All the anti-discrimination statutes make it clear that employers will be liable for an act of discrimination committed 'in the course of employment ... whether or not it was done with the employer's knowledge or approval'.

Employers' liability for discrimination 'in the course of employment' [3.17]

The phrase 'in the course of employment' has, over the years, been interpreted widely as the following case demonstrates:

Chief Constable of the Lincolnshire Police v Stubbs [1999] IRLR 81

Facts

Ms Stubbs, a police officer, had been subjected to a campaign of sexual harassment by her line manager over a period of 14 months. Two of the occasions on which Ms Stubbs suffered sexual harassment occurred away from the workplace and in the police officers' own time. On one of these occasions, police officers had met socially after work in a pub, and on the other she was accompanied by her boyfriend to another officer's leaving party which also took place in a pub.

Findings

The EAT held that the police officer who harassed Ms Stubbs was acting in the course of his employment within the meaning of the *Sex Discrimination Act* when he sexually harassed Ms Stubbs in the pub. They formed the view that, taking into account all the circumstances, the social occasions when the police officers met in the pub were in fact an extension of their employment. Although the fact that harassment takes place outside of working hours and away from the workplace will be key factors in determining employer liability, these are not the only relevant factors that need to be taken into account.

Implications

It follows from the *Stubbs* case that an employer may be held liable for acts of harassment that take place during all forms of business-related social events, for example residential training courses, business lunches, and office parties held away from the workplace.

Vicarious liability [3.18]

In cases of alleged harassment on grounds of sex, race, religion, sexual orientation or disability, the test for liability is wider than the common law vicarious liability test. Under the vicarious liability test, an employer will be vicariously liable for an employee's actions carried out 'in the course of employment' only if there is a close connection between the employee's act(s) and the nature of the job duties the employee is engaged to carry out. In cases of harassment, however, a wider test is now used, largely as a result of the case of *Tower Boot Co Ltd v Jones* [1997] (below).

The Tower Boot case [3.19]

Tower Boot Co Ltd v Jones [1997] IRLR 168

Facts

The applicant was a 16-year old boy of mixed parentage (his mother was white and his father black). During his employment as a last operator, he suffered extreme forms of physical and verbal racial abuse at the hands of two colleagues. His treatment included having his arm burned by a hot screwdriver, his legs whipped and metal bolts thrown at this head. He was also regularly called names such as 'chimp' and 'monkey'. Having resigned after only a month in the job, he brought a claim of race discrimination to tribunal. Criminal charges were also brought against the perpetrators of the abuse.

Findings

The tribunal and the EAT had no doubt that Mr Jones had suffered detrimental treatment on racial grounds, but, applying the common law test of vicarious liability, ruled that the employer could not be held liable for his treatment. This was because, the EAT could not 'by any stretch of the imagination' interpret such violent conduct as a mode of performing authorised job duties.

When the case was appealed, however, the Court of Appeal reassessed the phrase 'in the course of employment' and, taking a purposive approach, decided that it should be viewed broadly in cases of discrimination in order to give effect to justice. They decided that the phrase should be interpreted along the lines of the lay-person's normal understanding of the words. In taking this approach, the Court of Appeal, departing from the previous application of the common law principles governing vicarious liability in cases of harassment, overturned the tribunal's decision and held that the employer was liable for the racial harassment of Mr Jones.

Ignorance of the fact harassment is taking place [3.20]

Ignorance of the fact harassment is taking place is no defence against liability in law. The employer may be held responsible, and liable, for discriminatory acts whether or not management was aware of what was going on. Even in cases where the victim has not formally complained, the employer cannot escape liability by pleading ignorance. One case that demonstrates this point is *Driskel v Peninsula Business Services Ltd* (below).

Driskel v Peninsula Business Services Ltd & ors [2000] IRLR 151

The employee, an advice line consultant, was regularly subjected to sexual banter and vulgar comments by her manager, as were others in the department. Ms Driskel did not object at the time to these comments.

Having applied for a promotion, Ms Driskel was scheduled to attend an interview with her manager. On the day before the interview, her manager told her flippantly that if she wanted to be successful in her application for a promotion, she should come to the interview wearing a short skirt and see-through blouse showing plenty of cleavage. Ms Driskel complained about this incident after the interview, but her complaint was rejected after investigation. Despite this, Ms Driskel felt strongly enough about her manager's remarks to refuse to continue working alongside him. She was consequently dismissed, and brought a claim for sex discrimination to tribunal.

Findings

Ms Driskel's complaint of sexual harassment was upheld at appeal. The company tried to disclaim liability by arguing that they were unaware she found her manager's vulgar remarks offensive as she had not originally raised a formal complaint. The EAT judged, however, that, although sexist or vulgar remarks may not, when considered individually, be sufficient to found a complaint of sexual harassment, a collection of incidents may be enough to constitute unlawful discrimination irrespective of whether the employee has raised an objection.

The company also attempted to defend the claim by pointing out that, because the manager's remarks were made to everyone in the department, both men and women, Ms Driskel had not been treated less favourably than her male colleagues. The EAT held, however, that the effect on a woman of a man's sexual remarks is more intimidating than the effect of the same remarks on a man. Thus a woman subjected to remarks of a sexual nature will have been less favourably treated than a man in the same circumstances.

Implications

The outcome of this case was interesting because it showed that an employer cannot necessarily avoid liability by relying on the traditional comparative approach outlined in the discrimination Acts. In other words, it may be no defence to argue that others were treated equally badly when the conduct complained of involves extreme sexual or sexist remarks.

[The next paragraph is **3.22.**]

Lack of intent [3.22]

It has been clearly established through a long line of case law that lack of intent or motive will not reduce or prevent employer liability for acts of harassment. It is not the intent of the harasser that is the issue, but rather the effect on the victim. This principle emanated originally from the European Commission's definition of sexual harassment (see **3.28** below) which focuses on whether the treatment of an employee is offensive 'to the recipient'.

When individuals can be held liable for acts of harassment [3.23]

Individuals can also be held liable for acts of discrimination perpetrated against their colleagues, including harassment. Although an employee who wishes to bring a complaint of harassment to tribunal must cite their employer as the main respondent, it is open to them to cite one or more individuals as well as secondary respondents. If the complaint of discrimination is made out and compensation awarded, the tribunal may, if it judges it appropriate to do so, order an individual who was the perpetrator of the harassment to pay the victim compensation out of their own pockets.

In the high profile case of *Crofton v Yeboah* at the Court of Appeal in 2002, the Housing Director of London Borough of Hackney was ordered to pay £45,000 compensation (plus interest) to the Borough's former assistant chief executive of human resources (a black Ghanaian born West African). This followed a string of five complaints of race discrimination brought by the HR executive against the employer and the Housing Director personally on account of untrue allegations of corruption and improper conduct, all of which were found to be based entirely on the Housing Director's prejudice against West Africans.

The tribunal had found that the Housing Director was personally liable for the long series of false allegations and the campaign he had waged against the HR executive on account of his race and this was upheld on appeal. The award was in addition to the compensation ordered against the employer. In making the award, the Court of Appeal held that an employee can be held liable for race discrimination against a fellow employee irrespective of whether the employer succeeds in defending the claim against them, so long as the acts of discrimination are committed in the course of employment.

Compensation for harassment [3.23a]

Compensation for discrimination in the workplace (including harassment) is unlimited and can include various elements according to what the tribunal considers to be just and equitable. Compensation can include:

- loss of earnings (up to the date of the tribunal hearing and possibly into the future as well);

- injury to feelings;

- injury to health (ie personal injury).

It was held by the EAT in *Essa v Laing Ltd [2003] EAT 0697/01*, that if an employee suffers a psychiatric injury as a result of discrimination in the workplace, there is no requirement for the employee to prove at tribunal that the injury to their health was reasonably foreseeable in order to recover compensation for the injury. Instead, it is sufficient for the employee to show that the psychiatric injury was caused by discriminatory treatment.

How Employers can Reduce the Likelihood of Their Being Liable For Claims of Harassment   [3.24]

Clearly no employer can constantly be watching and monitoring employees' activities to make sure that their conduct never crosses the boundary from what is acceptable to what might be construed as sexual or racial harassment. Nevertheless, it is possible for employers to reduce substantially the chances of their being held liable for any acts of harassment that do occur in the course of employment. If the following steps are taken, then the employer may be able to avoid liability for claims of sexual or racial harassment.

1. Devise an equal opportunities policy to include within its ambit a statement that no form of harassment will be condoned or tolerated, including harassment by email.

2. Implement the policy, making sure it has full management backing. Articulately written policies will not serve to convince a tribunal that an employer's practices were not discriminatory in the absence of concrete evidence that specific steps have been taken to translate the policy into practice.

3. Provide equal opportunities awareness training for all staff, and additional training for managers and supervisors to make sure they are able to recognise all forms of harassment, including the types of conduct that might be interpreted as email harassment.

4. Introduce measures to ensure use of email and the internet is properly supervised and controlled (see **CHAPTER 9**).

5. Take steps to make sure all employees are aware of the potential for liability that can be created by misuse of email and the internet.

6. Design or re-design disciplinary procedures so that any form of harassment, including harassment by email, the downloading of material from the

internet that could be perceived as sexually explicit, sexist, homophobic, racist or religiously offensive and the distribution of such material, is defined as gross misconduct leading potentially to summary dismissal.

7. Devise and implement a complaints procedure so that any worker who is the victim of any form of harassment can raise a complaint in confidence in the secure knowledge that it will be investigated promptly and handled fairly, and that there will be no negative repercussions on account of their having raised such a complaint. Such a procedure should ideally be separate from the company's normal grievance procedure, so as to allow employees who may suffer harassment at the hands of their immediate manager the opportunity to complain to someone else within the organisation.

8. Promote the policy in such a way that managers and supervisors are encouraged to respond positively to complaints of discrimination, including harassment, and to be supportive towards employees in dealing with their complaints. The main aim of a complaints procedure should of course be to put a stop to the treatment that the employee finds unacceptable.

9. Make sure that the policy, the complaints procedure, and the penalties for harassment are clearly and unambiguously communicated to all who work within the organisation.

10. Make sure the policy and the procedure are applied consistently.

The thinking behind the above measures is that, if an employer can prove to a tribunal that they have taken all reasonable steps to prevent discrimination (so far as is reasonably practicable), this will form a statutory defence against liability. To have a chance of avoiding liability for claims of unlawful harassment, it is not enough to show a tribunal that all possible measures were taken to remedy a problem *after* it had arisen. To have a chance of escaping liability, the employer must be able to show that they took all the steps they reasonably could to *prevent* harassment from happening.

For example, in *Haringey Council v Al-Azzawi [2001]*, the EAT ruled that events that took place after an act of race discrimination had occurred were irrelevant when considering whether or not the employer had met the statutory defence contained in *section 32(3)* of the *Race Relations Act 1976*.

The issue of policies, rules and procedures for use of email and the internet is explored more fully in **CHAPTER 8**, with example policies and procedures provided.

Sample clauses [3.25]

An example of a clause that could be incorporated into an employer's disciplinary rules/procedure is:

> The company will regard the following types of behaviour as gross misconduct, leading potentially to summary dismissal:
>
> - Any form of bullying, harassment or intimidating behaviour. This includes harassment or inflammatory statements contained in email messages sent to colleagues;
>
> - The downloading of offensive material from the internet, or the distribution of such material whether in printed form or by email attachment.

[The next paragraph is **3.27**.]

Definitions and Meaning of 'Harassment'

New statutory definition of harassment [3.27]

The *Race Relations Act 1976*, the *Employment Equality (Religion or Belief) Regulations 2003* and the *Employment Equality (Sexual Orientation) Regulations 2003* each contain a statutory definition of harassment as a distinct form of unlawful discrimination. The definitions of harassment within each of these laws are consistent with one another. For example, the relevant provision in the *Race Relations Act* states that harassment occurs where on the grounds of the victim's race or ethnic or national origins, another person engages in unwanted conduct which has the purpose or effect of:

- violating that other's dignity; or

- creating an intimidating, hostile, degrading, humiliating or offensive environment for that other.

It is important to note that this definition of harassment means that:

- The motive of the sender of a discriminatory email is irrelevant, for example bombarding someone with lists of racist jokes that are intended to cause amusement might, if such conduct has the opposite effect, constitute racial harassment.

- So long as the conduct in question is unwanted by its recipient and is linked to race, religion, etc, it will be capable of constituting unlawful harassment.

- Conduct that is not directed at a particular individual may amount to harassment if it creates an uncomfortable or distressing working environment for that person. For example an employee with strong religious beliefs who regularly receives emails from a colleague containing derogatory banter about religious practices might be offended and consequently have a legitimate claim against the organisation for harassment on grounds of religion.

Codes of Practice [3.27a]

It will be helpful to employers if they follow the guidelines laid down in the Codes of Practice issued by the Equal Opportunities Commission (EOC) and the Commission for Racial Equality (CRE). Both codes contain sound advice. A further useful source of guidance is the EC Code of Practice on Measures to Combat Sexual Harassment (see **3.28** below).

The European Commission's definition of sexual harassment [3.28]

Although the *Sex Discrimination Act 1975* does not (as yet) contain a statutory definition of harassment, the EC Code of Practice on Measures to Combat Sexual Harassment defines sexual harassment as 'unwanted conduct of a sexual nature or other conduct based on sex affecting the dignity of women and men at work'. The Code also explains that sexual harassment may include physical, verbal or non-verbal conduct, and goes on to say that such conduct will constitute sexual harassment where it is 'unwanted, unreasonable and offensive to the recipient'.

This latter phrase means in effect that it is up to each individual to determine what types of sexual conduct they find unacceptable, irrespective of the view another employee might take. The new statutory definition of harassment incorporated into the UK's laws on race discrimination, religious discrimination and discrimination on grounds of sexual orientation mirrors the concepts contained in the EC Code and the principles that emanate from these concepts have been consistently upheld in practice by UK employment tribunals over a number of years.

The effect on the victim [3.29]

The definition of sexual harassment in the EC Code of Practice (see **3.28** above) makes it clear that the question of whether conduct of a specific kind constitutes harassment will depend on the effect of the conduct on the victim. As the EC Code of Practice points out, 'it is for each individual to determine what behaviour is acceptable to him or her and what he/she regards as offensive'. Thus the issue becomes subjective to an extent. This links in with the concept of detriment defined in the *Sex Discrimination Act*, i.e. in order for harassment to constitute unlawful discrimination, it must have caused some detriment to the individual who was its victim.

It follows that, when dealing with complaints of harassment, a manager should not substitute personal views for those of the employee raising the complaint. Making assumptions that, for example, an employee is over-reacting, or showing too much sensitivity, are unhelpful and may prevent a genuine complaint of harassment from being properly dealt with.

Example **[3.30]**

An employee distributes an email message that contains sexual innuendoes or jokes of a sexual nature, thinking that this will cause amusement amongst colleagues. The content of the email may be unwanted and offensive to one recipient, but be viewed as funny by another. In this case one person will have been the victim of sexual harassment, whilst the other will have suffered no detriment.

[The next paragraph is **3.32**.]

When Email Messages and Material From the Internet can Constitute Harassment

Offensive email messages **[3.32]**

Access to email facilities at work can, unfortunately for employers, provide employees with a readily available opportunity to harass or offend colleagues, even unintentionally.

If a message sent by email contains material that is inflammatory, sexually explicit, racially offensive, sexist/racist, homophobic or religiously offensive in content, the message is capable of amounting to harassment in the same way as the content of a written letter or memo, or a statement made verbally to a colleague directly. There is the added danger that email messages can (deliberately or accidentally) be distributed to a large and diverse audience, so that the unsuspecting click of a computer mouse can lead to the risk of serious offence being caused to large numbers of people. Furthermore, one or more of the recipients of an email message may then forward it on to others, both within and outside the organisation, thus widening the scope for offence to be caused.

In essence, the content of email messages is capable of forming the basis of a complaint of discrimination at an employment tribunal. Even jokes distributed by email, if they contain (for example) sexually explicit or racist wording, may cause offence to an individual thus causing them a detriment on grounds of sex or race. Similarly email attachments that contain sexually explicit pictures may constitute sexual harassment if the recipient finds them offensive. It is important always to bear in mind that the intention of the sender is irrelevant – it is the effect on the recipient that will determine whether the message constitutes harassment. It is all too easy for employees to send an email joke believing it to be funny and not realising that its content could be construed as detrimental to another person on grounds of sex, race, religion, sexual orientation or disability.

Case study [3.33]

The following case study demonstrates the type of problem that employers may encounter:

> *Case study*
>
> Jane and Jean both work in the accounts department of a major firm. The department consists of ten employees who work in reasonable close proximity in an open-plan area. Jane and Jean are the only two female employees in the department.
>
> The company has an email/internet policy in place banning personal use of its computer facilities during working time, but permitting reasonable personal use during employees' own time. There are no specific guidelines as to the definition of 'reasonable personal use'.
>
> Jane has noted that that one of her male colleagues, John, has recently started sending non-work related emails to the others in the department during lunch-times. Jane has been distracted by this because of the frequent outbursts of laughter amongst some of the men in the department and also because some of the email attachments (which consist of material downloaded from the internet) are large and have slowed the system down. Jane has noticed that the material circulating around the department includes images of a sexual nature and sexist jokes. On the whole, however, Jane is unperturbed by her colleagues' antics and has taken the view that what they do in their own time is their business. She has elected to ignore what they are doing.
>
> Jean, however, has confided in Jane that she is becoming more and more upset by John's conduct and in particular by the emails. Although she

realises that John has no malicious motive, she nevertheless finds the content of the emails and in particular some of the pictures (for example pictures of scantily-clad women) offensive and demeaning. It is virtually impossible to ignore the emails, because even if Jean deletes them immediately from her own computer, the pictures tend to be displayed regularly during lunch-hours on her colleagues' screens nearby. On one occasion Jean hinted to John that he should refrain from sending these emails or at the very least tone them down, but John retorted simply that she should 'lighten up' and claimed that the lunch-time amusement was simply a way of relieving the stress of a busy job for him and his colleagues. Jane, for her part, takes the view that Jean is over-reacting and would be better served to ignore the emails, although she nevertheless feels some sympathy for her. She has, however, advised Jean not to make a fuss in case the otherwise good working relationships in the department might (in her opinion) be damaged.

Would Jean have grounds to claim sex discrimination on account of the activities going on in her department?

Because of the way in which British courts view the issue of sexual harassment, it is likely that Jean could succeed in a claim for sex discrimination at tribunal. Conduct becomes sexual harassment at the point at which it is 'offensive, unwanted or unreasonable to the recipient'. This means that the question of whether a colleague's conduct amounts to sexual harassment is a subjective one, depending on whether the recipient of the conduct is genuinely offended by it. The fact that Jane is not offended by the same conduct is irrelevant. The point is that the working environment is uncomfortable for Jean on account of the sexually explicit material that is circulating and to which she is therefore subjected against her will.

Because the company has taken no steps to control the type of conduct that is going on Jean's department, they will be liable for sex discrimination and consequently to compensate Jean for any distress and upset that she has suffered as a result of the harassment. Additionally, if Jean decides to resign because of her colleagues' conduct, she may be able to succeed in a claim for constructive dismissal.

Offensive material from the internet [3.34]

The availability of pornographic material on the internet is another worry for employers whose employees need to access the internet during the course of their work. The display on screen, downloading or transmitting of sexually explicit or pornographic material may clearly cause serious offence to anyone seeing such material, whether on screen or in printed form. If such material is downloaded and distributed around the workplace, or attached to an email message sent to a colleague, then the employees receiving the information may have solid grounds to complain of sexual harassment. A check should therefore be kept on what is displayed on screens and screen-savers.

Single acts of harassment [3.35]

A single act of harassment is capable of amounting to discrimination provided it is sufficiently serious to constitute a detriment to the individual. In *Bracebridge Engineering Ltd v Darby* [1990] *IRLR 3*, the EAT held that there was no reason why a single incident, if serious enough, could not fall within the scope of the *Sex Discrimination Act 1975*.

A series of incidents amounting to unlawful harassment [3.36]

More commonly, however, a claim for discrimination may be the result of an ongoing series of incidents. Often the circumstances are such that, although no incident on its own would be sufficient to be classed as discriminatory treatment, a series of incidents when viewed collectively may be enough to amount to a detriment to the individual. Nevertheless, if pornographic material was downloaded from the internet, or sent to a colleague by email, a single incident could, if it genuinely caused serious offence to the recipient, found a valid complaint of sexual harassment against both the organisation and the sender of the email.

An example of when a series of discriminatory actions could collectively be held to amount to unlawful discrimination was dealt with in the case of *Hendricks v Commissioner of Police for the Metropolis* [2002]. In this case, the Court of Appeal judged that the interpretation of an act extending over a period of time need not be restricted to circumstances where a continuing policy, rule, practice, scheme or regime existed (as had previously been ruled by the courts), but could also include any 'ongoing situation' or 'continuing state of affairs' in which female or ethnic minority police officers were subjected to linked incidents of discrimination (as opposed to a succession of unconnected incidents). This case gave a broader interpretation to the concept of a continuing act of discrimination than had previously been held.

The creation of an uncomfortable working environment [3.37]

Furthermore, the transmission or downloading of offensive material may constitute unlawful discrimination even if it is not sent to or directed at a particular individual. The mere fact that such material is circulating around the workplace may create an uncomfortable or intimidating working environment which in itself could amount to a detriment to any employee forced to work in that environment. The following case demonstrates the risks.

Morse v Future Reality Ltd Case No 54571/95

Facts

Ms Morse worked in an office with several male colleagues. She found the working environment and atmosphere uncomfortable because the men spent an inordinate amount of time down-loading sexually explicit material and obscene images from the internet and circulating this material around the office. Eventually she resigned and complained of sex discrimination on the grounds of harassment, citing the pictures, bad language and general atmosphere of obscenity in the office as the basis for her complaint.

Findings

An employment tribunal upheld Ms Morse's complaint despite the fact that it was acknowledged that the activities that went on were not directed at her personally, and despite the fact that she had not raised a formal complaint with management whilst still employed. The point was that the working atmosphere was uncomfortable on account of sexually explicit material, bad language, etc. and this had a detrimental impact on her. The company was liable because of the harassment itself, and also because no action had been taken to prevent it.

Implications

Sexually offensive behaviour does not have to be directed at a specific employee in order for it to constitute unlawful discrimination. It will be enough that such behaviour creates an atmosphere at work which causes offence to a particular employee, or makes them feel uncomfortable. Thus a failure to control the use of email and the internet will increase the risk of the employer being liable for discriminatory actions by employees resulting from their use of these facilities.

Recognising the Distinction Between Office Banter and Harassment [3.38]

Whilst some types of behaviour may be so blatant or extreme that they obviously amount to harassment, other types of conduct may be perceived as borderline. Essentially the term 'harassment' can cover a wide range of conduct with one element in common – that the conduct in question makes its recipient feel uncomfortable, distressed, embarrassed, intimidated or degraded. Where this is the case, the individual will have suffered unlawful discrimination. Conduct thus becomes harassment at the point at which the person on the receiving end finds it unwelcome and offensive. A general test is whether the behaviour in question was such that a reasonable person might have felt disadvantaged in the circumstances and conditions of their employment.

Examples of unlawful harassment [3.39]

Certain types of conduct may or may not be serious enough to amount to unlawful harassment, depending on all the circumstances. For example messages sent by email may form the basis of a complaint of harassment if they contain:

- Sexual innuendoes.

- Sexist or racist terminology.

- Jokes of a sexual or racial nature.

- Remarks made about religious beliefs or practices that are derogatory or critical.

- Sexually provocative or suggestive remarks.

- Racial or religious insults.

- Speculation about another worker's private life and sexual activities.

- Derogatory remarks about a co-worker's sexual orientation or sexual preferences.

Similarly, material displayed on screen or downloaded from the internet may or may not be sufficient to constitute harassment. Harassment may, for example, include:

- Sexually suggestive pictures.

- Text containing sexist, racist or sexually explicit language.

- Messages, remarks or pictures likely to be offensive to people of a particular religion.

- Lewd comments.

- Text or pictures that are derogatory or demeaning to gay and lesbian people.

- Racist material.

Whenever the content of an email, or of material from the internet, contains a significant connection to sex, sexual orientation, race or religion, it may be capable of amounting to unlawful harassment of those who come into contact with it, whether by accident or not.

[The next paragraph is **3.41**.]

How Tribunals View Claims of Unlawful Harassment [3.41]

Applicants to tribunal do not need to prove 'beyond reasonable doubt' that they were subjected to unlawful harassment in the workplace. Tribunals operate according to the 'balance of probabilities' test, and are entitled to form their own view of whether a particular form of treatment was sufficient to amount to unlawful discrimination, and, where the facts are disputed, which party's evidence they find more credible.

The burden of proof in sex discrimination cases [3.42]

To conform with an EC Directive (Council Directive 98/52EC), the Government in October 2001 implemented new Regulations which reversed the burden of proof in cases of sex discrimination. Since this change was introduced, the burden of proof in claims for sex discrimination will lie with the employer rather than with the employee (as was previously the case).

To succeed in refuting an employee's claim for sex discrimination, the employer has to show that there has been no breach of the principle of equal treatment in relation to the employee in question. This will emphasise the need for proper equal opportunities policies, anti-harassment policies and effective complaints procedures to be in place, and for evidence to be available that concrete measures have been taken to implement the policies and procedures throughout the workplace (see **3.24** above).

The burden of proof in race discrimination cases [3.43]

The burden of proof in relation to complaints of discrimination on grounds of race, ethnic origins and national origins is now on the employer once the complainant has established facts that show that race discrimination may have occurred. This is the same principle as applies in cases of sex discrimination (see **3.42** above).

However, in relation to complaints under the *Race Relations Act* of discrimination on grounds of colour or nationality, the burden of proof technically lies with the complainant, although tribunals may, if they deem it appropriate to do so, draw an inference based on the facts presented to them that the conduct in question amounted to unlawful race discrimination. In practice it is often a question of whether the employer can present to the tribunal objective evidence to refute the employee's allegations of racial harassment, or show that there is a credible alternative explanation to the employee's version of events. If the employer fails to provide an explanation for the conduct complained of, or if the explanation put forward is, in the tribunal's view, inadequate, unsatisfactory or untrue, the tribunal is entitled to find in favour of the complainant.

The burden of proof in cases of discrimination on grounds of religion or belief and sexual orientation [3.43a]

The burden of proof in cases dealing with discrimination on grounds of religion or belief, or discrimination on grounds of sexual orientation, is the same as in cases of sex discrimination (see **3.42** above).

Forthcoming changes to the Equal Treatment Directive [3.44]

Sex discrimination is subject to EU law under the Equal Treatment Directive, the Equal Pay Directive and the Pregnant Workers Directive.
The European Commission has amended the Equal Treatment Directive so that it expressly defines sexual harassment at work as discrimination based on sex contrary to the Directive. The UK Government is obliged to implement the changes to the Directive into UK law and this is expected to take place in 2005.

The Directive in fact provides two definitions, one of 'sex-based harassment' and one of 'sexual harassment' as follows:

1. *Sex-based harassment* is 'where an unwanted conduct relating to the sex of a person occurs with the purpose or effect of violating the dignity of a person, and of creating an intimidating, hostile, degrading, humiliating or offensive environment'.

Thus sex-based harassment will include bullying or any intimidatory conduct directed at a woman for any reason related to the fact that she is a woman. The new definition of sex-based harassment is potentially very broad and could include sexist language, sexist jokes, banter and any unwanted conduct that is related in any way to gender. The structure of the new definition also indicates that there will be no need to show that offensive material was directed at a particular individual in order for it to constitute unlawful sex discrimination. So, for example, if offensive material is displayed on a computer screen, this will definitively be capable of amounting to sex discrimination whenever it has the effect of creating a working environment which is, in a general sense, intimidating, hostile, degrading, humiliating or offensive. This could be the case even if, for example, a female employee occasionally had to pass through an office where such material was visible on a computer screen.

The wording also means – importantly – that there will be no need for an employee who is being harassed to compare their treatment with someone of the opposite sex. Thus, for example where a manager regularly uses offensive sex-based language in an open-plan office such that all employees (men and women) are subjected to it, it will not be a defence for the employer to argue that the female staff were treated no less favourably than male staff. It will be enough for an employee to show that the language was sex-based and that it created an offensive working environment for them.

2. *Sexual harassment* is 'where any form of unwanted verbal, non-verbal of physical conduct of a sexual nature occurs, with the purpose or effect of violating the dignity of a person, in particular when creating an intimidating, hostile, degrading, humiliating or offensive environment'.

This definition is based on the widely followed EC Code of Practice on Measure to Combat Sexual Harassment. The word 'unwanted' reflects current practice. 'Purpose *or* effect' serves as a reminder that there is no need for the complainant to prove intention. The notion of a working environment that is intimidating, hostile etc, means that behaviour can be harassment where it is based on a series of incidents involving sexist banter, sex-related jokes, etc (whatever their means of communication).

The inclusion of two definitions of harassment in the revised legislation reflects the recognition that sexual harassment is not restricted to sexual conduct. Harassment of a woman often has nothing to do with sex, but instead can often be an expression of power or even hostility.

[The next paragraph is **3.48**.]

How Managers Should Deal With Complaints of Harassment [3.48]

If, despite policies being in place and despite other preventative measures having been taken, an employee is nevertheless subjected to harassment by email or via material obtained from the internet, the manager responsible for the employee should take immediate action to deal with the matter.

The main objective of any action in these circumstances should, of course, be to put a stop to the conduct which amounts to harassment. There may also be solid grounds to discipline or dismiss the perpetrator of the harassment (topics covered in **CHAPTER 11**).

The potential consequences of not dealing adequately with complaints of harassment [3.49]

Because the very nature of harassment can cause embarrassment, and because many managers are under high levels of work pressure already, it is too often the case that complaints are not properly dealt with. Not taking a complaint of harassment seriously or not dealing with it adequately is likely to compound the employee's feelings of offence and distress and may possibly give them even stronger grounds to complain of discrimination at tribunal. Such lack of support may also lead to a complaint of constructive dismissal based on breach of contract (see **3.54** below).

Apart from the possible legal consequences, a failure to deal adequately with any type of harassment may lead to low morale amongst employees, an atmosphere of fear, increased workplace stress, high levels of absenteeism and high turnover. These are very serious, and potentially costly, consequences.

Check-lists [3.50]

From the perspective of a line manager or human resource professional, there is a strong argument that it is much better to know if a problem exists, so that action can be taken to remedy it, than to remain blissfully ignorant that anything is wrong. It follows that managers should:

- adopt a positive attitude towards employees who come forward with a complaint of harassment, or a complaint about any form of misuse of email or the internet at work;

- give the matter priority and make sure the complaint is investigated and dealt with promptly;

- adopt a supportive attitude towards the employee who may be feeling distressed, embarrassed or worried;

- aim to resolve the matter as soon as possible by putting a stop to the behaviour that is causing offence and dealing fairly with the person who perpetrated the harassment.

Employers should have in place a specific procedure designed to deal with complaints of harassment and bullying. Irrespective of the structure and content of such a procedure, managers who are tasked with dealing with such complaints should:

- act impartially and objectively;

- do not assume or imagine the employee is somehow to blame for the incidents giving rise to the complaint;

- seek the assistance of HR department rather than acting in isolation;

- investigate the employee's complaint promptly and fully – aim to gather all the facts including, for example, information about whether other employees have been subjected to the same behaviour about which the employee is complaining;

- make sure the person accused of harassment is afforded the right to answer the complaint against them at an interview set up for that purpose;

- allow the alleged harasser to be accompanied by a colleague or trade union official (if they wish) at any interview set up to discuss the problem (this is in any event a legal requirement if the interview is one that might lead to formal disciplinary action against the interviewee);

- keep confidential records;

- monitor and follow up once the complaint has been dealt with.

Further guidelines are given in **CHAPTERS 9** and **11**.

Reasons why an employee may not formally complain [3.51]

Over and above the need to deal adequately with complaints of harassment, it is important to bear in mind that many employees may feel reluctant to complain, out of embarrassment, fear of retaliation or worry that the complaint will not be believed or taken seriously. This may be the case irrespective of the existence of a well-publicised complaints procedure.

Managers should not assume, just because no complaints are forthcoming, that no problems exist and that working relationships are happy and harmonious. It is advisable to be vigilant at all times to the range of behaviour that takes place between employees so that any suspected inappropriate behaviour can be identified and addressed quickly and any potential problem nipped in the bud.

The implied duty to provide redress for grievances   [3.52]

There is a duty under *section 3(b)(ii)* of the *Employment Rights Act 1996* to give employees a written statement defining whom they can apply to for the purpose of seeking redress for any grievance they may have relating to their employment. The duty to provide redress for grievances has also come to be regarded as an implied contractual duty as a result of the following case:

Goold (Pearmak) v McConnell [1995] IRLR 516

Facts

Mr McConnell and Mr Richmond, who were employed as jewellery salesmen, were paid on a salary plus commission basis. When the company changed their sales methods, the two employees' commission dropped considerably. Both employees raised a formal grievance about this with their manager, but nothing was done.

Later, a new managing director was appointed, and the two employees took their grievance to him. After some discussions, he said that nothing could be done immediately.

The employees then tried to speak to the company chairman, but were told by his secretary that a meeting would have to be arranged through the managing director. With all routes to redress effectively blocked, the two employees resigned and brought complaints of constructive dismissal to an employment tribunal.

Findings

The tribunal found that the employees' grievance had been left to 'fester in an atmosphere of prevarication and indecision', and that the way in which the employees had been treated amounted to a fundamental breach of contract. The EAT upheld this decision and found that there was an implied term in all employees' contracts of employment that employers would 'reasonably and promptly afford a reasonable opportunity to their employees to obtain redress of any grievance they may have'.

Implications

This ruling clearly reinforces the duty on employers, particularly in cases of harassment, to take employees' complaints seriously, and to deal with them promptly and adequately.

It can be seen from the *Goold* case above that there is an implied contractual obligation on employers to deal promptly and properly with any genuine complaint of harassment. It follows that any failure to do so may be a breach of contract.

The implied duty of trust and confidence [3.53]

There is also an implied duty of trust and confidence inherent in every contract of employment. This duty encompasses the concept of treating employees with respect, providing support and refraining from any type of conduct which would have the effect of making working life intolerable for a particular employee. Serious harassment in any form could in itself be sufficient to amount to a breach of the duty of trust and confidence, and hence a breach of contract. Furthermore, a manager's failure to deal promptly and adequately with a genuine complaint of harassment could also constitute a breach of contract provided the breach could be regarded as fundamental in all the circumstances of the case.

Employees' remedy for a fundamental breach of contract [3.54]

In the event of a fundamental breach of contract by the employer, an employee who has a minimum of one year's continuous service is entitled to resign (with or without notice) and bring a claim for constructive dismissal to tribunal. Such action must be taken promptly by the employee otherwise it can be argued later that the treatment about which the employee was complaining was not sufficient to make working life intolerable and that there was therefore no fundamental breach of contract.

In *Bracebridge Engineering Ltd v Darby* [1990] IRLR 3 (see **3.35** above), the EAT held that the sexual assault the employee had suffered amounted to a breach of contract, entitling the employee to resign and claim constructive dismissal.

An example of a more recent case follows below:

Reed and Bull Information Systems Ltd v Stedman [1999] IRLR 299

Facts

Ms Stedman worked as a secretary. During the course of her employment, she was repeatedly subjected to sexually provocative remarks and suggestive behaviour by her manager. She found this conduct disturbing and eventually resigned, bringing claims to tribunal for both sex discrimination and constructive dismissal.

Findings

The tribunal found that there was no individual incident which was sufficient when considered on its own to amount to a detriment, but that when viewed collectively, various incidents represented a course of conduct which constituted sexual harassment. This was despite the fact that Ms Stedman had never raised a formal complaint about the harassment with management. It was enough, the tribunal held, that she had made it clear to her manager through her own conduct that his behaviour was unacceptable to her. The tribunal specifically commented that the continuation of behaviour which any reasonable person would understand the victim to be rejecting could be regarded as harassment.

As well as being held liable for the manager's sexual harassment of the employee, the company was also held to be have discriminated against her by failing to investigate the matter. This, they held, also amounted to a breach of the duty of trust and confidence entitling her to resign and claim constructive dismissal.

Implications

Irrespective of whether behaviour is regarded as sufficient to amount to a detriment to an employee under the *Sex Discrimination Act*, a failure to investigate and deal with a genuine complaint could give rise to a fundamental breach of contract and a claim for constructive dismissal.

Thus, in addition to the risk of a claim for sexual harassment, the employer may face a claim for constructive dismissal if there is a blatant failure to deal adequately with a genuine complaint of harassment, whether by email or on account of any other type of conduct.

Conclusion [3.55]

Harassment in the course of employment can take many forms. Such conduct can give rise to claims from employees under the *Sex Discrimination Act 1975*, the *Race Relations Act 1976*, the *Disability Discrimination Act 1995*, the *Employment Equality (Religion or Belief) Regulations 2003 (SI 2003 No 1660)* or the *Employment Equality (Sexual Orientation) Regulations (SI 2003 No 1661)*. The employer will be liable for such harassment, and individual employees may also be held liable. An employment tribunal may order both the employer and the employee who perpetrated the harassment to pay compensation to the victim.

Email messages and material viewed on a computer screen or downloaded from the internet can amount to unlawful discrimination if such material is (for example) sexually explicit or racially offensive, or if it has the effect of making the working environment uncomfortable for a particular employee. It is thus very important for employers to introduce policies and procedures banning all forms of discrimination, including harassment and to make sure that these policies and procedures take into account the possibility of harassment by email or via the internet.

Questions and Answers [3.56]

Question

Which UK employment laws cover the issue of harassment?

Answer

The *Sex Discrimination Act 1975* and the *Disability Discrimination Act 1995* both contain a provision that it is unlawful to subject an employee (or job applicant) to a detriment on grounds of sex or on grounds related to a disability. Since harassment can be a detriment to the person who is its victim, it is capable of being regarded as discrimination. The *Race Relations Act 1976*, the *Employment Equality (Religion or Belief) Regulations 2003* and the *Employment Equality (Sexual Orientation) Regulations 2003* all expressly identify harassment as a distinct form of unlawful discrimination.

Question

If an individual suffers harassment on the grounds of their sexual orientation, can they bring a claim to tribunal for sex discrimination?

Answer

The term 'sex discrimination' in the Sex Discrimination Act 1975 has consistently been interpreted strictly to mean discrimination on the grounds of gender, thereby not encompassing discrimination on grounds of sexual orientation. However, Regulations outlawing discrimination on grounds of sexual orientation were implemented in December 2003 as a result of an EC Directive.

Question

Are all workers protected in law against harassment, or are some exempted?

Answer

All workers are protected against unlawful discrimination including, for example, home-workers, casual staff, agency temps and contractors. This is because all the anti-discrimination laws define 'employment' as 'employment under a contract of service or of apprenticeship or a contract personally to execute any work or labour'. There is no minimum service requirement. Job applicants are also covered by the Acts throughout the process of recruitment.

Question

Who is liable in law if an employee suffers harassment at work?

Answer

The employer is liable for any unlawful discrimination that occurs 'in the course of employment' whether or not management was aware of what was going on. Individual employees can also be held liable for their own discriminatory acts.

Question

How can an employer reduce the chances of their being held liable for acts of harassment perpetrated by their own employees against each other?

Answer

The prospect of being held liable can be reduced if the employer takes all reasonably practicable steps to prevent harassment from occurring in the first place. In practice this means introducing equal opportunities and anti-harassment policies and an effective complaints procedure, and providing proper training and detailed information for all staff in every aspect of harassment.

Question

How is sexual harassment defined?

Answer

The EC Code of Practice on Measures to Combat Sexual Harassment states that conduct will constitute sexual harassment where it is 'unwanted, unreasonable and offensive to the recipient'. This means in effect that it is up to each individual to determine what types of sexual conduct they find unacceptable, irrespective of the view another employee might take.

Question

In what circumstances can email messages constitute harassment of an individual?

Answer

If a message sent by email contains material that is inflammatory, sexually explicit, racially offensive, sexist/racist, homophobic or religiously offensive in content, the message is capable of amounting to harassment in the same way as the content of a written letter or memo, or a statement made verbally to a colleague directly. Even jokes distributed by email, if they contain sexually explicit or racist wording, may cause offence to an individual thus constituting harassment in law.

Question

In what circumstances could an employee claim sexual harassment on account of colleagues downloading sexually explicit material from the internet?

Answer

The transmission or downloading of sexually offensive material may constitute unlawful discrimination even if it is not sent to or directed at a particular individual. The mere fact that such material is circulating around the workplace, or visible on computer screens, may create an uncomfortable or intimidating working environment which could be discriminatory against an employee forced to work in that environment. This could lead to a legitimate claim of sex discrimination.

Question

What are the repercussions likely to be if a manager fails to deal adequately with an employee's complaint of email harassment?

Answer

Not dealing promptly and adequately with a complaint of harassment by email is likely to compound the employee's feelings of offence and distress and may possibly give them firm grounds to complain of unlawful discrimination at tribunal. Such lack of support may also lead to a complaint of constructive dismissal based on a breach of the implied duty of trust and confidence.

4 Confidentiality Issues

Introduction [4.1]

In an organisation where no restrictions are imposed on employees' use of email and the internet, there will be a substantial risk of breaches of confidentiality occurring. This may happen as a result of inappropriate handling of confidential information within the company or as a result of messages being inadvertently transmitted to people outside the organisation containing confidential or sensitive information. Because of the ease and speed with which email messages can be distributed to large numbers of people (some of whom may then forward the message and any attachments on to others), there is the further risk that confidential information accidentally or deliberately disclosed externally may find its way to a competitor company.

It is remarkably easy for a breach of confidentiality to happen accidentally as a result of a wrong email address being input, or a message being unthinkingly copied to someone who should not be privy to its contents. Furthermore, an innocent employee in a company with no guidelines on email use could inadvertently disclose something confidential in an email to a supplier. More seriously, a disgruntled employee (or ex-employee) may choose to disclose the company's trade secrets to an outsider, for example a competitor company or a new employer, perhaps because of a grudge against the company or resentment over perceived unfair treatment. Without appropriate safeguards in place, a departing employee could easily download sensitive information on to a couple of floppy disks, or transmit confidential data to their home computer by email before their departure.

Employers will need to take positive steps to protect:

- confidential information about the company's products and services, business plan, sales statistics, prices, contact details for customers;
- commercially sensitive information, e.g. new designs, formulae, manufacturing processes, marketing strategies, future plans;

- information about employees held in a personnel database or elsewhere. These will be subject to the provisions of the *Data Protection Act 1998* (see **4.30** below);

- confidential information held about clients and suppliers.

The duty to render faithful service [4.2]

Employers are protected by the common law against breaches of confidence by their employees. This is because every contract of employment contains an implied duty that the employee should render faithful service, which applies irrespective of whether there are written company rules governing the handling of confidential information. This duty to render faithful service means, amongst other things, that where information is confidential to the employer, employees are obliged to keep it that way, i.e. not disclose it to others without authority. Any breach of the duty can entitle the employer to take disciplinary action against the employee. Furthermore, any threatened or potential disclosure of misuse of confidential information could entitle the employer to dismiss the employee in question, as the following case reveals:

Winder v The Commissioners of Inland Revenue [1998] Case No 1101770/97

Facts

Mr Winder worked as a tax valuation officer for the Inland Revenue, a job which involved access to sensitive information held on the Revenue's computer system. The Revenue's rules on confidentiality stipulated that any information acquired by an employee in the course of their employment must not be misused or discussed outside the organisation.

It was discovered that Mr Winder had written a letter to the National Socialist Alliance (the NSA), a right-wing group, offering to provide them with certain confidential information from the Revenue's computer system that would be of assistance to them. Following this discovery, Mr Winder was dismissed for misconduct on the grounds that he had threatened to disclose protected information from records held on his employer's computer. He brought a claim for unfair dismissal to an employment tribunal. One of his arguments was that he had not actually disclosed any confidential information to the NSA, and thus had not committed any act of gross misconduct.

> *Findings*
>
> The employment tribunal held that Mr Winder's dismissal had been fair. Although no confidential information had actually been disclosed, the Revenue was entitled to form the view that an offer from one of their employees to disclose confidential information from their computer system to an outside organisation amounted to a breach of the duty to maintain confidence. The wording of Mr Winder's letter had been unambiguous and had indicated a clear intention to disclose confidential information.

The duty not to disclose confidential information applies throughout employment but will terminate when the employee leaves the company unless the employee has signed an appropriately worded restrictive covenant (see below in **4.15**). However, even after employment has ended, the obligation not to disclose information that amounts to a trade secret continues in force. The employer can seek to prohibit the disclosure of trade secrets by ex-employees by means of an injunction (see below in **4.21**).

Keeping Information Confidential [4.3]

The effective security management of confidential and sensitive information held on computer systems should be a key priority for employers. It is advisable to carry out reviews from time to time to identify the type of information that is sensitive, including information which, if it fell into the wrong hands, could cause damage to the company's business interests. Policy decisions can then be taken as to who in the organisation should have access to external email and the internet and what type of information should *not* be communicated by email.

A further very important aspect of confidentiality is to determine who in the organisation should have access to personal data held about employees, and any data obtained as a result of email and internet monitoring. Specific guidelines need to be drawn up to ensure that these employees understand their duties and responsibilities with regard to the confidentiality of personal data. Paragraph **4.46** provides further information.

Clearly training and communication will play an important part in ensuring that all employees understand how they should use email and the internet and how they should treat any confidential, sensitive or personal information to which they have access in the course of their work.

What information is confidential? [4.4]

The question as to what information can or should be regarded as confidential will depend on the nature of the employer's business. Generally, employers should seek to ensure their employees do not disclose information such as:

- personal data about employees of the company (see **4.6** below);

- trade secrets, for example, details of a new design, formula or a manufacturing process;

- any highly sensitive business information such as the details of the company's customers;

- confidential information about sales and pricing structures;

- any information which, if disclosed, would cause damage to the employer's business interests, especially if it could be used to the advantage of a competitor;

Under common law, information will not be confidential unless those to whom it is disclosed are informed that it is confidential. It follows that in the absence of notification about the confidentiality of specific information, the employer will lose the protection of confidentiality if that information is inadvertently communicated to a third party. Employers cannot simply stipulate that all information held within the company is confidential because protection against unauthorised disclosure by an employee will then not be enforced by the courts.

Employees' own knowledge [4.5]

In particular, information that can be attributed to an employee's own general skill and knowledge cannot be protected, even if this has been acquired as a direct result of the particular employment. Distinguishing between this type of information and confidential information relating to the employer's business can of course be difficult. Generally, knowledge of a the market for a product or service may constitute part of an employee's own knowledge, whilst knowledge of a specific business opportunity that the employer is pursuing could reasonably be regarded as confidential information. Another example could be the distinction between knowledge of the way a business is managed and organised, which cannot be regarded as confidential, and the precise details of the organisation's business trends or of manufacturing processes, which can be treated as confidential information.

Additionally, any information which is in the public domain or is available from public sources cannot be regarded as confidential.

Personal data about employees [4.6]

Every employer has duty under the *Data Protection Act 1998* to take appropriate steps to prevent unauthorised or unlawful access to, or interference with, personal data held about employees. The Act also prohibits employees who have access to personal data in the course of their work from obtaining or disclosing personal data unlawfully, i.e. without the consent of the employer. There is a small number of exceptions to this provision, for example if the disclosure is made in order to prevent or detect crime.

Further details of the *Data Protection Act* are to be found below at **4.30**.

Legal liability [4.7]

If an employer has in its possession confidential information belonging to a third party, for example a customer or supplier, it has the duty to keep that information confidential. If the employer is responsible for the inadvertent or deliberate disclosure of such confidential information, they will be legally liable for the breach of confidence and its consequences.

Employers also have legal liabilities towards their employees under the *Data Protection Act 1998* (see below at **4.34**).

Rules and procedures on confidentiality [4.8]

It is strongly advisable for employers to devise and implement clear rules and procedures governing the use of confidential information. This course of action will minimise the risks to the employer of breaches of confidentiality whilst at the same time educating employees about their individual responsibilities. This will be particularly important for employees who have access to sensitive information as part of their jobs. The particular responsibilities of such employees, for example those employed in HR department or IT department, will have to be spelled out unambiguously.

The advantages of rules and procedures on confidentiality [4.9]

Rules and procedures governing confidentiality will have five key advantages:

- they will clarify what information is to be treated as confidential;

- they will help employees to understand their obligations towards their employer;

- they can define employees' key responsibilities with regard to confidential information and specify rules as to how key information should be kept confidential (e.g. by keeping passwords secret, etc);

- they will reduce the risk of a breach of confidentiality occurring;

- they will allow the employer to enforce the rules on confidential information in the event of a breach by an employee.

The purpose and content of a procedure [4.10]

A company procedure on confidentiality should establish basic guidelines for employees and identify any prohibited practices so that a framework is established within which all employees can work. There should be internal controls to limit access to confidential information and to prevent the disclosure of sensitive data. Rules governing the choosing, changing and non-disclosure of passwords should be devised and implemented (see **10.15** below).

Rules governing use should also cover issues such as:

- the avoidance of email as a means of sending confidential or valuable information;

- the encryption of confidential information which is to be transmitted by email (see **10.19** below);

- disclaimers in external email messages (see **4.28** below);

- the intermittent breaking up of email messages that contain confidential information with a phrase such as 'confidential communication for intended recipient only';

- guidance on wrong delivery;

- a ban on forwarding emails sent by a third party without the original sender's express consent;

- a ban on sending email messages to large distribution lists;

- who may or may not be given details of any particular email address;

- a ban on information being transmitted by email to and from employees' homes;

- advice to employees to double-check the address of an intended email recipient before sending the message;

- the protection of computer data when the computer is logged on, i.e. a rule that workstations should not be left unattended;

- the protection of data held about employees and customers under the *Data Protection Act 1998*.

It is advisable to insert a clause such as the following into the organisation's policy on email use, or alternatively into the company's handbook:

'Employees should be aware that email is not a secure or confidential method of communication. Confidential or sensitive Company information should not therefore be transmitted by email or email attachment unless the file has been encrypted by IT department and a disclaimer attached'.

There may be a need for further more detailed rules and also for specific training for employees who, in the course of their jobs, have access to confidential or sensitive information. These will include staff in the HR department, finance department and of course those in IT department who may also be involved in monitoring employees' use of email and the internet.

Wrong delivery [4.11]

Every email message should contain a statement requesting the recipient not to open it or read it if it has been sent to them in error. The statement should also warn the recipient that if the message contains confidential information, use must not be made of the information and it must not be disclosed to anyone else. Sample clauses are given below in **4.27**.

For employees, there should be a rule stipulating that if a message is received in error, it should not be opened or read and should instead be redirected to the sender with a message explaining what has happened.

Confidentiality clauses in employees' contracts of employment [4.12]

In order to extend the implied duty to render faithful service owed by employees and increase the level of protection of the employer's business interests, there should be an express confidentiality clause in every employee's contract of employment. The precise wording of a confidentiality clause will depend on the nature of the employer's business and the employee's position. At the very least, however, the following issues should be covered:

- the type of information that is to be regarded as confidential;

- rules on confidentiality applicable to the employee during their employment;

- rules on keeping information confidential that will apply after the termination of the employee's employment.

Sample confidentiality clauses [4.13]

A sample confidentiality clause might read as follows:

Example 1

'You will not disclose to any person or organisation without the Company's consent any information concerning the trade secrets, inventions, processes, methods or procedures owned by or used by the Company, or any confidential information in any way related to the Company's business. This duty applies to you throughout your employment and subsequent to your employment.

After the termination of your contract of employment, you will not disclose or use any of the Company's trade secrets, its customer contact names and addresses, or any other information which is confidential to the Company'.

Example 2

'You must not at any time, other than in the proper performance of your duties, whether during or after your employment, disclose or misuse any information that is confidential to the Company. Confidential information includes any information of the Company or any of its customers, suppliers or agents which the Company treats as confidential and which is not part of your own general skill and knowledge. This includes (without limitation) any information about the Company's business plans, business opportunities, research and development, product formulae and processes, designs, sales statistics, pricing structures, and information about the Company's customers and potential customers. Such information is to be regarded as confidential whether it is recorded in documentary form, on computer or on disk or tape.'

Preventing unauthorised disclosure by employees who are leaving [4.14]

It is not an altogether uncommon phenomenon for an employee who is leaving their job to take information belonging to the company with them, and to use that information for their own purposes in a future employment. In the normal course of events, the consequences of this for the employer are likely to be negligible, especially where the employee has left the company of their own accord and has no grounds to bear the employer any ill-will. However, in the event that an employee is dismissed, whether for redundancy or for some other reason, there is a risk of resentment or even the desire for revenge on account of perceived unfair treatment. In these circumstances, an employee who has access to confidential or sensitive information in the course of their job duties could cause considerable damage to the employer's business interests, either by removing some of the information, or even destroying it, prior to their departure.

It may be prudent, therefore, to identify employees who could be in a position to cause damage of this kind, and put stringent measures in place to bar their access to the employer's computer system as soon as it is known that they are to be leaving the company. Normally this would mean asking an employee to leave the workplace immediately, rather than allowing them to work out their notice period. It may even be desirable to escort the person off the premises to make sure they cannot remove or damage any of the company's information systems This is of course a harsh and heartless course of action, especially where the employee has been a loyal and hard-working employee, but the risk of harm coming to the company's computer system is so serious that extreme measures may well be justifiable. If it is deemed necessary to take such an extreme course of action, the employer should make as much effort as possible to act discreetly and minimise any embarrassment or upset to the employee concerned.

Restrictive covenants [4.15]

A restrictive covenant is a clause in an employee's contract of employment designed to restrain the employee from undertaking certain defined activities after their employment has ended. Typically, a restrictive covenant may be drafted to prevent an ex-employee from joining a competitor company or setting up a business in direct competition with the employer for a defined period of time, to prevent the solicitation of the company's customers or to prevent the disclosure of confidential information.

As mentioned above, employees are under a duty not to disclose confidential information throughout their employment with the company, but unless the employee has signed an appropriately worded restrictive covenant, this obligation will terminate when the employee leaves the company (although the duty not to disclose trade secrets survives beyond the termination of employment). This means that it can be very important for employers whose employees have access to confidential or sensitive information to require them to sign a restrictive covenant preventing disclosure of such information.

The law on restrictive covenants is complex and the attitude of the courts towards them has tended to vary over time. Courts have frequently refused to uphold restrictive covenants in ex-employees' contracts if they consider them to be wider than is reasonably necessary to protect the employer's legitimate business interests. In particular, the period of time during which any restrictions apply and the geographical boundaries specified in the covenant will be key factors in determining whether the covenant is enforceable in law. If a restrictive covenant is too wide, the court may narrow its scope, but will not re-write the covenant for the benefit of the employer – a more likely outcome is that the court will rule that the covenant is unenforceable. Furthermore, if the covenant is drafted in a vague or ambiguous manner, a court may not enforce it.

Drafting restrictive covenants [4.16]

Employers should always seek legal advice before drafting restrictive covenants in order to ensure that they are drafted appropriately. There is no general wording that will be appropriate to every organisation's needs. Restrictive covenants should be individually tailored taking into account the type of work an employee, or group of employees, is employed to do and the type of information to which they have access. For example, the following points should be borne in mind:

- the nature of the employer's business;

- the type of products or services provided by the employer;

- the employee's job, status, level of responsibility and precise duties;

- the employee's relationship with the company's customers and suppliers;

- whether and to what extent the employee deals with customers and suppliers directly, and if so whether they have any tangible influence over them;

- whether and to what extent the employee has access to commercially sensitive information in the course of their job;

- the type of confidential that the employer wishes to protect.

It is essential, if a restrictive covenant is to be capable of enforcement, that it is drafted so as to be no wider than is reasonably necessary to protect the employer's legitimate interests. It will therefore be necessary to define closely the type of information that the employer wishes to protect (i.e. information which, if disclosed, would damage the employer's interests) and to check that the employee actually had access to that information during the course of their work. The aim should be to draft a restrictive covenant that is narrow enough to be considered valid whilst at the same time wide enough to provide sufficient protection to the employer's legitimate interests. Expert legal advice is essential.

The effect on restrictive covenants of termination in breach of contract [4.17]

One further very important point to bear in mind is that, if an employee's contract is terminated in a manner that constitutes a breach of contract (for example if the contract is terminated without proper contractual notice being given), the employer will not normally be able to rely on any post-termination clauses contained in the contract. Thus, if an employee is dismissed without proper notice, any restrictive covenant may be unenforceable following the dismissal. This is likely to be the case even if there is a statement in the contract to the effect that the restrictive covenant will still apply if the employer is in breach of contract.

Breaches of Confidentiality [4.18]

If confidential information is misused by employees or disclosed to an unauthorised person, considerable damage can be done to the employer's business. If, despite preventative measures, an employee of the company abuses confidential information, the employer will be entitled to take action against the employee. Any misuse or unauthorised disclosure of confidential information is likely to amount to a breach of contract on the part of the employee. This will be the case irrespective of the express terms in the employee's contract or the existence of any express policies and rules on the subject, as the employee will be in breach of the implied duty to render faithful service if they disclose confidential information without authority.

Breaches during employment [4.19]

It follows that where an employee has disclosed confidential information without authority, the employer may wish to take disciplinary action. The level of action that will be appropriate will depend on what type of information has been disclosed, to whom, and on whether the disclosure was deliberate or accidental. Other factors that will influence the level of disciplinary action to be taken will include:

- whether written guidelines were in place governing the handling of confidential information;

- the extent to which the employee understood these guidelines in relation to their job duties and responsibilities;

- the employee's job, level of seniority and the degree to which they could realistically be expected to keep information confidential;

- the reasons put forward by the employee for the breach of confidentiality and any mitigating factors;

- the consequences of the employee's conduct for the organisation, for example unfavourable press publicity or complaints from customers will render the incident more serious;

- whether the employee has previously committed any similar act of misconduct, whether or not warnings were given and whether any of these warnings are still 'in date'.

A serious breach of confidentiality on the part of an employee would normally constitute a potentially fair reason for dismissal. However, if the dismissal is to be fair, the employer will need to make sure that they follow a fair and reasonable procedure. This will involve a thorough investigation into the facts of the case and a properly convened interview at which the employee is given a full and fair opportunity to explain their conduct. Following the application of proper disciplinary procedures, the employer must have formed a genuine belief based on reasonable grounds that the employee was guilty of the breach in question. **CHAPTER 11** provides full details of disciplinary procedures and dismissal.

Breaches after termination of employment [4.20]

Where a breach of confidential information occurs after the termination of an employee's contract with the company, the company may be able to take legal action against the employee if:

- the employee signed a restrictive covenant covering the disclosure of confidential information; *or*

- the information disclosed by the ex-employee amounts to a trade secret.

In either of these circumstances, the employer will have a choice of several courses of action.

Injunctions [4.21]

The first would be to seek an injunction against the employee to stop the employee using the information and/or prevent further disclosures. If, however, the damage has already been done, a court will not normally grant an injunction. Equally, if the employer has delayed applying for the injunction or where the employer is in some way to blame for the disclosure, an injunction will not normally be granted.

Damages [4.22]

An alternative course of action for the employer in the event that confidential information has already been disclosed or misused, for example by an ex-employee, would be to sue for damages. However, this action would only be feasible if the information disclosed had caused financial loss to the business, which can be difficult to assess and to prove. There are further potential difficulties in that the employee may be unable to pay the damages ordered by the court and even if damages are paid, the sum in question may not be adequate in real terms to compensate the employer for the loss of confidentiality.

Account of profits [4.23]

Yet another possible remedy for an employer who has suffered a breach of confidentiality at the hands of a current or ex-employee is to ask a court to order the employee to account for the actual profits they have made by using the confidential information. In certain circumstances an account of profits could be extended to a third party. For example, if an employee had been paid a fee for disclosing documents to a newspaper, the employee would be ordered to pay the employer (or ex-employer) the equivalent of the fee paid to them by the newspaper. In addition, the newspaper could be ordered to pay the employer an amount of money equivalent to the extra profit they had made from increased sales attributable to the disclosed information.

Return of confidential documents [4.24]

Finally, an employer can ask a court to order the offending employee to return all confidential documents in their possession to the business.

Legal advice [4.25]

The law relating to confidentiality of information is complex and an employer should always seek proper legal advice if there are grounds to believe that an employee, or ex-employee, is misusing confidential information belonging to the company.

Model Clauses [4.26]

Under common law, information will lose its confidential nature unless those to whom it is disclosed are informed that it is confidential. Thus if confidential information is inadvertently communicated to a third party, that material may lose the protection of confidentiality. It is therefore very important that confidentiality clauses are included within all external email messages that contain, or may contain, confidential information.

Sample confidentiality clauses for emails [4.27]

Example 1

'This information is confidential and should be read by the addressee only. If you are not the intended recipient of this message, please do not read it or use it in any way. It would be appreciated if you would inform the sender of what has happened'.

Example 2

'The information contained in this email is confidential and may be legally privileged. It is intended solely for the addressee. Access to this email by anyone else is unauthorised.

If you are not the intended recipient, any disclosure, copying, printing, distribution or any action taken or omitted to be taken in reliance on this email is prohibited and may be unlawful.

Any views or opinions presented are those of the author only, and do not necessarily represent those of [Company name].'

Example 3

'This message is sent in confidence and is intended for the addressee only. The contents are not to be disclosed to anyone other than the addressee. Unauthorised recipients are requested to preserve this confidentiality and to advise the sender immediately of any error in transmission.'

Example 4

'This email message may contain confidential information and is protected by copyright. If you are not the named addressee, please notify us immediately, delete it, do not make any copies, and do not use it in any way.'

Example 5

'This email is strictly confidential and intended solely for the addressee. If you are not the intended addressee, you must not disclose, copy or take any action on account of this message.

Any views or opinions contained in this message are those of the author only, and do not necessarily represent the views or policies of [Company name].

If you have received this message in error, please notify the sender immediately and delete all copies.'

Example 6

'The information contained in this message and any attachments is confidential and may be legally privileged. It is intended only for the addressee. Rights to confidentiality and privilege are not waived. If you are not the intended recipient, any disclosure, copying, printing or distribution is prohibited and may be unlawful. Please advise the sender immediately if this message has been transmitted to you in error'.

Disclaimers [4.28]

It is advisable for all employers to take steps to minimise the risk of legal action being taken against them in the event that incorrect information is transmitted outside the organisation by email. All external email messages should therefore include a disclaimer, or alternatively a company policy could stipulate what types of email messages require a disclaimer.

The wording of a disclaimer can be the same as any wording currently in use in the employer's printed documentation. Disclaimers can range from a simple 'error or omission' statement through to a comprehensive and tailored disclaimer drawn up by a competent lawyer. Clearly the type of disclaimer that is appropriate will vary from organisation to organisation depending on the perceived level of risk and the potential consequences of mistakes being made.

Sample disclaimers [4.29]

Some examples of basic and simple disclaimers are as follows:

Example 1

'The information contained in this email is confidential and may be legally privileged. Any opinions or advice contained in this email are subject to [Company name's] terms and conditions of business'.

Example 2

This email and any files transmitted along with it are confidential, and are intended solely for the individual to whom the email is addressed. The views expressed are that of the author and may not necessarily reflect the views of [Company name].'

Example 3

Email is an informal means of communication and may be subject to data corruption, whether accidental or deliberate. For this reason it is inappropriate to rely on information or advice contained in an email without first obtaining written confirmation of its contents.'

Example 4

'Email is not a reliable form of communication. You should therefore not rely on any information or advice contained in this message and should not take any action on account of it. The views expressed are that of the author and may not necessarily reflect the views of [Company name].'

The Data Protection Act 1998 – A Summary of the Act as it Affects Employers' Rights to Monitor Employees' Communications [4.30]

If the employer keeps a record of any of the information that results from monitoring of employee communications, this information will constitute *'personal data'* as defined by the *Data Protection Act 1998*. The key difference between this Act and its predecessor (the *Data Protection Act 1984)* is that the 1998 Act covers personal data held manually as well as data held on computer.

Under the 1998 Act, personal data held in paper format, data stored on a computer system and data processed through email are all covered by data protection legislation, which strictly regulates the processing of data about individuals.

The Data Protection Act 1998 was implemented in March 2000 and will eventually completely repeal the *Data Protection Act 1984.*

The transitional provisions [4.31]

There are, however, some transitional provisions which apply to manual data that were already in existence prior to 24 October 1998. Such data will be exempt from the following provisions until 24 October 2007:

- certain aspects of the first data protection principle (see **4.41** below), although employers must still comply with the duty to provide certain key information to employees, including the purpose for which they intend to process data held about them;

- the second, third, fourth and fifth data protection principles (see **4.40** below).

It is important to note that these provisions are limited and do not apply to information that was created after 23 October 1998. This means that, although a personnel file that was in existence prior to 24 October 1998 will be exempt from some of the data protection principles until October 2007, a single piece of information added to the file after that date will be subject to the full provisions of the Act immediately.

Employers may therefore find it easier to adopt the approach that all personnel records should comply with all the data protection principles irrespective of when the particular part of the record came into existence.

Since 24 October 2001, all manual records (as well as computer records) are subject to the full provisions of the Act including the access provisions (see below in **4.36**).

Data [4.32]

'Personal data' for the purposes of data protection legislation means simply personal information held about an individual in a filing system in which the person is named or is otherwise identifiable. This includes:

- information that is held manually provided the file is structured by reference to the individual;

- information that is stored in a computer, and information stored in such a way that it can be fed into a computer;

- information about an employee contained in the text of an email;

- information stored on telephone logging systems, or on audio and video systems;

- information that forms part of an 'accessible record' This would include health records.

The Act specifically includes within its remit any expression of opinion about an individual and any indication of the intentions of anyone in respect of that individual. This would include, for example, a note written by a manager on an employee's personal file expressing the view that the employee was, or was not, suitable for promotion.

Where communications are monitored, but no record kept of the results of the monitoring exercise, then the restrictions under the *Data Protection Act 1998* will not kick in simply because no 'data' will have been created.

Data processing [4.33]

'Data processing' under the *Data Protection Act 1998* incorporates the collection, organisation, storage, retrieval, alteration, disclosure and destruction of both manual and computer information held about individuals. Thus all the routine aspects of handling personal information are covered within the scope of 'processing'.

Employees' Rights Under the Act [4.34]

Employees have considerable rights under the *Data Protection Act 1998*. The main rights are:

- to gain access to any personal data held about them (see below in **4.36**);

- to be informed in advance by their employer if personal data about them are being processed;

- to be given a description of the data;

- to be informed of the purposes for which the data are being processed and details of the persons to whom the data may be disclosed.

The right to be informed in advance if personal data are being processed is consistent with the duty on employers under the *Lawful Business Practice Regulations* to take all reasonable steps to inform employees that their communications may be intercepted. Monitoring employees' email or internet use without informing them that monitoring will take place will therefore be at risk of contravening both the *Lawful Business Practice Regulations* and the *Data Protection Act* (see **6.14** below for full information about the *Lawful Business Practice Regulations*).

Employees also have the right to ask their employer to correct or remove any inaccuracies on the file. If an employer fails or refuses (following an employee's request) to correct inaccurate information on an employee's personal file, the employee can take the employer to court. If the employee is successful, the court may order the employer to rectify, block, erase or destroy any information that contains an expression of opinion based on the inaccurate information.

The need for consent [4.35]

Under the first data protection principle (see below in **4.41**), an employer cannot process information about an employee unless the employee has given their consent or unless one of a list of other conditions has been met.

The right of access [4.36]

All employees have the right of access to manual files, computer files and email correspondence containing information about them personally. The Court of Appeal stated in *Durant v Financial Services Authority [2003]* that, in order to trigger the right of access, the information held must be biographical to a significant extent and should have the individual as its focus. This case suggests that the mere mention of a person's name in a document would not be sufficient to make the information 'personal data' for the purpose of access under the *Data Protection Act 1998*. Furthermore, where information is stored manually, it must be stored in a filing system 'by reference to employees or criteria relating to them' if it is to fall within the ambit of the access provisions.

Where the right of access is triggered, the information must be provided in an intelligible and permanent form within 40 calendar days, provided the employee has made a written request and paid the appropriate fee (see **4.38** below).

Employees therefore have the right to see documents such as appraisals, warnings held on file, statements about pay and expressions of opinion or intention about (for example) promotion prospects. They may also request access to information generated by computer systems involved in automated decision making on matters such as performance and conduct. Confidential references provided by the employer are, however, exempt from the Act (but not references received from another employer which are subject to the provisions of the Act – see also **4.37** below).

In requesting access to personal data held about themselves, employees may seek access to copies of any emails in which they are discussed. The Data Protection Code of Practice on Monitoring at Work (see **4.44** below) states that workers will not usually be entitled to be granted access to all emails just because they were the sender or the recipient, but that access would normally have to be granted to emails in which the employee was the subject of the email. If the employee's name was merely mentioned in the email, for example as one of a list of people who attended a meeting, it is unlikely that disclosure would be required under the Act. The *Durant* case (above) reinforced this principle. Employers should, however, if they receive an access request in relation to email correspondence, check sites that are reasonably likely to contain emails about the employee, for example the employee's manager's in and out-boxes.

Files that contain information about third parties [4.37]

If the file that the employee has requested contains information about another person such that the other person could be identified from it, then the employer has a choice of two courses of action:

- to blank out the details of the other person before making the file available to the employee who has requested it;

- to request permission from the other person to release the file to the employee who has requested it.

If neither of these options is possible, the employer may legitimately refuse the employee the right of access to the file in question.

Charging a fee [4.38]

Employers are entitled in law to charge a fee for the granting of access to an employee's personal file. The current maximum level of such a fee is £10. There is, however, no obligation to charge a fee and employers may elect to provide the relevant information free of charge if they wish to do so. One sound idea is to offer free access up to (for example) twice a year, but impose a charge of £10 for any further requests for access. Whatever policy is adopted, it should be clearly communicated and applied consistently.

Compensation [4.39]

If an employee suffers damage (for example loss of the opportunity for promotion) as a direct result of their employer's failure to comply with any part of the *Data Protection Act 1998*, they may take a case to court and claim compensation. Compensation may be awarded for any damage caused to the employee, and also for any distress the employer's breach has caused. The employer may be able to defend such a claim by proving that as much care as was reasonable in the circumstances was taken to comply with the provision of the Act that was breached.

The Data Protection Principles [4.40]

Apart from the fact that employees have the right to gain access to any personal data held about them, there are other aspects of the data protection legislation that are relevant to the monitoring of employee communications.

Employers are obliged under the *Data Protection Act 1998* to comply with eight data protection principles governing the processing of personal data. These read as follows:

1. Personal data shall be processed fairly and lawfully and, in particular, shall not be processed unless one of a list of conditions is met (this first data protection principle is dealt with separately in **4.41** below).

2. Personal data shall be obtained only for specified and lawful purposes, and shall not be processed in any manner incompatible with those purposes (see also **4.42** below).

3. Personal data shall be adequate, relevant and not excessive in relation to the purposes for which they are processed (see **4.43** below).

4. Personal data shall be accurate and, where necessary, kept up to date. The best way for an employer to achieve this is to adopt a policy of providing employees with a copy of any files held about them on a regular basis, asking them to bring any inaccuracies to their attention. This has the added advantage of creating trust and reassuring employees that the employer is not holding any 'secret' information about them.

5. Personal data shall be kept for no longer than is necessary for the purposes for which it is processed. Neither the *Data Protection Act*, nor the Code of Practice on Monitoring at Work lays down any time limits for the storing of data, but the employers should address this matter and develop their own policies.

6. Personal data shall be processed in accordance with the rights of data subjects (i.e. employees) under the Act.

7. Personal data shall be subject to appropriate technical and organisational measures to protect against unauthorised or unlawful processing and accidental loss, destruction or damage. This means (amongst other things) that the employer must take reasonable steps to ensure the reliability of all employees who have access to employee records in the course of their jobs (see **4.43A** below).

8. Personal data shall not be transferred to a country or territory outside the European Economic Area unless that country or territory ensures an adequate level of data protection.

Any personal information about an employee obtained as a result of monitoring (for example a computer print-out of the email addresses that a particular employee has corresponded with) will be classed as personal data under the *Data Protection Act 1998*. Consequently such data must be processed in a way that does not violate the data protection principles.

In relation to data held manually, however, a transitional period up to 23 October 2007 is in place for some of the data protection principles, namely part of number one (see **4.31** above and **4.41** below) and numbers two, three, four and five.

The duty to process personal data fairly and lawfully [4.41]

As can be seen from the above, the first data protection principle creates the obligation on employers to process personal data *fairly and lawfully*. It is feasible that even if the collection of data is *lawful* (either because the employee has consented to it, or because the purpose of recording the data falls under one of the provisions of the *Lawful Business Practice Regulations)*, it could still be *unfair.* If an employer was to take extreme measures to monitor employee communications, for example reading and recording an employee's personal emails without good cause, then this could potentially be deemed unfair under data protection legislation.

The first data principle also states that personal data must not be processed unless one of a number of conditions is fulfilled. One of these conditions is that the employee has given their consent to the processing. The most straightforward way of ensuring employee consent is to include a clause in all employees' contracts of employment authorising the employer to process personal data.

The document should, of course be signed by the employee. The other conditions in the list making data processing permissible are if the processing is necessary:

- for the performance of a contract, for example the processing of employees' wages;

- in order to ensure compliance with any legal obligation, for example information about an employee's working hours may be necessary in order to comply with the *Working Time Regulations*;

- to protect the vital interests of the employee, for example if disclosure of an employee's medical record was requested by a hospital in the event that the employee had suffered an accident and required urgent medical treatment;

- for the administration of justice or for public functions;

- for the purposes of legitimate interests pursued by the employer, for example if the business is about to be transferred.

The above restrictions would only come into play if an employee had not consented to the processing of personal information held about them. Thus where an employee's consent had not been obtained, data about that person could nevertheless be processed if the processing was necessary for one of the above purposes.

It is important to note the word 'necessary' used in this part of the *Data Protection Act 1998*. If the employee's consent has not been obtained, data about that person can be processed only if one of the above conditions is *necessary* for the business, and not just because (for example) management would find it convenient.

This raises the interesting question of whether random monitoring of employees' email and internet use is 'necessary' under the banner of 'performance of the contract'. It is highly unlikely that an employer would be able to assert in a general sense that monitoring of all employees' emails on a regular basis was necessary for the performance of an employee's contract, although it may (arguably) be necessary to monitor an individual employee's emails or internet usage following a specific complaint about the employee, or where there are reasonable grounds to suspect that the employee has been abusing the system. The general principle inherent in the *Data Protection Act* is that monitoring of employees' communications should only take place if it is proportionate in light of the employer's needs.

Nevertheless, employers are advised to gain employees' express consent to any monitoring they wish to carry out rather than relying on the assertion that monitoring is necessary for the performance of a contract. In requesting the employee's consent, the employer should clearly inform the employee who in the organisation will have access to the data obtained from monitoring, the purposes for which the data will be used and provide any other relevant information. The key to fairness in processing is transparency.

The duty to obtain and process data only for specified and lawful purposes [4.41a]

The second data protection principle imposes a duty on employers to specify clearly the purpose(s) for which they obtain and process data about employees and not to use the information for any purposes other than those specified. This means of course that employers must not put information gleaned from monitoring to any use other than that defined as the purpose of the monitoring. This restriction would appear to prevent employers from using information about an employee that was uncovered by chance as a result of monitoring for other purposes.

The duty to ensure that data is relevant and not excessive [4.41b]

This data protection principle means that employers should ensure that any personal information they hold about their employees is created and stored for a proper business purpose, and that, in relation to this purpose, this information is relevant, sufficient and not excessive.

This could be interpreted as a requirement for employers to use the least intrusive means possible to achieve their business aims, a principle that is put forward also in the Data Protection Code of Practice on Monitoring at Work (see **4.44** below). It may, for example, be excessive or irrelevant in relation to an employer's needs to monitor all employees' emails on a regular basis, where spot monitoring, or monitoring of selected employees' correspondence, would suffice to protect the interests of the business.

Data Regarded as 'Sensitive' for Which Processing may be Unlawful Unless the Employee has Expressly Consented [4.42]

The *Data Protection Act* limits the kind of information that can be processed about individuals. In particular, there is a provision which prevents the collection, holding or processing of data relating to an individual under any of the following headings:

- ethnic or racial origins;
- political opinions;
- religious or philosophical beliefs;
- trade union membership;
- physical or mental health or condition;
- sexual orientation;

- the commission or alleged commission of any offence.

Sensitive information can often be found in the content of employees' emails (even though the email may be work-related), and employers must take particular care to ensure that proper measures are in place to protect the data. For example, if the employer regularly monitors employees' emails, they may inadvertently come across information about:

- an employee's health, for example an employee may choose to disclose information about their health or about a disability to the employer's occupational health advisor or to a confidential counsellor;

- trade union membership or activities, for example in emails from an employee to their trade union official or deduced from the fact that the employee has made frequent visits to trade union websites;

- an employee's religious beliefs or political opinions made casually in an email to a colleague in the course of dealing with a work-related matter.

Conditions for processing to be lawful   [4.43]

The Act prohibits the collection of such data unless one of the following conditions is fulfilled:

- the employee explicitly consents to the information being collected;

- it is necessary to collect the data in order to comply with employment law, e.g. the processing of data on sickness absence will be necessary in order that the employer can comply with the legal obligation to pay statutory sick pay;

- the processing of the data is necessary on account of legal proceedings, e.g. defending a tribunal claim;

- processing is necessary for the administration of justice or to comply with a statute, e.g. the processing of information relating to an employee's criminal convictions may be necessary for the purpose of compliance with an attachment of earnings order;

- processing is carried out for the purposes of monitoring to ensure equality of opportunity as between individuals of different races or ethnic origins.

There are no other exceptions to this provision and it follows that, in most instances employers will have to ensure that employees' (and job applicants') express consent is obtained prior to gathering information for processing or monitoring purposes, if the information includes any of the types of sensitive information restricted by the *Data Protection Act 1998*.

Express consent in this context would have to be of a type that clearly indicated that the employee had agreed explicitly to the collection and processing of sensitive data by the employer. It will be necessary for the employee to have been clearly informed first of what personal information the employer wishes to collect and process and how that information will be used. The employee's signature will have to be obtained. Another requirement is that the employee's consent must be freely given, ie the employee must be in a position where they have a real choice as to whether or not to give consent to the sensitive data to be collected and used by the employer, and there must be no threatened or actual detriment to the employee if they refuse to give their consent. Processing of sensitive data without explicit consent (or without authorisation under one of the other headings above) will contravene the first data protection principle (i.e. the duty on the employer to process data fairly and lawfully).

Employees who have Access to Personal Information about Others   [4.43a]

One of the data protection principles (see **4.40**) is that employers must take appropriate measures to protect personal data against unauthorised or unlawful processing. This will lead to an inevitable need for careful recruitment, training and supervision of all employees whose jobs involve intercepting or monitoring the emails or internet activities of other staff in the workplace.

A number of principles will be important to ensure the proper and lawful processing of data, for example employers should:

- keep to a minimum the number of employees who have access to personal information about other staff obtained through monitoring;

- review carefully who in the organisation should be authorised to conduct monitoring, for example it may be more appropriate for HR professionals or IT specialists to carry out monitoring rather than employees' line managers;

- ensure all employees who may have access to personal data about other staff are properly trained so that they fully understand their obligations under the *Data Protection Act 1998*, in particular that data must be kept securely at all times and not misused or improperly disclosed;

- make it clear to employees engaged in monitoring activities that they must only use the information obtained as a result of monitoring for the purpose for which monitoring was introduced (unless in exceptional circumstances, for example where criminal activity came to light as a result of monitoring);

- communicate clearly to workers the likely consequences of any breach of confidentiality in relation to personal data obtained through monitoring, eg disciplinary action up to dismissal and possibly personal criminal liability;

- ensure all staff who are involved in monitoring activities are required to sign a confidentiality clause (see also **4.12**).

The Data Protection Code of Practice on Monitoring at Work [4.44]

The Information Commissioner published a Data Protection Code of Practice on Monitoring at Work in June 2003. The Code represents the Information Commissioner's interpretation of how the *Data Protection Act 1998* should be implemented with regard to monitoring the activities of employees at work. The Code, like other Codes of Practice, is not legally binding on employers, but a failure to follow its recommendations can be used in evidence against an employer in the event of a court or tribunal claim. In relation to monitoring of employees' email, telephone and internet usage, the Code highlights the threat such monitoring can pose to personal privacy and provides guidance on how employers can balance the requirement to protect employees' privacy against the need to pursue legitimate business interests.

One of the key recommendations of the Code of Practice is that employers should carry out an impact assessment to review the likely effect of monitoring on the privacy and other rights of employees, and to establish whether or not any adverse impact of monitoring on employees is justifiable when balanced against the needs of the employer. Impact assessments should be conducted to establish justification for monitoring in a general sense and also to review whether or not monitoring in specific circumstances would be justifiable.

The Code explains that an impact assessment involves:

- identifying the purpose(s) of any proposed monitoring and its likely benefits;

- identifying any likely adverse impact on employees of monitoring, for example the inevitable intrusion into employees' private lives that monitoring will cause;

- considering alternatives to monitoring or different ways in which monitoring might be carried out;

- deciding whether or not monitoring is justified.

There may, in any event, be considerable benefits for the employer in conducting a written impact assessment with regard to employee monitoring, for example:

- Conducting an impact assessment in an open and transparent manner will create trust between management and staff and hence enhance employee relations generally;

- The results of the assessment will help employees to understand why monitoring is necessary for the organisation;

- The assessment should also assist employees' general understanding of data protection issues and the parameters of workplace privacy;

- The measured and targeted approach required to conduct an impact assessment will ultimately save time and resources;

- If at any time legal action is taken against the employer in relation to workplace monitoring, the fact that the employer has conducted an impact assessment will put them in a stronger position to defend the action.

The Code of Practice stresses that workplace monitoring will be an intrusion into employees' privacy and may thus undermine employment relationships and damage the mutual trust and confidence that plays a key role in employment. The Code makes it clear that proportionality is the key to compliance with the *Data Protection Act*, i.e. the employer must design systems of monitoring that are linked to specific business needs and balance those needs against the reasonable rights of employees to be granted respect for their private lives and correspondence.

Another potentially negative factor that the Code identifies is the risk that confidential, private or otherwise sensitive information may be seen by the people who carry out the monitoring in circumstances where they do not need to know it, or have no right to know it. In general, the Code of Practice requires employers to recognise employee interests and provide real justification for any intrusive monitoring practices.

Although the obtaining of employees' consent to monitoring is an important and necessary prelude to monitoring, the Code of Practice points out that there are limitations as to how far consent can be relied on in an employment context to justify the processing of personal data generally. This is because consent must be 'freely given' in order for it to be valid under the *Data Protection Act*. In an employment relationship, the balance of power is not even and it may be that an employee feels that they have no choice but to agree to sign a document giving their consent to monitoring. The Code stresses that a better way forward for employers is to conduct a proper impact assessment, rather than relying on employee consent to authorise monitoring.

The Code of Practice and its accompanying supplementary guidance stress that employers should also consider alternatives to monitoring and cites as examples new methods of supervision or further training. The underlying message is that if there is an alternative, less intrusive, way of dealing with a particular situation, then monitoring should not be undertaken. Another suggestion is that employers should restrict monitoring, either by:

- targeting monitoring only at employees who work in jobs which pose a particularly high risk to the employer, rather than monitoring everyone;

- monitoring only workers about whom complaints have been made, or about whom there are reasonable grounds to suspect misconduct;

- conducting spot-checks rather than continuous monitoring;

- adopting a policy of analysing email traffic rather than monitoring the content of messages or reviewing whether traffic records can be used to narrow the scope of content monitoring;

- recording time spent on the internet rather than the sites visited or content viewed;

- using technology that prevents misuse (such as web-filtering software) rather than introducing systems designed to detect misuse after the event.

The Code stresses also that covert monitoring (defined in the Code as 'monitoring carried out in a manner calculated to ensure those subject to it are unaware that it is taking place') should not normally be undertaken. The only exception would be in circumstances were there were proper grounds for suspecting an employee of criminal activity or equivalent malpractice and it was reasonable to conclude that informing the employee that they were to be monitored would prejudice prevention or detection of the crime. In circumstances where covert monitoring is justified, the employer should ensure that any incidental information gathered about the employee that has nothing to do with their suspected wrongdoing is disregarded and subsequently deleted from the employee's file.

In relation to personal communications at work, the Code of Practice and supplementary guidance provide a number of suggestions for employers to:

- avoid reading emails that are clearly personal or private even where personal use of the email system is banned, but consider instead whether appropriate action can reasonably be taken against the employee for breach of the rules based on information available in the subject header or address of the email;

- provide secure lines of communication so that employees can transmit personal or sensitive information, for example an email to an occupational health adviser about a personal health matter or a message to a trade union official concerning a grievance;

- set up a system whereby private emails can be marked 'personal and private' and adopt a policy of not monitoring such emails unless the employee is genuinely suspected of serious wrongdoing;

- review (where a reasonable level of personal use is permitted) whether it is feasible to provide employees with two different passwords or methods of logging on depending on whether their internet access is work-related or personal;

- consider whether it is sufficient to record the time employees spend accessing the internet rather than monitoring the actual sites visited or the content viewed.

In essence, the Code recommends that emails which are clearly personal or private should not be intercepted, even in organisations that impose a complete ban on personal use of email and the internet. The supplementary guidance to the Code points out that although a ban is an important factor, it is not necessarily an over-riding one and the employer would have to be able to justify taking action to read a personal email by weighing up the intrusion into the employee's private life with the employer's need to know the content of the email. Some apparently personal emails may in any event be legitimate work-related messages, for example an email from an employee to an occupational health adviser concerning a personal health matter.

One key message inherent in the Code of Practice is that if there is a less intrusive method for an employer to establish facts that they need to know, then they should pursue that less intrusive method rather than intercepting an employee's email communications. The one exception would be where the employer had reasonable grounds to suspect that an employee had been involved in serious misconduct, for example harassing another employee by email, or criminal activity such as accessing child pornography on the internet. Ultimately, however, employers should only open an employee's private emails if there is no other reasonable alternative in all the circumstances.

It can be seen that the Code of Practice on Monitoring at Work goes much further than the *Lawful Business Practice Regulations 2000* which, broadly, make it lawful for an employer to monitor employees' communications provided monitoring is being done for one of the purposes specified in the Regulations (see **6.16**). The issue of privacy is a serious one and must be respected by employers.

Conclusion [4.45]

It is essential for all employers to devise appropriate restrictions on employees' use of email and the internet so as to avoid the risk of breaches of confidentiality. Breaches can occur as a result of inappropriate handling of confidential information within the company, or as a result of messages being inadvertently transmitted to people outside the organisation containing confidential or sensitive information.

The effective security management of confidential and sensitive information held on computer systems should therefore be a key priority for employers. It is advisable to take steps to identify the type of information that is sensitive and then make objective policy decisions as to who in the organisation should have access to external email and the internet.

Decisions also need to be taken on whether to introduce restrictive covenants into the contracts of employees who have access to sensitive or confidential information, and what disciplinary penalties should be in place to deal with any employee who breaches the organisation's confidentiality rules.

A further very important aspect of confidentiality is to determine who in the organisation should have access to personal data held about employees, and any data obtained as a result of email and internet monitoring.

In terms of adhering to data protection legislation, the key to staying within the law whilst at the same time ensuring fairness, is to adhere to the data protection principles and aim to strike a reasonable balance between the needs of the business to operate efficiently and lawfully, and the rights of employees to enjoy privacy and to be treated with respect. The level and nature of any monitoring should be proportionate to the employer's stated business needs, or to any specific problem that has been identified, for example an inordinate amount of time being spent by an employee visiting non work-related internet sites. Employees' explicit consent should be obtained before any data about them is collected, stored or used in any way.

Questions and Answers [4.46]

Question

What type of information should an employer regard as sufficiently confidential to merit the introduction of procedures and rules to limit employees' access and use?

Answer

Employers should take positive steps to protect confidential information about matters such as products and services, sales statistics, prices, contact details for customers, commercially sensitive information such as new designs, formulae and processes, information about customers and suppliers and personal data held about employees.

Question

To what extent is an employee obliged as part of their general obligations towards their employer not to disclose confidential information?

Answer

Every contract of employment contains an implied duty that the employee should render faithful service. This duty means, amongst other things, that where information is confidential to the employer, employees are obliged to keep it that way, i.e. not disclose it to others without authority. Even after employment has ended, the obligation not to disclose information that amounts to a trade secret continues in force. Despite this, it is strongly advisable for employers to devise and implement clear written guidelines on keeping information confidential.

Question

Can an employer simply state in a policy document that *all* information held by the company is to be regarded as confidential?

Answer

Employers cannot simply stipulate that all information held within the company is confidential because protection against unauthorised disclosure by an employee will then not be enforced by the courts. For example, information that can be attributed to an employee's own general skill and knowledge cannot be protected, even if this has been acquired as a direct result of the particular employment. Additionally, some company information may be available from public sources and cannot then be regarded as confidential. In any event, under common law, information will not be confidential unless those to whom it is disclosed are informed that it is confidential.

Question

What sorts of issues should be covered in an employer's procedure on confidentiality?

Answer

A company procedure on confidentiality should establish basic guidelines for employees and identify any prohibited practices so that a framework is established within which all employees can work. There should be internal controls to limit access to confidential information and to prevent the disclosure of sensitive data. Rules governing the choosing, changing and non-disclosure of passwords should be devised and implemented. There should also be rules banning (for example) the sending of confidential information by email (unless it is encrypted), the forwarding of emails sent by a third party without the original sender's express consent and the transmission of data by email to and from employees' homes.

Question

What practical steps can an employer take to protect confidential information from unauthorised or inappropriate disclosure by employees?

Answer

In order to increase the level of protection, employers should ensure that there is an express confidentiality clause in every employee's contract of employment. The precise wording of any confidentiality clause will depend on the nature of the employer's business and the employee's job, but should at least define the type of information that is to be regarded as confidential and lay down rules on confidentiality applicable during employment, together with rules on keeping information confidential that will apply after the termination of the employee's employment.

Question

What is a restrictive covenant?

Answer

A restrictive covenant is a clause in an employee's contract of employment designed to restrain the employee from undertaking certain defined activities after their employment has ended, for example disclosing information that the company has classified as confidential. Sound legal advice should be obtained before drafting restrictive covenants which should be tailored according to the type of work an employee, or group of employees, is employed to do and the type of information to which they have access.

Question

How should an employer respond if it is discovered that an employee has made an unauthorised disclosure of confidential information?

Answer

An unauthorised disclosure of confidential information may warrant disciplinary action. The level of action that will be appropriate will depend on a number of factors including the type of information that has been disclosed, to whom it was disclosed, whether the disclosure was deliberate or accidental and whether the employee has previously committed any similar act of misconduct. A serious breach of confidentiality may justify dismissal, but if the dismissal is to be fair, the employer will need to make sure that they follow a fair and reasonable procedure.

Question

What can an employer do if it is discovered that an ex-employee is using confidential information belonging to the company in breach of a restrictive covenant?

Answer

Where a breach of confidential information occurs after the termination of an employee's contract, the company may be able to seek an injunction to stop the employee using the information and/or prevent further disclosures, to sue the ex-employee for damages, to ask a court to order the employee to account for the profits they have made by using the confidential information and/or order the employee to return any confidential documentation to the company.

Question

How can an employer gain protection against liability for incorrect information being transmitted outside the organisation by email?

Answer

Employers can minimise the risk of legal action being taken against them in the event that incorrect information is transmitted outside the organisation by email by including a disclaimer in all external email messages. The type of disclaimer that is appropriate will vary from organisation to organisation depending on the perceived level of risk and the potential consequences of mistakes being made.

Question

To what extent does data protection legislation impact on the storing and processing of information held about individual employees' email and internet usage?

Answer

The *Data Protection Act 1998* strictly regulates the processing of personal information about individuals whenever an individual can be identified from the information. The Act covers information held about an employee in paper format, data stored on a computer system and data contained in emails. All the routine aspects of handling personal information (for example its collection, storage and amending) are covered within the scope of the term 'processing'. The Act contains eight data protection principles which employers must adhere to. One of these is that personal data must be processed 'fairly and lawfully' and must not be processed unless either the employee has consented, or one of a limited list of conditions is met. Another of the data protection principles is that information should be adequate, relevant and not excessive in relation to the purposes for which it is processed.

Question

What general rights do employees have under the *Data Protection Act 1998*?

Answer

Employees have the right under the Act to be informed in advance if personal data about them are being processed, to be given a description of the data, told the purposes for which the data are being processed and given details of the persons to whom the data may be disclosed. Employees also have the right to ask their employer to correct or remove any inaccuracies on the file. Finally and very importantly, employees have the right to be granted access to any personal data held about them.

Question

What specific rights of access do employees have to information held about them in their employer's manual or computer files?

Answer

Employees have the right to be granted access to manual files, computer files and emails containing information about them personally. This would of course include information about an employee's email and internet use. The information must be provided in an intelligible and permanent form within 40 calendar days of a written request being received from the employee, provided the employee has also (if the employer requests it) paid a fee (the maximum of which is £10).

Question

What steps need an employer take in relation to staff who have access to data obtained as a result of employee monitoring?

Answer

Employers must take measures to protect personal data against unauthorised or unlawful processing. This will lead to an inevitable need for careful recruitment, training and supervision of all employees whose jobs involve intercepting or monitoring the emails or internet activities of other staff in the workplace. It is advisable to require all staff who have access to data obtained from monitoring activities to sign a confidentiality clause.

Question

What is an 'impact assessment'?

Answer

The Data Protection Code of Practice on Monitoring at Work recommends that employers should conduct an impact assessment in order to establish the likely effect of monitoring on the privacy and other rights of employees and decide whether or not any adverse impact of monitoring on employees is justifiable when balanced against the needs of the employer. An impact assessment would involve identifying the purpose(s) of any proposed monitoring and its likely benefits, identifying any likely adverse impact on employees of monitoring, considering alternatives to monitoring or different ways in which monitoring might be carried out and ultimately deciding whether or not monitoring is justified.

Question

Is it likely that the reading of an employee's emails could infringe any of the provisions of the *Data Protection Act 1998?*

Answer

The first data protection principle creates the obligation on employers to process personal data *fairly and lawfully.* It is feasible that even if the collection of data is *lawful* (either because the employee has consented to it, or because the purpose of recording the data falls under one of the provisions of the *Lawful Business Practice Regulations),* it could still be *unfair.* If an employer was to take extreme measures to read an employee's emails, including for example reading and recording an employee's personal emails without good cause, then this could potentially be deemed unfair under data protection legislation. Reading employees' emails for no proper business reason could also be in breach of the Data Protection Code of Practice on Monitoring at Work, in particular if the emails in question contained personal or sensitive information. Employers should always gain employees' express consent to any monitoring they wish to carry out, and ensure that monitoring is not excessive in relation to its purpose.

5 The Employment Contract

Introduction [5.1]

A contract of employment forms the basis of the relationship between the employer and the employee. All the terms and conditions, rules, obligations and entitlements related to the employee's employment will be established by reference to the contract.

The law does not require a contract of employment to be in writing, although employers are under a statutory obligation to issue written particulars of the key terms and conditions of employment to every employee (including part-time employees) within two months of the employee starting work. These written particulars must include (amongst other things) start date, job title, rate of pay, normal hours of work, entitlement to sick pay and holidays, pension entitlements (if any), place of work and notice periods. Additionally, employers who have 20 or more employees must provide written details of any disciplinary rules that exist. Fuller details are given below in **5.19**.

A contract of employment comes into force as soon as there has been an offer of employment and an unconditional acceptance of that offer. This will be the case irrespective of whether all the specific terms of the contract have been agreed at that point in time, and irrespective of whether the offer and the acceptance were in writing or reached as a result of verbal agreement.

Once the terms of a contract of employment are agreed, they are legally binding on both parties. This means that none of the terms of the contract can be changed without the agreement of the other party.

The inter-relationship between contracts of employment and statutory obligations [5.2]

Employee rights that have been created by the passing of legislation are automatically incorporated into every contract of employment. It is not open to employers to attempt to exclude an employee's statutory rights. Any contractual clause purporting to deny an employee such rights will be unenforceable.

This means in effect that employees automatically have a range of employment rights conferred upon them by statute including, for example, rights under the *Data Protection Act 1998*, the *Sex Discrimination Act 1975*, the *Race Relations Act 1976* and the *Employment Rights Act 1996*.

Apart from any terms incorporated into a contract as a result of statute, a contract of employment is likely to consist of a range of terms, both express and implied.

The Express Terms of a Contract of Employment   [5.3]

The express terms of a contract of employment are those that have been specifically agreed between the employer and the employee, whether verbally or in writing. This notion of agreement is fundamental to the formation of the contract. Essentially anything that has been *agreed* between the employer and the employee will form part of the contract, whether or not the term is in writing. It follows that terms and conditions that are imposed unilaterally on an employee will not be contractually binding, unless and until the employee has agreed to them.

Express terms take precedence over implied terms in a contract of employment unless there are exceptional circumstances. Clearly this makes sense since the express terms represent what the parties have specifically agreed, whereas implied terms represent what the parties are taken to have agreed (see below in **5.8**).

Incorporated terms   [5.4]

Apart from statutory terms, certain other terms may be incorporated into employment contracts by means of reference to a separate document. Typically, disciplinary procedures and policies that are to have contractual effect may be incorporated in this way.

Employers may wish to insert a clause in their employees' contracts along any of the following lines:

> 'Details of the company's policy and rules on email and internet use are set out in the company handbook. This policy and the rules form part of the terms of your contract of employment'.

> 'It is a condition of your contract that you comply with the company's policy on email and internet usage, a copy of which has been provided to you. Breach of the policy may be regarded as gross misconduct, depending on the nature of the offence.'

'Rules governing the use of the company's communications systems, including telephones, email and the internet, are contained in the policies manual, a copy of which is enclosed. These rules form part of your contract of employment. Serious breach of any of these rules will be regarded as gross misconduct and may lead to summary dismissal.'

Whether policies and rules on email and internet use should be incorporated into employees' contracts [5.5]

Given the potentially serious consequences of employees misuse of email and internet facilities, it is advisable for employers to make sure that any policy and rules they have which govern uses of their communications systems are incorporated into employees' contracts.

Advantages and disadvantages of incorporation [5.6]

A policy that is not incorporated into contracts of employment will be regarded more as a management guideline indicating the employer's overall approach to the subject covered by the policy, and this will not give rise to contractually enforceable terms and conditions. This could mean that any breach of the rules on the part of an employee could not be viewed as a breach of contract, which in turn could limit the employer in enforcing the rules through their disciplinary procedures.

There are, however, certain disadvantages in introducing policies and rules that have contractual force. These are that:

- The employer (as well as the employees) will be contractually bound by the terms of the policy. If the employer fails thereafter to abide by the policy, there could be a claim for breach of contract against them. Realistically this is only likely to occur in the event that an employee is dismissed, since employment tribunals can only adjudicate on a breach of contract claim if it is associated with the termination of the employee's contract.

- If the employer wishes to change the policy or rules at a future date, the express agreement of all affected employees (or their representatives) will be required. It is not possible lawfully to change any of the terms of employees' contracts without their express consent. A policy document which consists only of a set of management guidelines on the other hand can be changed without the consent of the workforce.

One way to deal with this conundrum is to make the policy contractual, but include a clause within it stating that the employer may vary the content of the policy from time to time at the discretion of management.

It is important therefore that management weigh up the advantages and disadvantages of making their email and internet policy and rules contractual, and make it clear through the documentation itself whether or not any policy and rules on email and internet use form part of employees' contracts.

The subject of introducing new policies, rules and procedures is covered fully in **CHAPTER 9**.

Whether disciplinary procedures should be incorporated into employees' contracts [5.7]

The principles outlined above apply equally to disciplinary procedures. In most organisations, disciplinary procedures will form part of employees' contracts of employment, but this is not automatically the case. Again the advantages and disadvantages detailed above will apply. If the disciplinary procedure is contractual, the employer would be acting in breach of contract if they:

- failed to grant an employee a key entitlement under the procedure, for example refused to allow the employee the right to bring a companion to a disciplinary interview, or failed to offer a dismissed employee the opportunity to appeal against the decision to dismiss them;

- imposed a disciplinary penalty on an employee, for example suspension without pay, where the disciplinary procedure did not contain authority for the imposition of such a sanction;

- dismissed an employee without following the appropriate stages of the disciplinary procedure or without adhering to some key element of the procedure.

In this last example, the employee will have been dismissed in breach of contract, i.e. wrongfully dismissed. This topic is covered below at **5.43**.

A change to the law, set to be brought into force in October 2004 as a result of the implementation of the *Employment Act 2002,* will mean that all employers, irrespective of their size, will be obliged to introduce and operate minimum statutory dispute resolution procedures. The minimum procedures will be a statutory dismissal and disciplinary procedure (DDP) and a statutory grievance procedure (GP).

It is also proposed that these procedures will have to be in writing and will automatically form part of all employees' contracts of employment from day one of their employment. It is not clear, however, at the time of writing, whether this aspect of the new legislation will be implemented in October 2004 or at some later date.

Once the DDP provisions have been implemented, all employers will be obliged to ensure that they have a contractual disciplinary procedure in place for all their employees. Technically, however, there will be nothing to stop an employer from making only the statutory minimum procedure contractual and specifying that other aspects of their procedure which go beyond the statutory minimum are not contractual.

Further information about the future legislative provisions is provided in **5.21**.

The Implied Terms of a Contract of Employment   [5.8]

The implied terms of a contract of employment are those which are not spelt out in writing but are presumed to have been the intention of the parties when the contract was entered into. Even though nothing is in writing, implied terms are binding on both the employer and the employee.

How terms come to be implied into contracts   [5.9]

Terms may be implied into a contract in any of the following ways:

1. As a result of the conduct of the parties, i.e. both the employer and the employee act as if the term was agreed.

    If both the employer and the employee conduct themselves in a manner that is consistent with a particular term having been agreed, then the term may, by implication, come to form part of the contract. For example, if an employer imposed a pay cut on an employee and if the employee continued to work normally and accepted their normal pay at the end of the week or month, then the conduct of the employee would suggest that they had accepted the reduction to their pay.

    If over a period of time managers have openly condoned personal use of email and the internet, it could be argued that their conduct and that of their employees in using email and the internet for personal purposes has given rise to an implied term that personal use of these facilities is an entitlement.

2. Because they are necessary to give the contract 'business efficacy'.

    This means that the term is necessary in order to make the contract workable, or that it is common sense that the term should be implied. An example of a term implied in this way would be the requirement for an employee supplied with a company car to have a current driving licence.

3. Because they are so obvious that the parties took them for granted.

    An example of a term implied under this heading could be the requirement for an employee to be honest in their dealings with their colleagues.

4. As a result of custom and practice in the organisation or within the industry as a whole.

For a term to be implied into employees' contracts as a result of custom and practice, it must be:

*   Reasonable, i.e. fair and not arbitrary or capricious.

*   Certain, i.e. precisely defined.

*   Notorious, i.e. well known and established over a long period of time.

A term will only be implied into a contract on the basis of custom and practice if the practice has been regularly adopted in a particular company or industry over time. A single incident will not give rise to an implied term. The notion is that, because the term has regularly applied and employees have come to expect it, it has evolved into a contractual right.

There may, for example, be an implied right through custom and practice for employees to have reasonable use of email for personal or private purposes, if for a number of years they have been allowed reasonable use of workplace telephones for personal calls.

Implied terms that could impact on email and internet use [5.10]

Over a period of time, courts and tribunals have implied terms into employment contracts that impact on both employers' and employees' obligations. Those that could impact on employers with respect to their management of email and internet use are:

*   the duty to maintain trust and confidence in the employment relationship;

*   the duty to provide a reasonably tolerable working environment in which employees can perform their work;

*   the duty to enable employees to obtain redress for any grievance they may have.

These three terms are analysed further below.

The main relevant implied duties that apply to employees (in relation to email and internet use) are:

- the duty to obey lawful and reasonable instructions;
- the duty to exercise reasonable care and skill;
- the duty to maintain trust and confidence;
- the duty to render faithful service.

These implied duties are dealt with separately below.

Employers' implied duties [5.11]

The duty to maintain trust and confidence in the employment relationship

This wide ranging duty obliges employers not to treat employees arbitrarily or capriciously. The duty of trust and confidence encompasses the concept of treating employees with respect and maintaining a working relationship that is based on trust. The duty also incorporates providing support to employees when they need it and refraining from any type of conduct which would have the effect of making an employee's working life intolerable.

A blatant breach of an employee's right to respect for their privacy of correspondence (under the *Human Rights Act, Article 8*) could constitute a breach of the implied duty of trust and confidence. An example of such a breach could be if monitoring of employees' telephone calls, email messages and/or internet access was carried out without consent or forewarning. Monitoring is dealt with fully in **CHAPTER 6**.

A further example of a breach of the duty of trust and confidence could be a manager's failure or refusal to deal promptly and adequately with a genuine complaint of bullying or harassment by email (or by any other means).

Yet another example could be the sudden, unilateral introduction of restrictions on email and internet use without consultation or agreement.

The scope of the implied duty of trust and confidence is limitless, but a breach will only occur if the conduct of the employer is unreasonable to the extent that it makes continuing in the working relationship impossible or intolerable for the employee. In this respect the employer is liable for the behaviour of its managers. Interestingly, however, the EAT held in *Morrow v Safeway Stores plc EAT 275/00* (a case that involved unreasonable criticism of an employee in front of others) that where there has been a breach of the implied term of trust and confidence, this will always amount to a breach of the employee's contract.

In the case of *Stewart v Texas Homecare IT Case No 29209/91*, a tribunal held that there had been a fundamental breach of trust and confidence when a letter containing serious and false allegations against an employee (made by his supervisor) was left visible on a computer screen and was subsequently seen by both the employee and his colleagues. The tribunal ruled that the employee, who had resigned on account of the incident, had been unfairly constructively dismissed.

The duty to provide and monitor a reasonably tolerable working environment in which employees can perform their work [5.12]

This duty emerged from the case of *Waltons & Morse v Dorrington* [1997] *IRLR 488* reported below:

Waltons & Morse v Dorrington [1997] *IRLR 488*

Facts

Ms Dorrington had worked as a secretary for a firm of solicitors for eight years. She was a non-smoker. After an office reorganisation, she was moved to an open-plan area and began to suffer discomfort on account of cigarette smoking by colleagues. When she raised the matter with management, a policy was introduced banning smoking in the open-plan area where she worked. That did not resolve the problem, however, because smoke from nearby areas continued to affect the air quality and cause her discomfort. Having complained again and received an unsympathetic response, she resigned and brought a claim for constructive dismissal to an employment tribunal based on the allegation that her employer was in breach of her contract.

Findings

On assessing the evidence put forward, the tribunal concluded that the air quality had been intolerable for a non-smoker. On appeal, the EAT implied a term into the employee's contract that the employer must provide a reasonably tolerable working environment for employees to perform their work, and that the employer in this case was in breach of that duty. They also found that the employer was in breach of the implied term to provide

---

employees a reasonable opportunity to obtain redress for a grievance. Thus there had been a breach of contract entitling Ms Dorrington to resign, and she succeeded in her case.

Implications

Although the duty to provide a reasonably tolerable working environment was established in a case involving smoking, it could be applied to a much wider range of circumstances. One interpretation could be that it would also incorporate a duty to provide a working environment in which employees can perform their duties free from any form of bullying or harassment (including harassment by email). In a subsequent case, *Moores v Bude-Stratton Town Council [2000] IRLR 676*, the EAT held that the duty to provide and maintain a reasonably tolerable working environment applied to protect an employee from unacceptable treatment and behaviour and unauthorised interference with their work. The failure to prevent or control email harassment could therefore give rise to a constructive dismissal claim based on an alleged breach of the implied duty to provide a reasonably tolerable working environment.

The duty to enable employees to obtain redress for any grievance they may have [5.13]

The EAT, in the case of *W A Goold (Pearmak) Ltd v McConnell & anor [1995] IRLR 516,* implied a term into employment contracts that employers should 'reasonably and promptly afford a reasonable opportunity to their employees to obtain redress of any grievance they may have'. Thus, irrespective of whether the contract of employment contains express terms governing grievance procedures, employees are contractually entitled to have any genuine grievances dealt with by their management.

This has implications for managers who receive a complaint from an employee that another employee is misusing email or the internet, particularly if there is an allegation that the other employee's misuse of the system is causing them a detriment. A typical example would be a complaint that an employee had received an email from a colleague that contained words that amounted to sexual or racial harassment, or a complaint that a colleague had downloaded sexually explicit material from the internet that was offensive.

There are a number of serious implications in a case such as this. Apart from the duty to afford the employee an opportunity to obtain redress for the grievance, there is also the question of the employer's liability for sex or race discrimination in the event that the email message or material downloaded was genuinely offensive to the employee on the grounds of sex or race. The subject of sexual and racial harassment is dealt with fully in **CHAPTER 3**.

It follows that managers should always take any complaint from employees about misuse of email and internet facilities seriously and make sure the complaint is promptly and fully investigated and properly dealt with. This will avoid the possibility of a claim that the implied duty to provide redress for grievances has been breached.

As can be seen from the above, the right to obtain redress for a grievance has come about as a result of common law rather than statutory law. There is, at the time of writing, no statutory obligation on employers to operate a grievance procedure. However, as a result of the implementation of the *Employment Act 2002*, all employers (irrespective of size) will be obliged, as from October 2004, to introduce and operate minimum statutory dispute resolution procedures. The minimum procedures will be a statutory dismissal and disciplinary procedure (DDP) and a statutory grievance procedure (GP).

Once the GP provisions have been implemented, all employers will be under a duty to ensure that they have a contractual grievance procedure in place for their employees. The procedure will have to be incorporated into all employees' contracts of employment. The minimum procedure will contain three stages as follows:

- the employee will be entitled to present any grievance relating to their employment to their employer (this must be done in writing), making it clear what the basis is for the grievance;

- the employer will be under a duty to set up a meeting (within a defined timescale) to discuss the grievance with the employee and consider how it might be resolved;

- The employee will have the right to appeal against any decision that they consider unsatisfactory.

Employers will have to deal with every grievance lodged in writing through the GP, otherwise the employee may be able to resign and win a claim for automatically unfair constructive dismissal on account of the employer's breach of contract.

Employees' implied duties [5.14]

The duty to obey lawful and reasonable instructions

It is inherent in every contract of employment that employees should obey any lawful and reasonable instructions issued by their employer. This implied term must of course be read in the context of any express terms contained in the contract that define the nature and scope of the employee's job duties. If, however, an instruction is unreasonable (or unlawful), then the employee is under no duty to comply with it.

The duty to exercise reasonable care and skill [5.15]

There is an implied term in every contract that the employee must exercise reasonable care and skill in the carrying out of their duties. If there is a serious breach of this duty, this may justify dismissal, as in the case of *Taylor v. Alidair Ltd [1978] IRLR 82*. In this case, an airline pilot had landed his plane so badly that it was seriously damaged. The pilot was deemed to be in breach of the implied duty to take reasonable care and skill, and his dismissal (for one single incident) was ruled fair by a tribunal.

It is easy to see how this duty could be breached by an employee who used email carelessly and who, for example, accidentally sent confidential information by email to an outside source. Irrespective of the existence of any express terms governing employees' use of email, such careless action could be in breach of contract if the outcome of the employee's carelessness was sufficiently serious for the organisation.

The duty to maintain trust and confidence [5.16]

The duty of trust and confidence applies both to the employer and the employee. This means that the employee is contractually bound not to act in a way that fundamentally breaches the bond of trust that must exist in any employment relationship. Any act of very serious misconduct or blatant breach of company rules is likely to breach the duty of trust and confidence giving the employer the right to dismiss the employee summarily.

The duty to render faithful service [5.17]

Employees are under an implied duty to render faithful service, which includes the duty not to misuse or disclose confidential information belonging to their employer. This implied duty will apply whether or not there is an express clause in the contract governing confidential information. The duty not to disclose confidential information applies throughout employment. Even after an employee has left their employment, however, the duty not to disclose information that amounts to a trade secret continues in force.

Because of the ease with which email messages can be distributed to large numbers of people (some of whom may then forward the message and any attachments on to others), there is an inevitable risk that confidential information may (deliberately or accidentally) be disclosed to someone outside the organisation. For this reason, it is advisable for employers, despite the existence of the implied term, to introduce specific express rules governing the use of confidential information. This will be particularly important for employees who have access to sensitive information as part of their jobs. Express contractual terms governing confidentiality will have four key advantages:

- they will help employees to understand their obligations under the duty of confidentiality;

- they can clarify what information is to be treated as confidential;

- they can specify how employees should keep key information confidential (e.g. by keeping passwords secret, etc);

- they will help the employer to enforce the rules on confidential information in the event of a breach by an employee.

Further information on confidentiality as it applies to email use is provided in CHAPTER 4.

Communicating Contractual Obligations to the Employee [5.18]

As can be seen from the above provisions, employees' obligations in contract will depend on what has been agreed between the parties. Nevertheless, having reached agreement, it is up to the employer to communicate any rules, terms and conditions, duties and obligations to employees and it is always better for these to be in writing. The more information that is set out in writing, the less scope there will be for misunderstanding, misinterpretation or disagreement at a later date.

Committing policies, duties and obligations to writing need not restrict the employer because it is possible to incorporate discretion and flexibility into the terms of a contract, so long as any discretion is not subsequently applied irrationally or perversely. Employees also benefit from being given the maximum amount of information in writing because they then have a clear picture of what is expected of them and what their obligations and entitlements are.

The requirement to provide certain terms of employment in writing [5.19]

There is in any event a legal obligation on employers to communicate certain defined terms of employment in writing. Under the *Employment Rights Act 1996, s. 1*, an employer is obliged to provide all employees, including part-timers, a written statement setting out the main terms and conditions of their employment. This is known as the written statement of particulars of employment, or sometimes just as the written statement. Employees are entitled to receive a written statement within two months of the commencement of their employment.

The difference between a contract of employment and a written statement [5.20]

The difference between a contract of employment and a written statement is that the contract will consist of *all* the terms which have been agreed between the employer and the employee (including any terms agreed verbally), plus any implied terms, whereas the written statement is a document issued by the employer to the employee covering some of the terms of the contract. If the written statement contains terms to which the employee has not agreed, then these terms will not be legally binding even though they are included in the statement. Normally the terms contained in a written statement are consistent with what has been agreed as part of the contract, but in the event of a dispute, the written statement will not always be taken as proof of what was agreed (although it does provide evidence). The fact remains, however, that unless the employee agrees to the terms contained in the written statement, they will not be binding as part of the contract.

It is possible of course and indeed common for employers to formulate a written contract of employment that also contains all the information required for the written statement. This avoids the need to create a separate document containing written particulars of employment.

Terms that must be in writing [5.21]

The following information must, by law, be included within the written statement:

1. The names of the employer and the employee.

2. The date employment began, and whether any previous employment counts towards the employee's continuous service.

    Previous employment may count towards continuous service where there has been a transfer of the business in which the employee works to another employer (under the *Transfer of Undertakings Regulations 1981*), or where the employee has moved from one company to an associated company without a break in continuity.

3. The scale or rate of pay and the pay intervals (e.g. weekly, monthly).

    The rate of pay must not be below any minimum specified from time to time in the *National Minimum Wage Act*.

4. Any terms and conditions relating to hours of work.

    This should include terms relating to normal working hours and any overtime requirements. There is, however, no need to specify exact hours of work so long as the written statement makes it clear what the employee's obligations are. The clause governing hours may stipulate that the employee must be available to work any reasonable hours required for the performance of the job (subject to the working time restrictions laid down in the *Working Time Regulations*).

5. Entitlement to holidays, including public holidays, and holiday pay.

    This should include clarification of employees' entitlement to be paid for holidays accrued but not taken on termination of employment.

6. Any terms and conditions relating to sickness absence, including any provision for sick pay

    This provision relates to the provision of occupational sick pay, i.e. continuation of the employee's wage or salary during periods of sickness absence. The provision of statutory sick pay is a separate matter and is governed by statute.

7. Any terms and conditions relating to pensions and pension schemes

    The written statement should say whether or not an occupational pension scheme is in operation, and if so whether a contracting-out certificate is in force.

8. The length of notice which the employee is entitled to receive and obliged to give to terminate the contract of employment.

    Minimum notice periods are prescribed in law, but the written statement may impose longer periods on one or both parties.

9. The job title.

    Either the job title or a brief description of the work must be provided. There is no legal obligation on employers to provide a job description (although to do so represents good management practice). If a job description is provided, it is advisable to incorporate an 'any other duties' clause to ensure flexibility.

10. The likely duration of a period of temporary employment.

   If the temporary contract is for a fixed-term, the precise finish date must be stated. Alternatively, if the contract is to come to an end on the occurrence of a particular event, for example the return to work of another employee who is absent from work on maternity leave, this should be clearly notified in writing to the temporary employee.

11. The place of work.

   The employee's normal place of work, including the employer's address, should be stated. If there is a requirement for the employee to work at different places, this must also be specified.

12. Details of any relevant collective agreements which directly affect the employee's terms and conditions of employment.

   This must specify who the parties are to the collective agreement.

13. Details of overseas assignments.

   Where an employee is to be assigned to work overseas for a period of more than one month, they must be provided with written information on the duration of the assignment, the currency in which their salary will be paid, details of any special terms, conditions and perks relevant to the assignment and terms governing the employee's return to the UK.

14. The name or designation of the person to whom the employee should apply if they have a work-related grievance.

   This can either be the name or job designation of the appropriate person.

15. Disciplinary rules.

   The requirement to provide written disciplinary rules applies only to employers who have 20 or more employees.

There is no defined format or style for these terms and conditions of employment although the law states that certain terms should be contained within one document known as a 'principal statement'. Specifically, a single statement must include details of: the names of the parties, the date employment began, pay, hours, holiday entitlements, job title and place of work.

In October 2004, new legislation will come into force as a result of the implementation of the *Employment Act 2002*. Under the new provisions, all employers, irrespective of their size, will be obliged to introduce and operate minimum statutory dispute resolution procedures. The minimum procedures will be a statutory dismissal and disciplinary procedure (DDP) and a statutory grievance procedure (GP).

The DDP will contain three basic stages obliging employers to:

- set out the employee's alleged misconduct in writing and give or send a copy to the employee, inviting them to attend a meeting to discuss the matter;

- hold a meeting (within a defined timescale) in which the employee must be given a full and fair opportunity to explain their case prior to any decision being taken on whether to impose disciplinary action;

- allow a right of appeal against any decision to impose disciplinary action or dismissal.

Any dismissal implemented without the correct application of the DDP will be automatically unfair, provided of course that the non-application of the procedure was the employer's fault.

It is proposed that the new statutory procedures will have to be in writing and that they will automatically form part of all employees' contracts of employment from day one of their employment. It is not clear, however, at the time of writing, whether this aspect of the new legislation will be implemented in October 2004 or at some later date.

Once the DDP provisions have been implemented, all employers will be obliged to ensure that they have a contractual disciplinary procedure in place for all their employees and that this is included within the written statement. The exemption in relation to the provision of written disciplinary rules that currently applies to employers with fewer than 20 employees will be abolished.

The importance of ensuring employees understand their contractual obligations [5.22]

Over and above the requirement for the employer to provide the key terms of an employee's contract in writing, the employer may of course wish to specify additional written terms of employment. These may be provided in the written statement itself, in a separate document such as a company handbook, a policy manual or in a collective agreement. Such terms could cover, for example, medical examinations, personal and property searches, confidentiality clauses, restrictive covenants, safety, general security measures, equal opportunities, mobility, dress codes and of course, guidance and rules on the use of the employer's communications systems.

Where policies and procedures are provided in a document other than the written statement of particulars, it is important that the employer should make it clear whether or not the policy or procedure has contractual force (see above in **5.7**). A policy that is not incorporated into contracts of employment will be regarded more as a management guideline, and will not give rise to contractually enforceable terms and conditions.

Committing policies, procedures and rules on email and internet use to writing [5.23]

It is strongly advisable to formulate clear written policies, procedures and rules for employees' use of email and the internet. There is no legal requirement to do this, but the possible legal and practical consequences of not doing so are immense. Ultimately it is likely to be the employer who suffers the financial and other negative consequences of any misuse, whether deliberate or accidental.

The use of email and the internet at work is, for many employees, a relatively new experience and it is unrealistic to expect them to have knowledge or understanding of all the risks and liabilities involved. Many people have been accustomed for many years to using letters, faxes and the telephone for workplace communications. For most workers, these methods of communication will involve liasing with only one other person at a time, unlike email which allows the same message to be sent out to an infinite number of people at the same time at the single click of a computer mouse. Whilst it is relatively unlikely that an employee will send a letter to the wrong address, it is easy for a busy worker glancing quickly through a list of co-workers' email addresses on a computer screen, to hit the wrong one.

For these and many other reasons, it is advisable and arguably essential for employers to formulate written policies, procedures and rules governing the use of these modern systems of communication.

CHAPTER **8** covers this subject in depth, and provides examples of the sorts of policies, rules and procedures that an employer may wish to implement. The subject of introducing new policies and rules without being in breach of contract is also covered.

Breach of Contract Issues [5.24]

Unfortunately for employers and employees alike there is wide scope for both parties to inadvertently act in breach of contract on account of employees having access to email and the internet. Much will depend on the employer's policies and rules on the subject, or lack of them. Where an employee wishes to bring a claim for breach of contract to a court or tribunal, there is no minimum period of qualifying service required.

Under general contractual principles, where either the employer or the employee has committed a fundamental breach of contract, or indicated in words that they do not intend to honour future obligations under the contract (known as repudiation of the contract), the other party has the right to terminate the contract (if they so choose) immediately.

The alternative course of action for the aggrieved party is to affirm the contract, i.e. treat it as continuing. If, following a breach of contract by one of the parties, the party whose rights have been breached does nothing, but instead continues as normal, they will be deemed to have affirmed the contract through their conduct.

Typically, cases involving repudiatory breaches of contract by employees involve dishonesty, disobedience or serious negligence. Other actions by employees may also constitute a breach of contract provided the employer's policies and rules make this clear. This yet again demonstrates the importance from the employer's perspective of devising clear policies and rules on employees' use of email and the internet. Essentially it is up to the employer to clearly establish (and communicate) what sort of conduct will be regarded as a fundamental breach of contract leading to the employee's summary dismissal.

How employees can be in breach of contract through misuse of email and the internet [5.25]

The main areas that could give rise to a breach of contract on the part of the employee are:

- unauthorised access;
- breaches of confidentiality;
- inadvertent or deliberate harassment;
- use, or excessive use, of communications systems for personal or private reasons contrary to the employer's rules.

Unauthorised access [5.26]

Employees may be acting in breach of contract if they:

- gain access to a company computer without authorisation;

- use information held on a computer for unauthorised purposes;

- obtain and/or use another employee's password without authorisation;

- disclose their own password to another person without authority;

- access the internet without authority;

- use the internet for purposes prohibited by their contract;

- view pornography on the internet, whether or not any material is downloaded;

- use material downloaded from the internet in a way that could constitute a breach of copyright.

Key cases [5.27]

The following are two examples of cases in which employees were dismissed for unauthorised access to computer systems, one fair and one unfair:

Denco Ltd v Joinson EAT [1991] ICR 172

Facts

Mr Joinson and his daughter both worked for the same company. Mr Joinson had authority to gain access to certain files held on his employer's computer system, for which purpose he had been issued with a password. Other parts of the computer system were not available to him. However, having learned the password for access to another part of the computer system from his daughter, Mr Joinson proceeded, out of curiosity, to access certain sensitive data that was held there. When the employer discovered that Mr Joinson had entered the computer system with an unauthorised password and accessed data to which he had no entitlement, they dismissed him, taking the view that such unauthorised access amounted to gross misconduct. Mr Joinson brought a claim for unfair dismissal to an employment tribunal.

Findings

Overturning the employment tribunal's original decision, the EAT held that Mr Joinson's dismissal was fair in all the circumstances. Although the evidence suggested that he had no improper motive for accessing the sensitive data, the employer's contention that his conduct constituted gross misconduct was justified. This was because Mr Joinson had deliberately

---

used an unauthorised password knowing that the part of the computer system he was about to access contained information that he was not entitled to see. This, the EAT, was gross misconduct justifying summary dismissal.

Implications

The EAT also commented in this case that employers should take appropriate steps to make it clear to employees that any unauthorised access to information held on computer will be regarded as gross misconduct.

British Telecommunications plc v Rodrigues EAT [1995] (854/92)

Facts

Mr Rodrigues had worked for British Telecommunications plc for many years when he obtained access to data held on the employer's computer system by using and modifying the passwords of other employees who had authority to access the data. Although Mr Rodrigues was not authorised to access the data in question via the computer, his reasons for doing so were linked to valid work-related purposes. Furthermore, he would have been able legitimately to obtain the same information over the telephone.

When the employer discovered Mr Rodrigues' activities on the computer, he was summarily dismissed on account of unauthorised access to the data. He complained of unfair dismissal at tribunal.

Findings

The EAT upheld the employment tribunal's decision that Mr Rodrigues' dismissal was unfair on the grounds that the employer had acted unreasonably in all the circumstances. This was partly because neither the employer's disciplinary procedure nor any other company documentation stated that conduct involving misuse of the employer's computer facilities would be regarded as gross misconduct leading to summary dismissal. Mr Rodrigues' dismissal was therefore not within the range of reasonable responses open to the employer.

Implications

It is not enough for an employer's policy on computer access to stress the need for security. Employers should make it abundantly clear to employees if unauthorised access to their computer system, or part of the system, will result in summary dismissal. The same principle should be applied to use of confidential passwords.

The level of seriousness of a breach [5.28]

The level of seriousness of an employee's conduct that involves unauthorised access to computer systems, and whether the conduct amounts to a fundamental breach of contract, will depend on a number of factors including:

- whether the employer has introduced a policy and rules covering access to email and the internet;
- the extent to which the employee was aware of the policy and rules;
- how other employees who have committed similar offences have been dealt with in the past;
- whether the employee's use of email or the internet involved any unlawful activity, for example a breach of copyright;
- the reasons put forward by the employee for their unauthorised access to a computer or to the internet, and any mitigating factors;
- whether there is evidence to suggest that the employee was not to blame, for example, if they accessed a particular internet site by accident;
- whether the employee has previously received any warnings for misconduct and whether these warnings are still 'in date';
- the employee's length of service and general record.

Essentially, any serious breach of the company's policy or rules on access to email and internet facilities is likely to amount to a breach of the implied duty if trust and confidence (see **5.11** above). Managers should not, however, jump to hasty conclusions before they have established all the relevant facts of the individual case.

Breaches of confidentiality [5.29]

Any fundamental breach of confidentiality, or unauthorised disclosure of confidential information is likely to amount to a breach of contract on the part of the employee. This will be the case irrespective of the express terms in an employee's contract or the existence of any express policies and rules on the subject, because there is an implied duty in every contract that the employee should render faithful service to the employer (see **5.17** above).

Factors for the employer to take into account in dealing with an employee who has inadvertently or deliberately disclosed confidential information by email would include:

- whether written guidelines were in place governing the handling of confidential information;

- the extent to which the employee understood these guidelines in relation to their job duties and responsibilities;

- whether the breach of confidentiality was deliberate or accidental;

- how serious the breach of confidentiality is, for example the disclosure of one item of confidential information to a colleague by mistake is not in the same category as the deliberate disclosure of a trade secret to a competitor company;

- the reasons put forward by the employee for the breach and any mitigating factors;

- the consequences of the employee's conduct for the organisation, for example unfavourable press publicity or complaints from customers will render the incident more serious;

- whether the employee has previously committed any similar act of misconduct, whether or not warnings were given and whether these warnings are still 'in date';

- the employee's job, level of seniority and the degree to which they could realistically be expected to keep information confidential.

If an unauthorised disclosure of information was accidental, it may not be in breach of the employee's implied duty to render faithful service, but may nevertheless constitute a breach of the implied duty to exercise reasonable care and skill. Clearly, in the event of a deliberate breach, the implied duty to render faithful service will have been breached.

Inadvertent or deliberate harassment [5.30]

Any bullying or harassment of another employee by email (or by any other means) should be regarded by the employer as serious misconduct. Irrespective of any policies and procedures governing bullying and harassment at work, such conduct may be regarded as a breach of the implied duty of trust and confidence on the part of the employee, and hence a breach of contract.
It is important, however, that this type of conduct is spelt out in writing by

means of a policy on harassment, and also classified as misconduct in the organisation's disciplinary procedure. Because harassment may occur in many forms, and in varying degrees of seriousness, it will be difficult for an employer to deal effectively with any incidences of it unless clear policies and rules are in place.

The subject of unlawful harassment is dealt with fully in **CHAPTER 3**.

Use or excessive use of communications systems for personal or private purposes contrary to the employer's rules [5.31]

If all personal use is banned

If the employer has a policy in place that stipulates that email and the internet are to be used strictly for business purposes only, and that all personal and private use is forbidden, then any instance of an employee using these facilities for non-business related reasons without specific authority could be regarded as misconduct. Examples could include:

- playing computer games;
- sending lists of jokes to colleagues or friends by email;
- surfing the net for information about holidays, vacant jobs, etc;
- viewing sexually explicit material on the internet.

If the employer's policy bans all personal use, such conduct will be in breach of the duty to obey lawful and reasonable instructions. This does not mean that an employee can be summarily dismissed for such a breach as the degree of seriousness may not warrant such action.

Case study [5.32]

The following case study demonstrates the possible consequences of an over-harsh approach towards an employee's breach of policy.

Patrick has been employed as a materials controller in a moderately sized family firm for the last seven months. During the course of his work, he uses email on a regular basis to correspond with suppliers, and occasionally uses the internet to research new products and check prices. His job is a busy one with little time for any ancillary activities.

Patrick has been issued with a contract of employment which includes the contractual right to four weeks notice in the event that his employment is terminated. The company also has a set of disciplinary rules and a disciplinary procedure, both of which are incorporated into all employees' contracts of employment. In relation to use of email and the internet, the disciplinary procedure states that 'excessive or inappropriate personal use of email and the internet' will be regarded as misconduct justifying the issuing of a written warning. The procedure also contains a list of the types of conduct that are to be regarded as gross misconduct. This list includes (amongst other items) 'using email or the internet for illegal purposes' and 'accessing, viewing or downloading pornography from the internet'. Any employee found to have been guilty of gross misconduct is to be dismissed summarily, i.e. without notice or pay in lieu of notice.

The department in which Patrick works has recently been taken over by Patricia, a manager with a strongly authoritarian approach who believes that discipline in the department is lax and the employees there need closer supervision to ensure they spend their time working diligently rather than (as Patricia perceives it) frittering time away on unimportant activities. She holds the view that browsing the internet is, in most cases, an inappropriate and time-wasting activity.

It has come to Patricia's attention, after a few weeks in the job, that Patrick has on several occasions used email to send personal messages to friends outside the organisation. There is also evidence that his internet browsing has not been entirely for work-related purposes. On checking Patrick's personnel file, she learns that he has only worked for the company for seven months' and would therefore not be eligible to bring a claim of unfair dismissal to an employment tribunal in the event that his employment was terminated (for a full discussion of the law on unfair dismissal, see **CHAPTER 11**).

Having made a decision that Patrick's use of the company's communications system is inappropriate, Patricia calls Patrick into her office, informs him that he is guilty of serious misconduct through his personal use of email and the internet, and that the company has decided to dismiss him for that reason. The dismissal is to be effective immediately and will be without notice or pay in lieu. Patrick is stunned.

> *Given that Patrick does not have sufficient service to bring a claim of unfair dismissal, what, if any, legal remedy might he have in these circumstances?*
>
> Patricia has applied the disciplinary procedure to Patrick in a way that is in clear breach of his contractual terms. The procedure, which forms part of his contract, describes the types of email/internet abuse that are to be regarded as misconduct (leading to a written warning) and the types of behaviour that will be viewed as gross misconduct (leading to summary dismissal). Patrick's use of his employer's communication facilities may possibly amount to misconduct, but by no stretch of the imagination accords with the company's definition of gross misconduct.
>
> Patrick would therefore be able to take a claim to tribunal for wrongful dismissal (*see* **5.43**) based on the argument that he was entitled in the circumstances to four weeks pay in lieu of notice on termination, as per the terms of his contract of employment. There is no minimum length of service for this type of claim.

Appropriate action [5.33]

The appropriate action to take following an employee's breach of contract will depend on:

- the extent to which the employee had been informed about the policy and rules;

- then the employee used email or the internet for personal purposes, for example whether it was during a lunch hour or late in the evening after several hour of overtime had been worked that day;

- the amount of time spent and the type of material communicated or accessed;

- whether the employee's use of email or the internet involved any unlawful activity;

- how other employees who have committed similar offences have been dealt with in the past;

- the explanation put forward by the employee for their conduct, and any mitigating factors;

- whether the employee has previously breached the rules on email and internet use, whether or not warnings were given and whether these warnings are still 'in date';

- the employee's position within the organisation and the extent (if any) to which they could be expected to set an example to others;

- the employee's length of service and general record.

If reasonable use is permitted [5.34]

If an employer's policy and rules on email and internet use allow reasonable personal use, then the employer needs to view the employee's conduct objectively in order to determine whether it is sufficient to constitute a breach of contract. Clearly if the amount of time spent surfing the net or sending personal emails has been excessive in relation to the number of hours the employee is contracted to work, then the matter can be regarded as a breach of contract. This clearly is a matter for objective judgement and it is important therefore that the manager dealing with the employee should act impartially and reasonably.

If no policy or rules are in place [5.35]

In the event that an employer does not have a policy or rules in place governing use of email and the internet, an employee's excessive use of email and the internet for personal purposes could still be in breach of the implied duty to maintain trust and confidence in the working relationship. The absence of rules on the matter would, however, hamper management in attempting to deal fairly and objectively with such an employee.

How employers can be in breach of contract through misuse of email and the internet [5.36]

There are three main ways in which an employer can breach an employee's contract of employment:

1. By indicating in words that they do not intend to honour future obligations under the contract (this is known as repudiation of the contract).

2. By taking an action that fundamentally breaches one of the express or implied terms of an employee's contract. Omission to take a specific action could in certain circumstances have the same effect, for example a failure to deal adequately with a genuine workplace grievance raised by an employee;

3. By terminating an employee's contract in a way which is in breach of contract. This is known as wrongful dismissal (see **5.43** below).

As stated above, once the terms of a contract of employment have been agreed between employer and employee, they can be altered only with the consent of both parties. This is because the terms of a contract of employment, like those of any other type of contract, are legally binding on the parties.

Obtaining agreement to changes to contractual terms [5.37]

It follows that any attempt on the part of the employer to alter one or other of the key terms of an employee's contract unilaterally will constitute a breach of contract. The unilateral imposition of new policies and rules where these were to form part of employees' contracts would thus be in breach of contract. To avoid breach of contract, the employee's agreement must be obtained. Agreement can be secured in three ways:

- By inserting a flexibility clause into employees' contracts at the start of their employment giving the employer authority to vary a particular term of the contract, for example a clause stating that the employer has the right to vary its policy on email and internet use. The existence of such a flexibility clause means in effect that the employee has agreed in advance that the employer may alter a specific aspect of the contract, as defined in the flexibility clause. It should be noted, however, that a universal flexibility clause, purporting to give the employer the right to alter any of the terms of the contract at any time, is unlikely to be enforceable.

- By means of a clause in a collective agreement with a recognised trade union, the terms of which are binding on individual employees.

- By securing the employee's agreement to a change at the time it is proposed.

The seriousness of the employer's breach [5.38]

Not every breach of contract will be serious enough to allow the employee to succeed in legal action. Whether or not a breach is fundamental will depend on a number of factors. These will include:

- The specific nature of the employer's actions.

- The impact the employer's actions have on the employee, for example a change to an email policy introducing a complete ban on all personal emails might seriously disadvantage an employee who relied on the facility to communicate occasionally with their child-minder.

- The reason for the change, e.g. whether there is a sound business reason necessitating the change, or whether it is introduced to accord only with administrative convenience or the autocratic views of a particular manager.

- The manner in which the employer proceeds to introduce the change.

In the event that the employer unilaterally introduced a policy or rules governing email and internet use which had the effect of restricting or limiting employees' use of these facilities (where unrestricted use was previously allowed), this could amount to a breach of contract.

Breach of implied terms [5.39]

A fundamental breach of contract may also occur as a result of a breach of one of the implied terms in an employee's contract, such as the duty of trust and confidence. A breach of trust and confidence may occur as a consequence of a single incident, or a series of incidents which, when considered together, have the effect of destroying trust and confidence, for example:

- bullying, victimisation or harassment – whether by email or by some other means;
- constant unfair criticism by email or other means;
- placing wholly unreasonable requirements on an employee in terms of workload, deadlines, use of facilities etc;
- seeking to apply an express contractual term in a manner which makes it impossible for the employee to comply;
- humiliating or degrading treatment;
- falsely accusing the employee of misconduct or unsatisfactory job performance;
- unfair or discriminatory application of any discretionary policy;
- treating the employee in any way calculated to force them to resign.

Employee's' potential remedies following a breach of contract on the part of their employer [5.40]

Where there is a breach of contract by an employer, the employee has a choice of courses of action:

1. If the breach involves a financial loss to the employee, to sue the employer for damages for breach of contract in an ordinary civil court. The employee does not require any minimum period of service to take this course of action.

2. If the breach involves a pay-cut, to make a claim for unlawful deduction of wages under the *Employment Rights Act 1996*. Again, no minimum period of service is required.

3. To resign and claim unfair constructive dismissal. For this to succeed, the breach must be fundamental and go to the very root of the contract of employment. Employees need a minimum of one year's continuous service to take this course of action. Constructive dismissal is dealt with fully in **CHAPTER 9**.

4. To do nothing, and continue to work under the contract, in which case acceptance of the new terms will, after a reasonable' period of time, be implied.

5. To inform the employer in writing that they are continuing to work under protest, i.e. to make it clear they have not agreed to the change.

If the employee continues to work without expressing any objection, they will lose the right to claim both constructive dismissal and breach of contract, because in effect they will be taken to have agreed to the change on account of their action (or rather inaction). Stating they are continuing to work under protest will allow a breach of contract claim to proceed at a later date (but not one of constructive dismissal which requires a prompt response from the employee).

Altering terms of employment [5.41]

Obviously it is necessary for employers to alter terms of employment from time to time, and to introduce new policies and rules, in order to cope with changes in their business activities. It is, however, very important that fair procedures are observed when this is being done. Essentially, provided that an employer has sound business reasons for wishing to introduce a new policy or rules, then they may do so through a process of consultation. This subject is covered fully in **CHAPTER 9**.

An employer's failure to deal with a genuine complaint from an employee about misuse of email or the internet [5.42]

As stated earlier, there is an implied term in all employees' contracts of employment that employers should provide reasonable opportunity for them to obtain redress for any grievance they may have (see **5.13** above).

It follows that a manager who is approached by an employee who has a genuine complaint or grievance concerning misuse of the employer's communications systems (or indeed any other legitimate work-related grievance), the manager is under a contractual duty to deal with the matter reasonably and promptly. A failure to tackle the problem, or a refusal to do so without good reason, may amount to a breach of the employee's contract.

It follows that if a manager receives a complaint from an employee that another employee is misusing email or the internet, the manager should:

- take the complaint seriously and resolve to deal with it promptly;

- seek the assistance of HR department rather than acting alone;

- establish the exact nature of the complaint, for example harassment by email, unauthorised use of another employee's password, and try to identify some specific examples;

- consider whether the alleged abuse is causing the employee who is complaining about it a detriment (for example if the employee is the victim of harassment);

- consider the possibility that the report may be a malicious or vexatious complaint from an employee who bears a grudge against their colleague for some personal reason;

- carry out a thorough investigation into the matter, keeping an open mind at all times;

- notify the employee who is alleged to have committed the offence in writing of the allegations against them and invite them to attend a meeting to discuss the matter;

- conduct a confidential interview with the employee, allowing them the right to be accompanied at the interview by a fellow worker or a trade union official. This in any event is a legal requirement if the interview is one that might lead to formal disciplinary action being taken against the employee (see **11.18** below). The aim of the interview should be to afford the employee a full and fair opportunity to respond to the complaint against them and put forward their version of events and any explanation for their behaviour;

- act impartially and objectively in dealing with both the employee who raised the complaint and the employee who is alleged to have committed the offence;

- keep confidential records of all interviews held;

- after the investigation and the interview are complete, decide whether it is appropriate to take disciplinary action against the employee, and if so what level of action, taking into account the precise provisions of the employer's disciplinary procedure. any policies and rules on use of the employer's communications systems and the extent to which these have been breached;

- (where disciplinary action is taken against the employee) allow the employee the right of appeal against the action taken;

- monitor and follow up once the complaint has been dealt with in order to make sure that the original problem has not recurred and that no further problems (for example victimisation of the person who complained) has arisen.

Wrongful dismissal [5.43]

Termination of an employee's contract in a way that is in breach of contract is known as wrongful dismissal. Wrongful dismissal is a completely different concept to that of unfair dismissal. The differences are that:

* unfair dismissal is concerned with the reason for the dismissal, whether the employer has acted reasonably in dismissing the employee for the stated reason and whether they have followed fair procedures (see **CHAPTER 11**);

* wrongful dismissal is simply dismissal an element of which amounts to breach of contract. Overall reasonableness is generally irrelevant to a claim for wrongful dismissal.

The most common forms of wrongful dismissal are:

* where an employee is dismissed in breach of the provisions contained in a contractual disciplinary procedure;

* where the employee's contract is terminated with insufficient contractual notice;

* where the contract is terminated with no notice (i.e. summary dismissal) in circumstances where the employee was entitled to notice.

Key case [5.44]

An example of the third type of breach of contract occurred in the case below:

> ### Case Study
>
> *Humphries v V H Barnett & Co [1998] Case No 2304001/97*
>
> #### Facts
>
> Mr Humphries worked for a family firm which had no procedure in place setting out what types of workplace conduct would be regarded as gross misconduct leading to summary dismissal. When it was discovered that Mr Humphries had used the firm's computer facilities to download obscene

pornography, he was asked to leave. Instead of dismissing him summarily, however, the employer placed Mr Humphries on paid suspension for a month pending the expiry of his notice period. During the notice period, the employer made further discoveries regarding Mr Humphries' activities on the computer from which they formed the view that he had misused working time and company equipment to such an extent that his conduct amounted to gross misconduct. At that point he was summarily dismissed. He brought a claim for wrongful dismissal to an employment tribunal arguing that his summary dismissal for misuse of company resources was in breach of contract (i.e. that such misuse did not constitute gross misconduct).

Findings

The tribunal judged that, in view of the objectionable nature of the downloaded pictures (some of them involved sex acts with animals), Mr Humphries' conduct in downloading such material must inevitably be viewed as gross misconduct sufficient to breach the contract. However they went on to hold that the employer had not viewed these activities as gross misconduct at the time since they had not summarily dismissed him (they had instead allowed him the period of notice due to him under his contract). This meant that the employer had in effect waived Mr Humphries' repudiatory breach of contract. Thereafter his eventual summary dismissal had been on account of misuse of working time and company equipment.

The tribunal ruled that in the absence of terms specifying the types of conduct that would constitute gross misconduct, the employer was not entitled to regard the use of the internet for unauthorised purposes as sufficient to justify summary dismissal. The tribunal therefore held (reluctantly) that the dismissal had been wrongful.

Implications

It is important to have clear policies and rules in place defining what is and is not regarded as gross misconduct. A further very important point is that an employer should not act inconsistently, i.e. if conduct is to be viewed as gross misconduct, then it should lead to summary dismissal (following the application of proper procedures) and not to dismissal with notice. Otherwise mixed messages may be conveyed to a tribunal.

Conclusion [5.45]

A contract of employment forms the basis of the relationship between the employer and the employee, and once its terms are agreed, they are legally binding on both parties and so cannot be altered unilaterally by the employer.

It is strongly advisable to set up the organisation's policy, procedure and rules on email and internet use in such a way that it is clear that they form part of all employees' contracts of employment. In this way any breaches of contract involving misuse of email or the internet can be dealt with more effectively and efficiently. Examples of breach of contract on the part of employees could include unauthorised access, breaches of confidentiality, inadvertent or deliberate harassment by email and excessive use of communications systems for personal or private purposes contrary to the employer's rules.

Employers themselves must take care not to breach the terms of employees' contracts, an in particular not to act in breach of the implied duty of trust and confidence which is inherent in every contract of employment. A blatant breach of an employee's right to respect for their privacy of correspondence could, for example, constitute a breach of trust and confidence. Equally, managers should take seriously any genuine complaint from an employee about a colleague's alleged misuse of email or the internet, and take appropriate steps to investigate.

Questions and Answers [5.46]

Question

Can an employer limit an employees' statutory rights by means of clauses in the contract of employment?

Answer

Employee rights that have been created by the passing of legislation are automatically incorporated into every contract of employment. It is not open to employers to attempt to exclude an employee's statutory rights. Any contractual clause purporting to deny an employee such rights will be unenforceable.

Question

How can the employer make sure that their policy and rules on email and internet use are made part of employees' contractual obligations?

Answer

Policies and rules such as an employer's email and internet policy can be incorporated into employment contracts by means of a clause in the contract itself referring to the policy document and stating that the policy forms part of the contract. In this way the policy is forms part of employees' terms and conditions and is binding on both parties.

Question

Is it advisable to incorporate email and internet policies into employees' contracts?

Answer

Given the potentially serious consequences of employees' misuse of email and internet facilities, it is, on balance, advisable for employers to make sure that any policy and rules they have which govern uses of their communications systems are incorporated into employees' contracts.

Question

What are implied terms in a contract of employment, and what types of implied terms could impact on the management of employees' use of email and the internet?

Answer

The implied terms of a contract of employment are those which are not spelt out in writing but are presumed to have been the intention of the parties when the contract was entered into. Even though nothing is in writing, implied terms are binding on both the employer and the employee. The implied terms that could potentially impact on the employer in relation to the management of employees' email and internet use are the duty to maintain trust and confidence in the employment relationship, the duty to provide a suitable working environment in which employees can perform their work and the duty to enable employees to obtain redress for any grievance they may have.

Question

Is it possible for employees to contend that they have a right to use email for personal purposes at work on the grounds of custom and practice?

Answer

Yes, it is possible, but only if the practice is one that has been regularly adopted over a long period of time. The notion is that, if a particular term has regularly applied and employees have come to expect it, it may have evolved into a contractual right. However, the right to reasonable use of email at work for personal purposes could also be argued if, for a number of years, employees have been allowed reasonable use of workplace telephones for personal calls.

Question

What sorts of actions on the part of the employer (in relation to employees' email and internet use) could breach the implied duty of trust and confidence?

Answer

A blatant breach of an employee's right to respect for their privacy or correspondence, for example if monitoring of employees' telephone calls, email messages and/or internet access was carried out without consent or forewarning could constitute a breach of the implied duty of trust and confidence (and a breach of *Article 8* of the *Human Rights Act 1998* as well). Another example could be the sudden, unilateral introduction of restrictions on email and internet use without consultation or agreement.

Question

How could the implied duty to allow employees to obtain redress for any grievance they may have impact on any complaints from employees about email and internet use?

Answer

Managers should always take any complaint from employees about use or misuse of email and internet facilities seriously and make sure the complaint is promptly and fully investigated and properly dealt with. This will avoid the possibility of a claim that the implied contractual duty to provide redress for grievances has been breached.

Question

If an employee has, due to carelessness, sent confidential information by email to someone who should not have been allowed to see the information, how should the employer react?

Answer

Irrespective of the existence of any express contractual terms governing employees' use of email, such careless action could be in breach of contract (under the implied duty on employees to exercise reasonable care and skill). This would be the case in particular if the outcome of the employee's carelessness was sufficiently serious for the organisation. The appropriate action to take will depend on the seriousness of the breach, and the provisions of the employer's disciplinary procedure.

Question

Is it really necessary to devise written rules and procedures on employees' use of email and the internet?

Answer

It is strongly advisable to formulate clear written policies, procedures and rules for employees' use of email and the internet because the possible legal and practical consequences of not doing so are immense for the employer. Both employers and employees will benefit from clear written rules and policies. Employees will be able to understand what is, and is not, acceptable use of email and the internet, and the employer will have a framework for dealing fairly with any accidental or deliberate misuse.

Question

What are the most likely forms of breach of contract that an employer may have to deal with relative to employees' email and internet misuse?

Answer

The main areas that could give rise to a breach of contract on the part of the employees are unauthorised access, breaches of confidentiality, inadvertent or deliberate harassment by email and excessive use of communications systems for personal or private purposes contrary to the employer's rules.

Question

In the absence of any specific rules on the subject, what action should the employer take in the event that an employee has grossly misused their access to the internet, for example by using the internet during working hours to look for another job?

Answer

Irrespective of the existence of any company rules on the subject, any serious misuse of internet facilities is likely to amount to a breach of the implied duty of trust and confidence on the part of the employee. It is important, however, to establish the degree of the employee's misuse and how serious it really is. Dismissal of the employee for a first offence of this nature would be likely to be unfair and the manager should in any event not jump to hasty conclusions. The appropriate action to take will depend on the amount of time the employee spent on the job search, the explanation put forward, any mitigating factors and whether the employee has previously breached any of the company's rules on email and internet use.

Question

If an employer's policy and rules on email and internet use allow reasonable personal use, how should a manager judge when an employee's use has become excessive to the point that it becomes a breach of the rules?

Answer

The employer needs to view the employee's conduct objectively in order to determine whether it is sufficient to constitute a breach of contract. Clearly if the amount of time spent surfing the net or sending personal emails has been excessive in relation to the number of hours the employee is contracted to work, then the matter can be regarded as a breach of contract and appropriate disciplinary action taken. This clearly is a matter for objective judgement and it is important therefore that the manager dealing with the employee should act impartially and reasonably.

Question

Is it essential to procure employees' agreement prior to changing the company's rules on the how employees may use email and the internet?

Answer

The unilateral imposition of new or different rules where any existing rules form part of employees' contracts would be a breach of contract. To avoid this, the employees' agreement to the changes must be obtained through a process of consultation. For new employees, future agreement can be assured by inserting a flexibility clause into their contracts at the start of their employment which states that the employer has the right to vary its policy on email and internet use at its discretion.

6 Monitoring Telephone Calls, Email and Internet Use

Introduction [6.1]

No-one would doubt that modern means of communication such as email and the internet have brought huge benefits to organisations in every sector of business activity. However, the very nature of such technological advances is that they are largely unregulated, and the scope for misuse is unfortunately very wide. There is considerable potential for legal liability on the part of employers (see **2.2** above). In light of the many problems associated with employee use of email and the internet, employers may wish to regulate and control such use by introducing a system for monitoring telephone calls, email messages and access to internet sites.

New legislation has, however, had a major impact on the right of employers to monitor, and care needs to be taken not to breach employees' rights.

The sensitive nature of monitoring [6.2]

Any type of surveillance of employees will clearly be a sensitive issue, and one that needs careful handling by the employer. Some employees may resent the idea of their employer listening in to their telephone conversations, or accessing their emails. The view may be held that such activities amount to an unacceptable infringement of privacy. Some employees may view monitoring as oppressive or demeaning. Whatever employees views are, they should be taken into account by the employer and full consultations should be carried out before any system of monitoring is introduced, or existing procedures changed.

The Need to Monitor [6.3]

Despite the above concerns, and because the potential consequences of *not* monitoring employees' use of the employer's communications systems are so serious, it could be argued that a degree of monitoring is a business necessity for many employers. For others, where the nature of employees' jobs is such that they have little cause to use email or access the internet, the need will not be so great, if indeed it exists at all.

A key recommendation contained in the Data Protection Code of Practice on Monitoring at Work (see **4.47**) is that employers should carry out an impact assessment to establish whether or not any adverse impact of monitoring on employees is justifiable, and review the likely effect of monitoring on the privacy and rights of employees. An impact assessment will involve:

- identifying the purpose(s) of any proposed monitoring and its likely benefits;

- identifying any likely adverse impact on employees of monitoring;

- considering alternatives to monitoring or different ways in which monitoring might be carried out;

- deciding whether or not monitoring is justified in all the circumstances.

Another point to note from the Code of Practice is its recommendation that employers should not monitor their workforce just because a customer or client demands it. Even if a customer insists that the employer must monitor employees' communications as a condition of business, this will not be an adequate justification for monitoring as it will not override the requirements of the *Data Protection Act 1998*. The employer must take the appropriate steps to satisfy themselves that monitoring is justified under all the circumstances.

The Code and its accompanying supplementary guidance stress that employers should consider alternatives to monitoring, and cites as examples new methods of supervision or further training. The underlying message is that if there is an alternative, less intrusive, way of dealing with a particular situation, then monitoring should not be undertaken. If despite such considerations, the employer concludes that monitoring is necessary for their business, they should review whether it can be restricted, for example by targeting monitoring only at employees who work in jobs which pose a particularly high risk to the employer, or by monitoring only workers about whom complaints have been made or about whom there are reasonable grounds to suspect misconduct.

Striking a balance [6.4]

Employers should aim to strike a reasonable balance between their need to monitor the use employees make of telephone, email and internet facilities at work as judged against employees' rights in contract, including the mutual duty of trust and confidence (see **6.28** below), and the right to privacy under the *Human Rights Act 1998* (see **CHAPTER 7**). Arguably, monitoring should be carried out only where it is necessary and relevant to the business, and where the legitimate business needs of the employer outweigh the inevitable intrusion into employees' privacy. These principles are consistent with the provisions of the *Data Protection Act 1998* which requires that any adverse impact on employees caused by monitoring must be justified by the genuine business needs of the employer (see **CHAPTER 4** for information on the *Data Protection Act*). It is all too easy for employers in today's technological world to conduct monitoring without considering whether it is really necessary. The temptation to do so without first weighing up the business need against the privacy rights of the employees should be avoided.

The legal issues relating to restrictions on monitoring should also be weighed up against the legal risks of a failure to monitor. Whilst no employer would wish to be perceived as 'big brother', most employees will be capable of understanding the need to conduct a reasonable amount of monitoring (provided of course that managers explain the employer's position, and the reasons for monitoring, clearly).

The purposes of monitoring [6.5]

An employer may legitimately wish to monitor employees' use of communication systems for any of the following reasons:

- to provide a record of transactions capable of forming contractual agreements, whether by telephone, email or through business deals conducted on the internet;

- to ensure employees who deal with customers on the telephone conduct themselves in a professional and consistent manner and in a way that meets the quality standards of the organisation;

- to identify whether there is a need for training, or further training, of employees, particularly those who communicate with customers by telephone or email;

- to gain access to telephone or email messages relevant to the business whilst an employee is absent from work, for example on holiday or off sick. Clearly it may be important for the business that the sender of the message receives a prompt response to their query, instead of having to wait indefinitely until the employee returns;

- to check emails and email attachments for offensive material;

- to guard against loss of confidential information;

- to guard against computer viruses;

- to ensure security of the system and of data;

- to make sure that employees are not using the employer's telephones or email system for purposes that are prohibited in the company's policy or rules;

- to make sure that employees are not spending an inordinate amount of time surfing the net, or sending emails to their friends, thus costing the employer a lot of money in terms of lost productivity.

The objective of monitoring [6.6]

As a general principle, the objective of monitoring should be identifiable as one that is clearly associated with a genuine need of the business. Systems of monitoring should be specifically designed to achieve that need and be in proportion to the need. The aim should be to conduct monitoring sensibly, and not oppressively.

The nature of monitoring [6.7]

The monitoring of employee communications can take many forms. At one extreme, the employer may decide that it is sufficient to conduct an occasional spot-check on the telephone numbers, email addresses and internet sites that are being accessed generally in the organisation, without pinpointing which employees are accessing which numbers and sites. Then (and only then), if a problem is identified, an investigation can be instigated, the employee interviewed and if necessary, further monitoring carried out.

Alternatively, the employer may wish to carry out specific checks on individual employees' use of the employer's communications network by reviewing each person's access to telephone numbers, email addresses and internet sites individually. Once again, if a problem was identified, or inappropriate use suspected, the employee could be interviewed in order to establish the legitimacy or otherwise of their use of the systems.

The next stage in monitoring, going beyond this type of general checking, would be to monitor employees' telephone calls and email messages. Monitoring in this context would involve listening to employees' calls and reading through their email messages. Clearly this is much more intrusive than carrying out general checks and would be subject to legal provisions governing interception. The possibility of an infringement of individuals' rights to privacy in their correspondence would also arise and the provisions of the *Human Rights Act 1998* would have to be taken into account (see **CHAPTER 7**).

The third stage would be to create records of the communications that had been monitored. This could, for example, involve recording telephone conversations, or creating a file on a particular employee's email and internet activities. Such records would be subject to the provisions of the *Data Protection Act 1998* (see **4.30**) and the Data Protection Code of Practice on Monitoring at Work.

The Data Protection Code of Practice on Monitoring at Work (see 4.47) specifies that if there is a less intrusive method for an employer to establish facts that they need to know, then they should pursue that less intrusive method rather than intercepting an employee's email communications. The one exception would be where the employer had reasonable grounds to suspect that an employee had been involved in serious misconduct, for example harassing another employee by email, or criminal activity such as accessing child pornography on the internet.

Clearly it is up to each employer to decide what, if any, type of monitoring they wish to conduct and how much detail, or intrusion, they feel is appropriate. As stated above, monitoring should be carried out only where it is necessary and relevant to the business. Equally, the type of monitoring should not be excessive in relation to the needs of the business. There is a major difference between carrying out occasional spot checks on the one hand and the regular interception of actual communications on the other. These matters will need to be carefully thought through by management before any decisions are taken. The workforce should, of course, be consulted before any new or different provisions for monitoring are introduced.

Monitoring personal communications [6.7a]

Further recommendations exist in the Data Protection Code of Practice on Monitoring at Work (and the supplementary guidance that accompanies it), that are relevant to the potential monitoring of employees' personal communications. These include recommendations that employers should:

- set up a system whereby personal or private emails can be marked 'personal and private' and adopt a policy of not monitoring such emails unless the employee is genuinely suspected of serious wrongdoing;

- provide secure lines of communication so that employees can transmit personal or sensitive information, for example an email to an occupational health adviser about a personal health matter or a message to a trade union official concerning a grievance;

- review (where a reasonable level of personal use is permitted) whether it is feasible to provide employees with two different passwords or methods of logging on depending on whether their internet access is work-related or personal;

- consider whether it is sufficient to record the time employees spend accessing the internet rather than monitoring the actual sites visited or the content viewed.

The Code recommends that emails that are clearly personal or private should not normally be monitored, even in organisations that impose a complete ban on personal use of email and the internet. The supplementary guidance to the Code points out that although a ban is an important factor, it is not necessarily an over-riding one and the employer would have to be able to justify taking action to read a personal email by weighing up the intrusion into the employee's private life with the employer's need to know the content of the email. Thus, even where an employer had a blanket ban on personal use of email and the internet and a contractual term or policy that authorised them to monitor the content of all emails and internet use, opening messages that were obviously personal or private would not (unless in exceptional circumstances) be legally permissible according to the Code of Practice. This is because the principle of proportionality (as interpreted by the Information Commissioner) limits the lengths to which the employer can legitimately go in their monitoring practices (see also **4.47** above and **7.35** below).

Irrespective of the recommendations contained in the Code of Practice, employers may wish to consider the potentially damaging effects of creating a working environment in which employees fear that their private lives might be subject to intrusion through the reading of their personal email correspondence or the reviewing of the internet sites they have visited. Monitoring personal and private communications would have a detrimental impact on the employee's dignity and well-being, risk stifling the employee's creativity and have considerable potential to demotivate. These negative effects are, of course, in addition to the risks an employer would run of breaching the employee's right to privacy under the *Human Rights Act 1998* (see **CHAPTER 7**) and (if the data is recorded) the provisions of the *Data Protection Act 1998*. The only reasonable conclusion to this debate is that employers should not open emails that are clearly personal or private, unless there are exceptional circumstances justifying such a course of action.

Telephone Monitoring [6.8]

In some types of business, routine monitoring and recording of telephone calls has been common practice for some time. One example is stockbroking, where it may be necessary to check the terms of a deal that has been agreed on the telephone.

Another is monitoring of the telephone calls of employees working in call centres, particularly in the financial services sector, both from a regulatory perspective and in order to ensure standards of customer service are maintained. The employer may legitimately wish to assess employees' performance in order to make sure that quality standards are upheld.

The Regulation of Investigatory Powers Act (RIP Act) [6.9]

The *Regulation of Investigatory Powers (RIP) Act 2000,* implemented in October 2000, established a legal framework to protect the confidentiality of communications and govern their interception in the course of their transmission on public and private tele-communications systems. The Act, which replaced the Interception of Communications Act 1985, was introduced to protect the confidentiality of communications generally and provide a framework to ensure the relevant investigatory powers are used in accordance with human rights legislation.

The main thrust of the *RIP Act* was to enable the police to access email and internet traffic, and gain access to encryption information. Some of the provisions of the Act, however, apply to employers who monitor their employees' telephone calls, email messages and internet access.

Section 1 of the *RIP Act,* which deals with unlawful and authorised interceptions, states that:

> 'It is unlawful for a person, without lawful authority, intentionally to intercept a communication in the course of its transmission by way of a public or private telecommunications system'.

Unlike the earlier Act, the *RIP Act* covers private telecommunications systems. 'Private telecommunications system' is defined in the explanatory notes accompanying the Act as:

> 'any telecommunication system which is not a public telecommunication system; but is attached to such a system. This means that an office network, linked to a public telecommunication system by a private exchange, is to be treated as a private system. ... An entirely self-standing system, on the other hand, such as a secure office intranet, does not fall within the definition'.

Private telecommunications systems (for the purpose of the *RIP Act*) would therefore include internal telephone systems and any computer network or intranet linked to the outside world by means of a dial-up or fixed-line connection.

What the RIP Act covers [6.10]

The RIP Act covers:

- interception of communications;

- The acquisition of communications data;

- Intrusive investigative techniques;

- Access to encrypted data.

The *RIP Act 2000, s1(3)* also creates a separate civil liability for unlawful interception on a private telecommunications network. The Act in effect gives both the sender and the recipient (or intended recipient) of a communication the right to claim damages against the system operator if their communication is unlawfully intercepted.

Under the *RIP Act*, there will be 'lawful authority' to intercept communications in any of the following circumstances:

- where there is an interception warrant;

- *where an existing statutory power is used in order to obtain stored communications*;

- where the reason for interception falls within the ambit of the *Telecommunications (Lawful Business Practice) (Interception of Communications) Regulations 2000 (SI 2000 No 2699)*;

- where both the sender and the recipient (or intended recipient) have expressly consented to the interception.

Only the latter two grounds for interception are relevant to employers.

Gaining employees' consent to monitor [6.11]

Although the Lawful Business Practice Regulations authorise the interception of employee communications in a wide range of circumstances relevant to the business (see **6.16** below), it is nevertheless strongly advisable for employers to obtain their employees' consent to monitoring. This removes the margin of doubt and clarifies for everyone that monitoring of all forms of communication is carried out by the company. An employee who has signed a document giving their free consent to monitoring will not be in a position to assert or complain that monitoring conducted in line with the employer's policy was unlawful or in breach of contract.

Consent can be obtained in one of two ways:

- drafting a clause for insertion into all employees' contracts of employment; *or*

- preparing a separate consent form.

In either case, the document must be signed by the employee, otherwise they will not be taken to have consented to monitoring. It is important to bear in mind that, even if policies governing permitted uses of email and the internet are in place, these alone are unlikely to be interpreted as employee consent.

It is important to note, however, that even if employees' consent is gained to monitoring, this does not provide the employer with the unfettered right to intercept every communication sent or received. Under the *RIP Act*, the consent of both the sender and the recipient of a communication is required before monitoring can take place, unless the purpose of the interception is one of those specifically allowed for under the Lawful Business Practice Regulations.

A further consideration is the restrictions imposed by the *Data Protection Act 1998*. The Data Protection Code of Practice on Monitoring at Work (which is the Information Commissioner's recommendations as to what employers must do to comply with the *Data Protection Act*) points out that there are limitations as to how far consent can be relied on in an employment context to justify the processing of personal information. This is because consent must be 'fully informed' and 'freely given' in order for it to be valid under the *Data Protection Act*. In an employment relationship, the balance of power is not even and it may be that an employee feels that they have no choice but to agree to sign a document giving their consent to monitoring. The Code stresses that a better way forward is to conduct a proper impact assessment, rather than relying entirely on employee consent to authorise monitoring (see **4.47**).

Example of a consent form [6.12]

An example of a consent form is provided below:

Company Name:

The Company has a policy of monitoring employees' communications in order to protect its business interests. We therefore request your consent so that we may carry out such monitoring

A copy of the policy is available from ....

Employee Name:

I hereby give my full consent to permit *Company Name* to monitor and/or record all telephone communications, voice mail messages, pager messages, email communications (including email attachments) and paper mail (including faxes) that I may send or receive. These include both internal

---

and external communications. I also consent to the Company monitoring and/or recording the internet sites I access during my employment with the Company.

Signed

Date

The Lawful Business Practice Regulations [6.13]

The *Telecommunications (Lawful Business Practice) (Interception of Communications) Regulations 2000 (SI 2000 No 2699),* made under the *RIP Act 2000, s 4(2)* and implemented in October 2000, essentially authorise certain interceptions of employee communications on the employer's business network (whether private or public) which would otherwise be prohibited by the *RIP Act 2000, s 1.* The overall objective of the Regulations is to ensure that any monitoring of communications is carried out in compliance with the *EC Telecommunications Data Protection Directive (No 97/66)* (see **CHAPTER 4**) and the European Convention on Human Rights (see **CHAPTER 7**).

The Regulations cover both public and private communications networks, but do not cover payphones installed in employers' premises where the payphones are provided for employees' personal use rather than business use. Specifically, the Regulations provide for a number of circumstances in which it is lawful for businesses (and public authorities) to intercept, monitor and record communications without the consent of sender, recipient or caller. These are detailed below in **6.16**.

The Regulations do not apply to interceptions to which employees have already consented since these are not prohibited by the *RIP Act.*

Informing potential users that interception may take place [6.14]

In order for monitoring to be lawful under the Lawful Business Practice Regulations, the employer must have taken all reasonable steps to inform potential users that interceptions may be made. Notification in individual contracts of employment, a staff handbook, or a statement in the company's internet/email policy will suffice for the purpose of informing employees. A summary statement might say:

'The company has adopted a policy of monitoring employees' use of telephones, email and the internet. Monitoring is carried out only for business purposes authorised by the Lawful Business Practice Regulations. You should therefore be aware that the telephone calls you make or receive, your incoming and outgoing email messages, and the internet sites you access during the course of your work may be intercepted by management. Full details of the policy and the rules are available in the employee handbook/company policy manual, a copy of which has been provided to you/is available from HR department.'

It will be very important, when informing employees about their intentions to monitor, that the employer states clearly:

- the purposes for which monitoring is to be carried out;

- when monitoring will be carried out;

- how the information obtained from monitoring will be used;

- who will have access to the information obtained from monitoring.

It will be equally important for employers to notify employees whenever there is any change to the employer's policy on monitoring or methods of monitoring.

Informing incoming callers or individuals who may choose to send emails to employees might require more inventive measures. Such measures could include, for example:

- an automated, recorded telephone message played to all incoming telephone callers;

- a statement contained in all outgoing emails to the effect that incoming communications are subject to monitoring by the organisation;

- printing warnings in any advertising or customer literature used by the organisation making it clear that telephone calls and email messages may be intercepted by the employer.

It is difficult to envisage how outside parties who initiate email correspondence with employees can be informed, prior to sending an email, that interception of their message may take place. It should be remembered, however, that the Regulations stipulate that employers must make 'all reasonable efforts' to inform users that interception may take place. It follows that there is no legal obligation to invent a 'crystal ball' and anticipate everyone who might conceivably choose to send an email message to an employee of the company. The phrase 'reasonable efforts' does not include the impossible or the highly impracticable!

The distinction between informing and gaining consent   [6.15]

It is important to be clear about the distinction between *informing* users that interception may take place (as is required under the Lawful Business Practice Regulations) and obtaining users' *consent*, which is required if the purpose of monitoring falls outside the scope of the Regulations.

Although the Lawful Business Practice Regulations authorise the monitoring and recording of employee communications in a wide range of circumstances, it is nevertheless advisable for employers to have documented authority from all their employees to allow them to carry out monitoring, including interception and recording of all employee communications. This can be achieved either by including a standard clause in all contracts of employment, or by asking each employee to sign a separate consent form (see **6.11** above). It is also a good idea to remind employees from time to time that monitoring that takes place. Better still, the employer should conduct an impact assessment (see **4.47**) to:

- identify the purpose(s) of monitoring and its likely benefits;

- identify any likely adverse impact on employees of monitoring;

- consider alternatives to monitoring or different ways in which monitoring might be carried out;

- decide whether or not monitoring is justified.

The Circumstances in Which it is Lawful for an Employer to Monitor Employees' Communications Without Their Consent   [6.16]

If interception is carried out for one of the reasons detailed below, it will be lawful, under the *Telecommunications (Lawful Business Practice) (Interception of Communications) Regulations 2000, Reg 3(1)*, with or without employee consent.

To establish the existence of facts relevant to the business   [6.17]

It is justifiable for an employer to monitor and record telephone calls or email messages where the business of the company is conducted largely by these methods of communication, for example to record evidence about commercial contracts or other business transactions.

An example could be where there is a dispute over the exact terms of a deal agreed on the telephone and the employer wishes to provide evidence to the other party as to what was actually said.

To ascertain compliance with regulatory and self-regulatory practices or procedures that are relevant to the business [6.18]

This clause is potentially very wide in its scope. It would include compliance with Regulations, Codes of Practice and guidelines issued by bodies such as ACAS, the Equal Opportunities Commission, the Commission for Racial Equality and the Health and Safety Executive (for example), and potentially anything issued by any EU-based organisation that has amongst its objectives the publication of codes of practice or standards. An example would be the interception of telephone conversations to ensure compliance with the statutory or non-statutory rules in the financial services sector.

To ascertain or demonstrate standards that employees achieve or ought to achieve when using the employer's systems of communication [6.19]

This allows employers to monitor and record employees' communications for the purpose of ensuring that the company's quality standards (for example standards of customer care) are being met, or to demonstrate standards that should be met as part of a training programme. Recording could also be used to identify areas in which there may be a training need for a particular group of employees.

For example if the employer of a group of workers in a call centre had trained those workers to use key words or phrases when dealing with queries on a particular topic, it would be legitimate to record a cross-section of calls and use them to identify which employees needed further training (perhaps because they were not consistently remembering to use the required words) or as examples on a training programme for new staff to demonstrate the 'right' and 'wrong' way to handle a telephone call.

In the interests of national security [6.20]

In this case only certain specified public officials may make the interception.

To prevent or detect crime [6.21]

It would be lawful, for example, to intercept employee communications for the purpose of protection against hacking. Another example could be monitoring for the purpose of detecting fraud or corruption.

To investigate or detect unauthorised use of the system [6.22]

Employers may monitor employee communications if the purpose of doing so is to establish whether any unauthorised use of the system is taking place.

For example, if a company policy states that email is provided strictly for business use only, then general monitoring could be carried out to establish whether there was any evidence of personal use.

It is important to note, however, that although monitoring may be conducted for the purpose of detecting unauthorised personal use of the employer's computer system, this will not entitle the employer to read through the content of an employee's personal emails. The supplementary guidance to the Data Protection Code of Practice on Monitoring at Work (see 4.47 above) points out that an employer would have to be able to justify taking action to read a personal email by weighing up the intrusion into the employee's private life with the employer's need to know the content of the email. It may, in any event, be enough for the employer to detect from addresses and subject headers that personal emails have been sent by the employee. The employer can then set up a meeting with the employee in order to discuss the matter and establish whether unauthorised use of the system has in fact taken place.

If the company policy is that reasonable personal use of the telephone, email and the internet is permissible, monitoring could be carried out to establish whether, on the whole, employees are confining their personal use of the communications systems to within the bounds of reasonableness. Clearly it is helpful in these circumstances if the employer can provide specific examples of what is regarded as reasonable personal use (see **8.34** below).

To ensure the effective operation of the system [6.23]

It is legitimate to monitor the computer system to check for potential viruses or other threats to the system such as hacking.

In addition, monitoring, *but not recording*, is permissible for the following purposes:

To determine whether received communications are relevant to the employer's business [6.24]

This provides employers with authority to check employees' voicemail and email in-boxes whilst they are absent from work (for example if they are on holiday or absent on account of sickness) if the purpose of so doing is to identify business communications that need to be dealt with. Only monitoring is authorised, not recording. Clearly employees must be properly informed that communications addressed to them will be opened in their absence.

It should be noted that it is only incoming communications that can be monitored under this heading. Although an employee on holiday or off sick will obviously not be making business telephone calls or sending emails on the employer's telecommunications system, outgoing emails sent prior to the employee's absence may still be in the system (if they have not been deleted). Monitoring of these outgoing emails will be permissible only if the purpose of such monitoring is in compatible with one of the *other* purposes contained in the Lawful Business Practice Regulations, or unless the employee has expressly consented.

Even if the employee's express consent has been obtained to all forms of monitoring, checking up on an employee's emails whilst the person is on holiday or off sick may be viewed as suspect and underhand. Managers may wish to consider the benefits of monitoring in a way that is up-front and transparent, rather than carrying out checks when the employee is absent.

The meaning of 'relevant to the business' [6.25]

The phrase 'relevant to the business' is further defined in Reg 2(b) as:

(a) 'a communication:

   (i) by means of which a transaction is entered into in the course of that business; or

   (ii) which otherwise relates to that business; or

(b) a communication which otherwise takes place in the course of the carrying on of that business.'

It is apparent therefore that any telephone calls or email messages that are personal or private in nature and unrelated to the employer's business will fall outside the scope of the Regulations. Employers should not therefore be tempted, in normal circumstances, to open or read any of their employees' incoming or outgoing email messages that are obviously personal.

Upon closer reading of the wording, however, there may (arguably) be limited exceptions to this principle. For example, if a personal message sent by email is in clear breach of a company policy governing acceptable use of the employer's communications systems, the communication may well be 'relevant to the business'. Examples could include:

● the unauthorised transmission of confidential information by email to an outsider;

● the forwarding of pornographic material as an email attachment from one employee to another;

● an email message containing a defamatory statement about a competitor company.

Provided there were proper grounds (and not for example just a vague whimsical suspicion based on a purely personal view) to believe that an employee's personal telephone messages or email communications were 'relevant to the business' in this way, then monitoring of those personal messages could potentially be justified. This is in contrast with monitoring of communications that are obviously private and unrelated to the business, which would not conform with the provisions of the *Telecommunications (Lawful Business Practice) (Interception of Communications) Regulations 2000* and which would risk being in breach of the employee's right to privacy under the Human Rights Act 1998 (see **7.31** below).

To identify calls being made to anonymous counselling or support help-lines [6.26]

This category includes the monitoring of calls to confidential or welfare help-lines in order to protect or support help-line staff.

Under the Regulations, the employer must be acting for one of the above specified purposes in order for monitoring and/or recording to be lawful. *Reg 3(2)* states that the interception must be 'solely for the purpose of monitoring or (where appropriate), keeping a record of communications relevant to the [business].' Thus employers are not permitted to use these purposes as a shield for monitoring that is in reality for a different purpose. Monitoring for any other purpose, for example out of curiosity, will be unlawful.

The Possible Effects of Unlawful Monitoring [6.27]

Under the *RIP Act 2000, s.1*, it will be illegal for an employer intentionally to intercept their employees' communications in the course of transmission unless they have lawful authority to do so. Extensive lawful authority is provided in the *Telecommunications (Lawful Business Practice) (Interception of Communications) Regulations 2000* (see **6.16**), but monitoring or recording which does not fall within the scope of the Regulations will be a criminal offence unless the sender and recipient (or intended recipient) have consented to interception.

There is also a potential civil liability under the *RIP Act 2000* which gives both the sender and the recipient (or intended recipient) of a communication the right to claim damages against the system operator (e.g. the employer) if their communication is unlawfully intercepted.
It follows that the employer must either:

● gain employees' express consent to interception; *or*

● make sure they conduct interception only for purposes that are relevant to the business and that are expressly covered in the Telecommunications

(Lawful Business Practice) (Interception of Communications) Regulations 2000.

If neither of these two conditions is fulfilled, the employer may be prosecuted and may also be sued for damages by both their own employees and any outsiders whose communications have been unlawfully intercepted.

When monitoring without consent or forewarning can constitute a breach of the mutual duty of trust and confidence [6.28]

A more immediate risk is that if employees' communications are monitored without consent or forewarning, this may constitute a breach of the implied duty of mutual trust and confidence that is inherent in every contract of employment.

The duty of trust and confidence encompasses the concept of treating employees with respect and maintaining a working relationship that is based on trust. Engaging in any activity that clearly breaches that trust, for example reading personal or private email messages without a proper reason and without proper authority, could undermine the employment relationship at its roots and thus constitute a fundamental breach of contract.

In the event that the employer acts in any way that is in fundamental breach of the employee's contract, the employee so affected is entitled (if they so choose) to resign and take a claim for constructive dismissal to an employment tribunal. This right is, however, dependent on the employee having a minimum of one year's continuous service with the employer. (See also **5.11** above.)

Claiming constructive dismissal [6.29]

In order to succeed in a claim of constructive dismissal, an employee must be able to show the tribunal that:

- the employer's actions amounted to a breach of contract; *and*

- the breach was fundamental (and not minor); *and*

- it was the employer's actions (and not some other factor) that caused the employee to resign; *and*

- there was no delay in resigning (a delay would imply that the employee had accepted the employer's breach and affirmed the contract).

The underlying principle of the concept of constructive dismissal is that some action on the part of the employer breaches the terms of the contract and is so fundamentally unacceptable to the employee that the option of continuing in the employment relationship is intolerable. Thus there is no alternative for the employee but to resign. In effect, the employee is released from all further obligations under the contract as a result of the employer's actions, and is thus entitled to resign, either with or without notice.

The concept of constructive dismissal was established in the case of *Western Excavating (ECC) Ltd v. Sharp [1978] IRLR 27*. In this case, the Court of Appeal held that:

> 'If the employer is guilty of conduct which is a significant breach going to the root of the contract of employment, or which shows that the employer not longer intends to be bound by one or more of the essential terms of the contract, then the employee is entitled to treat himself as discharged from any further performance. If he does so, then her terminates the contract by reason of the employer's conduct. He is constructively dismissed.'

Breach of the right to privacy [6.30]

Monitoring employees' private mail, telephone calls or emails where there was no legitimate business need to do so would in all likelihood be in breach of the employee's right to respect for privacy of correspondence under *Article 8* of the *Human Rights Act 1998* – (see **7.31** below).

Claims to tribunal [6.31]

Traditionally employment tribunals have not been prevented from accepting evidence from employers just because the evidence was obtained unlawfully. Tribunals, however, like all courts, are obliged to interpret legislation (including employment law) in a way that is compatible with the rights contained in the European Convention on Human Rights (and by extension the *Human Rights Act 1998*). The effect of this potentially is that employees may be able to use the provisions of the *Human Rights Act 1998* to support any existing legal claim they may have at tribunal, for example a claim for unfair dismissal.

Example [6.32]

An employee is suspected of fraudulent activity by his employer. In an attempt to establish proof of the employee's guilt, the employee's manager listens in on the employee's private telephone calls, and, whilst the employee is out of the office, reads his private emails. One of those emails contains information that points to the employee's involvement in the fraudulent activities of which he is already suspected. The company has no rules in place prohibiting employees from using the employer's telephone or email systems for personal or private communication.

Following the interception of the email, the employee is interviewed and subsequently dismissed for gross misconduct.

A tribunal hearing an unfair dismissal claim from an employee in these circumstances would normally be entitled to allow the employer to present whatever evidence they wished, including evidence contained in the relevant email communications. The employee, however, could argue that, since the interception of the email in question was in clear contravention of *Article 8* of the *Human Rights Act 1998* (the right to respect for private and family life, home and correspondence), the tribunal must exclude this evidence in order to achieve compatibility with the rights contained in the *European Convention on Human Rights*. The tribunal may well feel obliged to agree with the employees' assertion in these circumstances. This would place the employer in the unenviable position of having to defend the unfair dismissal claim without the evidence obtained from the email.

Another simpler interpretation of the same set of facts could be that, in obtaining evidence by monitoring private emails without the employee's consent, the employer had failed to follow a fair procedure prior to dismissal. This would render the dismissal unfair (see **11.15** below for further information about dismissal in connection with employees' misuse of email and the internet).

The Impact of the Data Protection Act 1998 on Employer' Rights to Monitor Employee Communications [6.33]

Whenever an employer keeps a record of any of the information that results from monitoring of employee communications, this information will constitute 'personal data' as defined by the *Data Protection Act 1998*. Personal data about individuals are covered under the Act whether they are held in paper format, stored on a computer system or contained in the body of an email. Thus personal information about an employee obtained as a result of monitoring (for example a computer print-out of the internet sites that a particular employee has accessed from their workplace computer) will be classed as personal data under the *Data Protection Act 1998*. Consequently such data must be processed in a way that does not violate the provisions of the Act. 'Processing' in the context of the *Data Protection Act 1998* includes all the routine aspects of handling personal information about employees, for example collating the information, storing it and refining it in any way.

Employers are obliged under the *Data Protection Act 1998* to comply with eight data protection principles governing the processing of personal data.

These include a duty to process personal data fairly and lawfully, to obtain and use personal data only for specified and lawful purposes and to ensure that personal data are adequate, relevant and not excessive in relation to the purposes for which they are processed. This means that employers must ensure that any personal information they hold about their employees is created and stored for a proper business purpose, and that, in relation to this purpose, the information is sufficient, but not excessive.

Under the first data protection principle (the duty to process data fairly and lawfully), an employer cannot process information about an employee unless the employee has given their consent, or unless one of a list of other conditions has been met. Although the question of whether data processing is *lawful* is largely governed by the *Telecommunications (Lawful Business Practice) (Interception of Communications) Regulations 2000* (see **6.13** above), the first data protection principle also creates the obligation on employers to process personal data *fairly*. It is quite conceivable that the processing of data for a specific purpose could be lawful (if it was carried out for one of the purposes authorised by the *Telecommunications (Lawful Business Practice) (Interception of Communications) Regulations 2000*), but still be unfair if, for example, a manager was to carry out unnecessary or over-intrusive monitoring of a specific employee's use of email or the internet without an objective reason for doing so. The general principle inherent in the Data Protection Act 1998 is that monitoring of employees' communications should only take place if it is proportionate in light of the employer's business needs.

Fuller details of the *Data Protection Act 1998* appear in **CHAPTER 4** at **4.30**.

Conclusion [6.34]

The laws in this area are relatively new and will no doubt develop over the coming years as a result of cases being brought before courts and tribunals. Many of the provisions in the legislation depend on the consent of the individual employee being obtained. It is vital, therefore that employers should take the appropriate steps to obtain employees' consent for any monitoring and recording of data that they wish to carry out, as well as implementing an email/internet policy. Another vital course of action is to conduct an impact assessment on the need to monitor and the effects of monitoring. Employers are advised to address these important issues as a matter of urgency in order to avoid exposing themselves to the many risks associated with employees' use of the telephone, email and the internet.

Questions and Answers [6.35]

Question

How should an employer decide whether or not to monitor the use employees make of email and internet facilities?

Answer

Employers should aim to strike a reasonable balance between their need to monitor the use employees make of telephone, email and internet facilities as judged against employees' rights in contract (including the mutual duty of trust and confidence) and the right to privacy under the *Human Rights Act*. To do this, they should conduct an impact assessment. Arguably, monitoring should be carried out only where it is necessary and relevant to the business, and where the legitimate business needs of the employer outweigh the inevitable intrusion into employees' privacy.

Question

What is an impact assessment?

Answer

The purpose of an impact assessment is to establish the purpose and benefits of monitoring and whether or not monitoring is justified. The assessment should identify the likely adverse effects of monitoring on the privacy and rights of employees and consider whether these effects are justified when weighed against the business needs of the employer.

Question

Is it lawful for an employer in the course of monitoring to read an employee's personal email correspondence, in particular where the employer has imposed a ban on personal use of the computer system?

Answer

Emails that are clearly personal or private should not normally be monitored, even in organisations that impose a complete ban on personal use of email and the internet. The employer would have to justify taking action to read a personal email by weighing up the intrusion into the employee's private life with the employer's need to know the content of the email.

Question

To what extent is an employer prevented from monitoring employees' communications by dint of the RIP Act?

Answer

Monitoring will be lawful under the Act if either the sender and the recipient (or intended recipient) have expressly consented to the interception, or if the reason for interception falls within the ambit of the Lawful Business Practice Regulations.

Question

Should employers seek employees' consent to monitoring in any event even if the type of monitoring they carry out is authorised by the Lawful Business Practice Regulations?

Answer

Although the Lawful Business Practice Regulations authorise the interception of employee communications in a wide range of circumstances relevant to the business, it is nevertheless advisable for employers to obtain their employees' consent to monitoring. An employee who has signed a document giving their free consent to monitoring will not be in a position to assert or complain that monitoring was unlawful or in breach of contract.

Question

In what circumstances can it be lawful for an employer to monitor employees' communications without their consent?

Answer

The Lawful Business Practice Regulations provide for a number of circumstances in which it is lawful for businesses to monitor communications without the consent of sender, recipient or caller. These include: monitoring for the purpose of establishing facts relevant to the business; ascertaining compliance with regulatory and self-regulatory practices or procedures; for quality control or training purposes; preventing or detecting crime; investigating or detecting unauthorised use of the system; and determining whether received communications are relevant to the employer's business. In these circumstances, employees must still be informed that monitoring will take place.

Question

Is it lawful for an employer to read the emails of an employee who is absent from work on holiday?

Answer

It is permissible under the Lawful Business Practice Regulations for an employer to check employees' email in-boxes whilst they are absent from work on holiday (or for some other reason) if the purpose of so doing is to identify business communications that need to be dealt with.

Question

If an employer should intercept an employee's email messages or record their access to internet sites without proper lawful authority, what recourse might the employee have?

Answer

If employees' communications are monitored without consent or forewarning, this may constitute a breach of the implied duty of mutual trust and confidence that is inherent in every contract of employment, giving the employee the right to resign and complain of constructive dismissal (depending on a minimum of one year's service with the company). There may also be a breach of the right to privacy in these circumstances. Furthermore, under the RIP Act, both the sender and the recipient (or intended recipient) of a communication will have the right to claim damages against the employer if their communication is unlawfully intercepted.

7 The Implications of the Human Rights Act on Employers' Right to Monitor

Introduction [7.1]

The *Human Rights Act 1998*, which came into force in the UK in October 2000, implemented the rights contained in the European Convention on Human Rights into UK domestic law. The European Convention on Human Rights (which is a treaty of the Council of Europe) was originally ratified by the UK Government in 1951 and brought into force in 1953. The *Human Rights Act* mirrors the language and philosophy of the European Convention in most respects.

The *Human Rights Act 1998* was designed to supplement and improve upon the legal provisions that already existed in the UK. Its implementation in the UK did not confer any new rights on anyone, but simply made legal action taken on account of a perceived infringement of the rights contained in the Convention more accessible. As a result of the implementation of the Act, individuals who believe their rights have been breached can raise legal action in the UK courts instead of having to take their case to the European Court of Human Rights in Strasbourg, as was previously the case.

The *Human Rights Act 1998* is not an employment law, and it therefore does not confer any specific new employment rights on individuals. However, many of the rights contained within the Act are relevant to employment law and likely to give employees additional grounds to claim 'rights' in an employment context. In particular, the right to respect for privacy impacts directly on employers who wish to carry out monitoring of their employees' use of communication systems.

Rights conferred by the Human Rights Act [7.2]

Essentially the Act gives private individuals the right to take a public authority to court if they believe that one of their rights, as defined in the Act, has been infringed by that authority. This means that employees of public authorities can take a direct claim against their employer in court or tribunal if any of their rights under the Act is infringed by the employer.

Although the Act does not confer any similar benefit on private sector employees, there is a separate provision which obliges courts and tribunals (as public authorities themselves) to interpret legislation (including employment law) in such a way as is compatible with the rights contained in the European Convention (and by extension the *Human Rights Act 1998)*. Thus private sector employers are affected, albeit indirectly.

Claims brought directly under the *Human Rights Act 1998* must be brought within one year of the date of the act complained of. Courts and tribunals do have discretion to extend that time limit if they believe it is equitable in all the circumstances to do so.

The Human Rights Act 1998 – A Summary of the Act and its Inter-Relationship With Employment Law   [7.3]

The *Human Rights Act 1998* contains a range of rights and freedoms for individuals as follows:

Article 2:   The right to life.

Article 3:   The right not to be subjected to torture or to inhuman or degrading treatment or punishment;

Article 4:   Prohibition of slavery and forced labour.

Article 5:   The right to liberty and security.

Article 6:   The right to a fair trial.

Article 7:   The right not to be punished without law (i.e. the right not to be held guilty of a criminal offence when none has been committed).

Article 8:   The right to respect for private and family life, home and correspondence (This is the area that impacts upon employers' monitoring of employee communications).

Article 9:   The right to freedom of thought, conscience and religion.

Article 10:   The right to freedom of expression.

Article 11:   The right to freedom of assembly and association.

Article 12:   he right to marry and found a family.

Article 14:   The right to enjoy the rights and freedoms in the Convention without discrimination on any ground.#TableE

Key principles underlying the Human Rights Act   [7.4]

There are three key principles underpinning the application of the rights contained within the *Human Rights Act 1998*. These are:

1.   The principle of proportionality.

2.   The margin of appreciation.

3.   The notion of being a 'victim'.

The principle of proportionality [7.5]

The principle of proportionality contained in the European Convention on Human Rights means that a balance must be struck between the rights of individuals as defined in the Act and the general interests of the community at large. In *Soering v United Kingdom* [*1989*] *11 EHRR 439*, the European Court of Human Rights described the principle of proportionality as:

'the search for a fair balance between the demands of the general interest of the community and the requirements of protection of the individual's fundamental rights'.

Thus the rights contained in the Convention and in the *Human Rights Act 1998* are not absolute rights that can be insisted upon irrespective of everyone and everything else. An individual's rights must be balanced proportionally against the interests of the community, i.e. the rights of others (including the rights of the employer). Thus, for example, if an employer applies a policy or procedure that appears to restrict the rights of employees under one of the Articles of the *Human Rights Act 1998*, this may be justifiable provided the policy or procedure is:

● necessary in a democratic society;

● designed to achieve a legitimate business aim;

● likely to achieve that aim in practice;

● proportionate to the achievement of that aim.

The margin of appreciation [7.6]

The second principle underpinning the rights contained in the Convention is the margin of appreciation. This, in effect, allows each Member State a measure of discretion in the way in which it takes public policy decisions.

The meaning of 'victim' [7.7]

Thirdly, an individual can, as a general rule, only take a public authority to court for an alleged breach of one of the rights contained in the Convention if they are personally the victim of the breach. Representative actions are not generally allowed, although an exception to this rule would be made where the relevant representative body could show that the individuals they represented were directly affected by a breach of one of the Convention rights, and could produce evidence of their authority to represent those individuals.

As a general rule therefore, an individual has to be directly affected by an action (or omission) of a public authority before they can claim to be a 'victim'. Thus although trade unions, for example, can act on behalf of their members in relation to a claim, they are prevented from bringing general representative claims on their own initiative unless they can identify one or more of their members who have been directly affected by the measure they claim is in breach of one of the Convention rights. A trade union cannot claim to be a victim itself just because it represents the interests of a defined group of employees.

An individual does not, however, have to have suffered an actual breach to bring a claim to court. For example in *Campbell and Cosans v UK (1982) 4 EHRR 293*, a successful case was brought before the European Court of Human Rights on behalf of children who attended a school where corporal punishment took place. The children in question had not been personally subjected to corporal punishment; it was enough that they attended the school and were thus potential victims.

The inter-relationship between the rights contained in the Human Rights Act and the contract of employment [7.8]

Most contracts of employment contain terms which define and/or restrict employees' freedoms whilst at work. If an employee has agreed as part of their contract of employment to do something, then it cannot be a breach of that person's 'rights' for the employer to expect them to fulfil that part of the contract. One example would be a term defining specific hours of work. Thus, for example, if an employee's contract specifies hours of work from 09.00 am to 5.00 pm Monday to Friday, then it is not unreasonable for the employer to expect the employee to work those hours. An employee cannot legitimately argue later that a refusal on the employer's part to grant time off during those hours is a breach (for example) of the right to freedom of expression or the right to manifest their religion. This does not, of course, preclude the employer from granting time off, but simply means that the employee does not have an unfettered right to the time off by dint of the *Human Rights Act 1998*.

Note: Care should be taken if an employee requests time off for religious reasons, as an unreasonable refusal to grant such time off may be in breach of the *Employment Equality (Religion or Belief) Regulations 2003* (see **7.14** below).

Waiving rights under the Act [7.9]

It is feasible in effect for employees to agree contractually to waive their rights under the *Human Rights Act* in an employment context. Examples include:

- (as in the example above) a contractual agreement that the employee will work set hours will act to limit that person's right to take time off work during those hours;

- agreement to adhere to a dress code that formed part of a contract of employment would act to prevent the employee insisting on a right (under the right to freedom of expression) to wear unconventional clothing to work;

- a clause in the contract that the employee will agree to submit to a medical examination by a company nominated doctor at the request of the employer negates the argument that such medical examinations are an infringement of the employee's right to privacy;

- express agreement that the employer has contractual authority to monitor the employee's email messages and internet access which would in effect debar the employee from claiming that their right to privacy in their correspondence had been infringed (see **7.32** below).

The rights contained in the *Human Rights Act 1998* do not therefore alter an employee's contractual duties nor do they turn the employment relationship around and create an automatic right for employees to refuse to comply with the terms contained in their contract.

Remedies under the Human Rights Act [7.10]

When determining claims against public authorities under the *Human Rights Act 1998*, courts and tribunals have authority to grant remedies and make orders within the limits of their existing powers according to what they consider 'just and appropriate'. Thus, depending on the type of case and which court or tribunal is hearing it, the court or tribunal might award damages, issue an injunction or make a declaration. Exemplary damages (i.e. an amount of money imposed on the employer as a punishment) are not, however, permitted.

Areas of the Human Rights most likely to impact on employees' rights [7.11]

Aspects of the *Human Rights Act 1998* that are particularly relevant to the employment relationship are summarised below.

Article 3: The right not to be subjected to torture or to inhuman or degrading treatment or punishment [7.12]

This could potentially be interpreted to mean that an employee working for a public authority who is severely bullied in a way that is degrading could bring a complaint directly against their employer on account of a breach of their right not to suffer such treatment. Since there is no specific anti-bullying law in the employment arena, this could be a significant development.

Article 8: The right to respect for private and family life, home and correspondence [7.13]

The impact of this Article on employers' monitoring of employee communications is dealt with separately below at **7.31**.

Other areas in which *Article 8* may impact include the searching of employees and their personal property, medical examinations and questionnaires and drugs screening programmes. The principle of proportionality contained in the Convention may, however, permit these activities, i.e. if the employer can show that their policies are designed to achieve a legitimate business aim and are proportionate to that aim.

It has already been ruled by the European Court of Human Rights that unfavourable treatment of individuals on the grounds of homosexuality is in breach of the right to respect for private life.

Article 8 also provides for the right to family life. This may have an impact on the issue of work–life balance and could provide ammunition for employees who wish to achieve a reasonable balance between the number of hours they spend at work and the amount of time spent with their family.

Article 9: The right to freedom of thought, conscience and religion [7.14]

This includes the right for individuals to manifest their religion or belief. This would be a relevant consideration for employees whose religion means that they need to pray at regular intervals, or have time off to practise their religion.

Because it is permissible under the *Human Rights Act 1998* for employees to agree contractually to waive their rights, a contractual agreement that the employee will work set hours may act to limit that person's right to take time off work during those hours for religious (or other) purposes.

A further important consideration relevant to this subject is the *Employment Equality (Religion or Belief) Regulations 2003*, implemented into UK law in

December 2003. Broadly, the Regulations give all workers the right not to suffer discrimination or harassment (see **CHAPTER 3**) on grounds of 'any religion, religious belief or similar philosophical belief'. A refusal without proper justification to grant an employee reasonable time off for religious reasons would be likely to be in breach of the Regulations. A detailed analysis of these Regulations is, however, outside the scope of this book.

Article 10: The right to freedom of expression [7.15]

This right includes freedom for individuals to hold opinions and to receive and impart information and ideas without interference by a public authority. It could also potentially give employees the right to wear clothing to work (or even sport a tattoo) which has religious or other relevant significance.

If, however, employees have expressly agreed to a dress code as part of their contracts of employment, this would restrict their ability to argue that their rights under the *Human Rights Act 1998* had been breached.

Article 11: The right to freedom of assembly and association [7.16]

This includes the right to form and to join trade unions, although all employees in the UK already had this right prior to the implementation of the *Human Rights Act 1998* by dint of existing domestic legislation. Case law from the European Court of Human Rights shows that *Article 11* does not create the right to strike.

Article 14 – The principle of non-discrimination [7.17]

Article 14 of the *Human Rights Act 1998* also states that the enjoyment of the rights and freedoms set out in the European Convention must be applied to everyone without discrimination on any ground such as sex, race, colour, language, religion, political or other opinion, national or social origin, association with a national minority, property, birth or other status. The 'other status' referred to may be interpreted as including (for example) sexual orientation.

It is important to note that *Article 14* does not create a free-standing right to freedom from discrimination, but simply means that individuals have the right to enjoy the other rights contained in the Convention without discrimination.

The Obligation on Courts and Tribunals to Interpret Existing Legislation in a Way that is Compatible with Rights Contained in the European Convention on Human Rights [7.18]

There is a specific provision in the *Human Rights Act 1998, section 3* which obliges courts and tribunals to interpret legislation (including employment law) in such a way as is compatible with the rights contained in the European Convention (and by extension the *Human Rights Act*) so far as it is possible to do so. This provision applies irrespective of when the legislation under review was enacted.

Decisions of the European Court of Human Rights [7.19]

In addition, *section 2* of the *Human Rights Act 1998* provides that courts and tribunals must take account of decisions, declarations, judgements and opinions of the European Court of Human Rights insofar as the decision in question is relevant to the proceedings before them. This would include not only UK cases but also decisions and judgements from any State that has ratified the Convention.

The *Human Rights Act 1998* does not go so far as to stipulate that the decisions of the European Court of Human Rights are binding on courts and tribunals, but instead the Court's decisions are to be viewed as persuasive.

Limitations [7.20]

The principle that courts and tribunals must interpret existing legislation in line with the Convention rights is limited by the clause 'so far as it is possible to do so'. If a provision in existing legislation is ambiguous, courts and tribunals must interpret it so as to uphold the Convention rights. In contrast, if it appears to a court or tribunal that a specific provision in primary legislation is completely at odds with one of the Convention rights, the court or tribunal does not have the authority to change it by interpreting its wording in a way that is clearly contrary to its intended meaning. Primary legislation can only be changed by Parliament. Certain courts (but not employment tribunals) have authority under *section 4* of the *Human Rights Act 1998* to address this dilemma by issuing a 'declaration of incompatibility' if they believe that existing legislation cannot be reconciled with the rights contained in the Convention.

Thus courts and tribunals have no choice but to enforce unambiguous primary legislation irrespective of its inter-relationship with the *Human Rights Act 1998*. However, where a provision contained in secondary legislation, i.e. statutory instruments, is clearly incompatible with one of the Convention rights, the court or tribunal can disapply it (unless of course the provision is also governed by primary legislation).

In the Government's White Paper on the *Human Rights Act*, these provisions were succinctly described as:

> '… [enabling] the courts to take the Convention into account in resolving any ambiguity in a legislative provision. The courts will be required to interpret legislation so as to uphold the Convention rights unless the legislation itself is so clearly incompatible with the convention that it is impossible to do so'.

The effect of the obligation [7.21]

This duty on courts and tribunals to interpret legislation in line with the rights contained in the *Human Rights Act* is the underlying ingredient that allows private sector employees who believe their rights are being infringed by their employer to enforce their rights, albeit indirectly (see **7.25** below).

A similar provision in the *Human Rights Act 1998* allows courts and tribunals to disregard any earlier ruling handed down by a higher court if that ruling is inconsistent with Convention rights. Thus for example an employment tribunal could disregard a binding precedent formed by the Court of Appeal in an earlier case if the Court of Appeal's decision was perceived by the tribunal to be incompatible with one of the rights contained in the Convention.

The Rights of Public Sector Employees Under the Human Rights Act [7.22]

There is a clear differentiation in practice between the impact of the *Human Rights Act 1998* on public sector employers and the effect on private sector companies.

Because the *Human Rights Act 1998* allows individual citizens to sue a public authority for damages if that authority has infringed one of their Convention rights, individuals who are employees of a public authority can take their employer to court or tribunal if any of their rights in the Act have been breached by the employer. Thus public sector employees have a direct or 'vertical' right under the Act to bring legal proceedings against their employer.

Definition of 'public authority' [7.23]

'Public authority' is unfortunately not exhaustively defined in the *Human Rights Act 1998*. *Section 6* states that a public authority includes 'a court or tribunal, and any person certain of whose functions are functions of a public nature'. Thus in order to qualify as a 'public authority' for the purposes of the Act, an organisation does not need to be one that exclusively carries out public functions.

Clearly the term 'public authority' will include obvious public authorities such as central government departments, local councils, the police, schools, the Inland Revenue, Customs and Excise, health authorities and organisations such as the Health and Safety Executive, the Commission for Racial Equality, etc.

Quasi public authorities (also sometimes referred to as 'hybrid' public authorities) whose functions include a mixture of public and private services are also likely to be caught within the definition of 'public authority' for the purposes of the Act. Examples include organisations that were once public authorities but have been privatised, such as water utilities, and organisations part of whose functions are public in nature. The list would also include, for example, the BBC, doctors in general practice and any private organisation that provided a public function such as a privately owned school. Private companies could also be caught if they provided a service under contract to a public authority, for example a contract to provide security services to a prison.

Clearly the drafting of the Act in this respect creates some doubt over which employees can claim directly against their employer in the event that the employer acts in breach of one of the rights in the *Human Rights Act 1998*. Ultimately it will be up to a court or tribunal to determine (where the matter is challenged) whether or not an organisation is a public authority, or whether the individual's employment forms part of the organisation's public function or private function, and (depending on what is decided) whether a direct claim under the Act can legitimately proceed.

Organisations that fulfil mixed functions [7.24]

If an employee works for an organisation that fulfils mixed functions (both public and private), a direct claim under the Act is only likely to be admitted if the person works in the part of the organisation that provides a public service. Clearly this distinction could lead to the peculiar anomaly that one employee within a particular organisation would be able to bring a claim to a tribunal directly under the *Human Rights Act 1998* whilst a colleague working in a different part of the same organisation would not.

The Rights of Private Sector Employees Under the Human Rights Act [7.25]

The *Human Rights Act 1998* does not confer any right for private sector employees to take their employer to court on account of an alleged breach of the rights and freedoms contained in the European Convention on Human Rights. The impact of the Act will thus be much greater for public sector employers than for wholly private organisations. This does not mean, however, that private sector employers can relax and ignore the provisions of the *Human Rights Act*. This is because private sector employees can use the Act's provisions indirectly. This is due to the provision in *section 3* of the Act which obliges courts and tribunals to interpret legislation in such a way as is compatible with the rights contained in the European Convention (and by extension the *Human Rights Act*) unless they cannot do so by dint of existing primary legislation (see **7.18** above).

Private sector employees can therefore rely indirectly on the provisions of the Act to support any existing legal claim they may have. The duty on courts and tribunals to interpret employment laws in line with Convention rights applies irrespective of whether the organisation accused of unlawful behaviour is a public or private sector employer. The difference is that private sector employees have to 'hang' their human rights claim on to another claim for example a claim for unfair dismissal or unlawful discrimination.

An example could be an employee dismissed for expressing views publicly who would be able to use the human rights argument (under *Article 10*, the right to freedom of expression) in support of a claim for unfair dismissal.

Equally, in an unfair dismissal claim, if it is shown that the employer obtained information about the employee's conduct by monitoring private correspondence or telephone calls without the employee's consent (and without authorisation under the *Telecommunications (Lawful Business Practice) (Interception of Communications) Regulations 2000*), then the tribunal may well conclude that the employer failed to follow a fair procedure. This of course would make the dismissal unfair.

Constructive dismissal on the grounds of a breach of the right to privacy [7.26]

It is also likely that if a public or private sector employer acted in blatant breach of one of the rights contained in the *Human Rights Act 1998*, this would give the employee who was the victim of such treatment grounds to resign and bring a complaint of constructive dismissal to an employment tribunal on the grounds that the employer's conduct was in breach of the implied duty of trust and confidence (see **7.40** below). This type of claim requires the employee to have a minimum of one year's continuous service.

General Limitations and Restrictions on the Rights Contained in the Act [7.27]

The majority of the rights contained in the *Human Rights Act* are not absolute rights, as they are subject to certain qualifications. This means that individuals' rights can be limited or restricted by their employer provided the employer can show that there is proper justification for such limitations. This is based on the principle of proportionality (see **7.5** above) that seeks to achieve a fair balance between the rights of individuals and the general interests of the community. In an employment context this means that the rights of the employer to run their business effectively and efficiently can be balanced against the rights of their employees as defined in the *Human Rights Act*.

Thus if an employer applies a policy or procedure that in practice restricts the rights of employees under one of the Articles of the *Human Rights Act 1998*, this may be justifiable provided the policy or procedure is:

- designed to achieve a legitimate business aim;

- likely to achieve that aim in practice; *and*

- proportionate to the achievement of that aim (i.e. not excessive).

Most of the Articles of the *Human Rights Act 1998* are subject to certain defined limitations or exceptions (although not, notably, *Article 3*).

Limitations on Article 9 [7.28]

For example, rights under *Article 9* (the right to freedom of thought, conscience and religion) are limited in the following circumstances (*Article 9.2*):

- In the interests of public safety.

- For the protection of public order.

- For the protection of health or morals.

- For the protection of the rights and freedoms of others.

The term 'others' used in this context would include the employer of an employee bringing a claim, and the employee's colleagues.

Key case [7.29]

Thus, for example, if an employee wished to take an excessive amount of time off work for religious purposes to the extent that this would have an adverse effect on the employer's business, the employer would not be required under the Act to grant such time off. The following case demonstrates this point:

Case Study

Stedman v United Kingdom [1997] EHRLR 544

Facts

Ms Stedman was engaged by a travel agency. She was asked to sign a new employment contract, the terms of which included Sunday working. Because Ms Stedman held strong views that Sunday was a day that should be devoted to family and religious activities rather than commercial gain, she refused to agree to Sunday working. She was consequently dismissed. She did not have sufficient service to bring a complaint of unfair dismissal to tribunal. Instead she applied to the European Commission of Human Rights arguing that her dismissal was in breach of her rights under *Article 9* (the right to freedom of thought, conscience and religion) since her refusal to work on Sundays was on account of the expression of her Christian faith. She also argued that the requirement for her to work on Sundays was in breach of *Article 8*, the right to family life.

Findings

The European Commission declared her case inadmissible. Their analysis was that her dismissal was caused by her refusal to work certain defined hours, rather than on account of her religious beliefs. Although her refusal to work on Sundays was motivated by her religious beliefs, this was insufficient to give rise to a legitimate claim under *Article 9*.

In relation to the *Article 8* argument, the Commission held that the requirement to work five days per week including Sundays did not amount to an infringement of the employee's right to a family life.

Implications

In dealing with the *Stedman* case, the European Commission referred to an earlier decision involving the dismissal of an employee in Finland on account of his refusal to work after sunset on Fridays. This refusal was in line with the employee's religious beliefs as a Seventh day Adventist. It was held in this case that the reason for the employee's dismissal was his failure to adhere to his employer's working hours, rather than the expression of his religious beliefs.

Employers should note, however, that since these cases were determined, the UK has implemented the *Employment Equality (Religion or Belief) Regulations 2003.* These Regulations give all workers the right not to suffer discrimination on grounds of 'any religion, religious belief or similar philosophical belief'. A refusal without proper justification to grant an employee reasonable time off for religious reasons would be likely to be in breach of the Regulations. For a refusal to be justified, the employer would have to show that it was proportionate to the achievement of a legitimate aim, in other words that the provision underpinning the refusal was necessary and appropriate to a genuine business need.

Limitations on Article 10 [7.30]

Exceptions to *Article 10*, the right to freedom of expression exist in the following circumstances:

- in the interests of national security, territorial integrity or public safety;

- for the prevention of disorder or crime;

- for the protection of health or morals;

- for preventing the disclosure of information received in confidence;

- for maintaining the authority and impartiality of the judiciary;

- for the protection of the reputation or rights of others.

Article 10 does not, however, prevent employers from imposing reasonable restrictions on employees' dress or appearance, provided the restrictions are necessary from a business standpoint and can be shown to be proportionate to their desired aim. Dress and appearance restrictions could thus be imposed legitimately on the grounds of health and safety, or to create a professional image in the eyes of the company's customers, so long as the rules were not excessively restrictive in relation to their aim.

Equally, if an employee claimed the right to wear unconventional clothing to work in contravention of an employer's (reasonable) dress code, and if doing so would cause damage to the employer's reputation, or would be likely to offend others, the employer could legitimately refuse permission for the employee to do so, or discipline them for any breach of the dress code.

Article 8 – The Right to Respect for Private and Family Life, Home and Correspondence [7.31]

The much publicised *Article 8* of the *Human Rights Act 1998* provides for the right to respect for private and family life, home and correspondence. 'Correspondence' in this context would include telephone calls, voicemail, pagers, faxes, letters, memos, emails and internet use.

There are also potential implications for employers who use CCTV for surveillance purposes where the siting of a camera means that employees may be caught on film. This, arguably, could be an infringement of the employee's right to a private life. Additionally, if an employer elected to use photographs of employees at work for inclusion on their website, there could be an arguable infringement of privacy unless the employees' consent had first been obtained.

Article 8 brings into sharp focus the whole issue of monitoring and recording employee communications, and surveillance and security measures taken by employers.

Employees for their part may assume that any personal emails they send or receive will be accorded a similar degree of privacy as, for example, a letter arriving for them addressed as private or personal. Some may even believe that using their employer's telephone or email system for personal purposes is an unassailable right. This is particularly likely if the employer has not introduced any policies or rules on employees' use of these facilities.

The opposite view, i.e. a view that when an employee is at work, their right to privacy is suspended, is unsupportable in light of the *Human Rights Act 1998* and the *Data Protection 1998*. Even though people are (to one degree or another) under the control of their employer whilst at work, it is not possible for the intrinsic human need for privacy to be completely relinquished during working hours. Although it is fair and reasonable for an employer to seek to exercise a reasonable degree of supervision and control over what their employees do in the workplace, this will not entitle them to expect employees to put up with arbitrary or intrusive monitoring that breaches their right to privacy. All types of monitoring will potentially impact on employee privacy (some more than others) and some forms of monitoring will be obviously objectionable. For example, if a line manager was to read an email clearly marked personal in an employee's in or out-box for no reason other than personal curiosity, this would be an unjustifiable intrusion into the employee's privacy.

Another factor to consider is that the traditional nine-to-five working day is no longer the norm in today's 24/7 society, and working patterns often extend into evenings as well as weekends. Many people work long hours and dedicate large chunks of their lives to their employer, perhaps assenting to considerable flexibility over when they work and how long they work. In these circumstances it would – arguably – be unrealistic to expect an employee not to engage in some private communications during the course of their working time. Employees may in reality have little choice but to carry out some personal business during working hours, for example they may only be able to contact their lawyer or doctor between the hours of 9.00 am and 5.00 pm. The employer should aim therefore to strike a balance between the reasonable needs of their employees in relation to their private lives and correspondence as measured against their reasonable business needs, rather than attempting to deny employees the right to privacy altogether during working time.

How an employee's right to privacy interrelates with the employer's right to monitor communications [7.32]

The inter-relationship between employees' right to privacy and correspondence contained in *Article 8* of the *Human Rights Act* and the employer's right to monitor employees' communications presents a complex picture. There are a number of factors to take into account:

- any policies, procedures and rules in place which define or limit the purposes for which employees may use the telephone, email or the internet;

- any policies in place specifying that employees' communications may be subject to interception;

- whether employees have a reasonable expectation of privacy (which in turn will depend on the employer's policies and on whether they have been properly communicated);

- Whether employees have consented to interception (in which case they cannot reasonably expect privacy) or have been informed that interception may take place;

- The provisions of the *Regulation of Investigatory Powers Act 2000 (RIP Act)* – see **6.9** above for full details;

- Whether any monitoring and/or recording of employee communications is done within the bounds of the *Lawful Business Practice Regulations 2000* (see **6.13** above for full details).

The starting point for an analysis is that where an employee's communications are monitored and/or recorded this will patently amount to a breach of that person's right to respect for their private life and/or a breach of their right to privacy in their correspondence. However, laws introduced in 2000 expressly authorise employers to carry out monitoring and recording in certain defined situations.

The effect of the RIP Act [7.33]

The *Regulation of Investigatory Powers (RIP) Act 2000* established a legal framework to protect the confidentiality of communications and govern their interception in the course of their transmission on public and private tele-communications systems. The Act gives both the sender and the recipient (or intended recipient) of a communication the right to claim damages against the system operator if their communication is unlawfully intercepted. However, the Act provides also that there will be 'lawful authority' to intercept communications where both the sender and the recipient (or intended recipient) have expressly consented to the interception, or where the reason for interception falls within the ambit of the *Telecommunications (Lawful Business Practice) (Interception of Communications) Regulations 2000.*

It follows that if an employee has expressly consented to monitoring, such monitoring will be lawful and unlikely to be in breach of the individual's right to privacy.

The effect of the Lawful Business Practice Regulations [7.34]

The *Lawful Business Practice Regulations 2000* provide for a number of defined circumstances in which it is lawful for employers to intercept, monitor and record communications on their own business network without the consent of sender, recipient or caller and which would otherwise be prohibited by the *RIP Act s.1.* The underlying principle of the Regulations is that, for interception to be lawful, it must be for a purpose relevant to the business. The defined lawful business purposes for monitoring and recording employees' communications are:

- to establish the existence of facts relevant to the business;
- to ascertain compliance with regulatory and self-regulatory practices or procedures that are relevant to the business;
- to ascertain or demonstrate standards that employees achieve or ought to achieve when using the employer's communications systems (i.e. for quality or training purposes);
- in the interests of national security;
- to prevent or detect crime;
- to investigate or detect unauthorised use of the system, for example if the

purpose of monitoring is to establish whether any unauthorised use of the system is taking place;

- to ensure the effective operation of the system;

- to determine whether received communications are relevant to the employer's business (for example when an employee is absent on holiday and their incoming communications may have to be dealt with). Only monitoring is authorised under this heading, and not recording;

- to identify calls being made to anonymous counselling or support help-lines (in order to protect or support help-line staff). Again only monitoring, and not recording is authorised.

Monitoring for any other purpose will be unlawful unless both the sender and recipient of the communication have expressly consented, as required by the *RIP Act 2000*.

Whether the interception of private or personal communications is likely to be lawful [7.35]

The monitoring, interception or recording of telephone calls or email messages that are personal or private in nature and unrelated to the employer's business will therefore generally fall outside the scope of the *Telecommunications (Lawful Business Practice) (Interception of Communications) Regulations 2000.* This will be the case unless the sending of personal messages by email is in clear breach of company policy. In this case it could be argued that the monitoring of personal emails would fall within the scope of the provision in the Regulations that allows employers to monitor communications for the purpose of investigating or detecting unauthorised use of their system. The sending of personal emails or access to the internet for personal purposes would then, arguably, be relevant to the employer's business in the sense that such activity represented a breach of the employer's rules. It should be noted, however, that the monitoring of personal or private email messages could still be regarded as a breach of *Article 8* of the *Human Rights Act 1998* and as unfair under the data protection principles (see **4.41** above). In particular, the Data Protection Code of Practice on Monitoring at Work (and its supplementary guidance) recommends that employers should avoid intercepting emails that are clearly personal or private even where personal use of the email system is banned. The Code of Practice is not legally binding on employers, but its provisions are capable of being taken into account by courts and tribunals.

The supplementary guidance to the Data Protection Code of Practice suggests that the employer would have to be able to justify taking action to read a personal email by weighing up the intrusion into the employee's private life with the employer's need to know the content of the email. Some apparently personal emails may in any event be legitimate work-related messages, for example an email from an employee to an occupational health adviser concerning a personal health matter. Instead of reading the content of the emails, the employer should consider whether appropriate action can reasonably be taken against the employee for breach of the rules based on information available in the address and/or subject header of the email.

One key message inherent in the Data Protection Code of Practice is that if there is a less intrusive method for an employer to establish facts that they need to know, then they should pursue that less intrusive method rather than intercepting an employee's email communications. The one exception would be where the employer had reasonable grounds to suspect that an employee had been involved in criminal activity or serious misconduct at work.

It can be seen that the Data Protection Code of Practice on Monitoring at Work goes much further than the Lawful Business Practice Regulations 2000. The issue of privacy is a serious one and must be respected by employers.

The precedent set in the Halford case [7.36]

The leading case on the question of employees' rights to privacy of correspondence was that of *Halford v United Kingdom* [*1997*] *IRLR 471*. This case was dealt with prior to the introduction of the *Human Rights Act* and consequently the only route available to the complainant was to take the case to Europe.

Case Study

Halford v United Kingdom [1997] IRLR 471

Facts

Ms Halford, who at the time was an Assistant Chief Constable of Merseyside Police, had brought a complaint of sex discrimination against her employer on account of lack of promotion. Whilst the claim was outstanding (it was later settled), she applied to the European Court of Human Rights complaining that private conversations from a telephone provided by her employer for her private use had been intercepted and that this was in breach of *Article 8* of the European Convention on Human Rights. She claimed that her employer had deliberately intercepted her calls on the private telephone line in order to gather information that could be used against her in the sex discrimination proceedings, and that

---

this interception was in breach of her right to privacy under *Article 8* of the European Convention on Human Rights.

Findings

The European Court of Human Rights accepted that the interception of telephone calls made from work, as well as from home, were covered by the notions of 'private life' and 'correspondence' contained in *Article 8*. The Court upheld Ms Halford's claim, judging that the interception of her calls by her employer without her knowledge amounted to an unjustifiable interference with her right to respect for her privacy and correspondence. They rejected the UK Government's contention that employers should be able to monitor their employees' telephone calls made at work without their prior knowledge. Ms Halford was awarded compensation of £10,000 plus expenses and costs.

Implications

There were two key features of the case which were instrumental in its success. The first was that Ms Halford had not been told that calls made using the telephone provided to her were liable to be intercepted by the employer. The second point, which flows from the first, was that she was able to show that she had 'a reasonable expectation of privacy' in using the telephone. The fact that she had two telephones in her office, one of which was specifically provided for her private use (including use for the purpose of preparing her sex discrimination claim), reinforced her argument.

Although the *Halford* case dealt with the unauthorised interception of an employee's private telephone calls and the breach of *Article 8*, the outcome of the case is directly relevant to the interception of other forms of communications such as email.

Reasonable expectation of privacy [7.37]

Although *Article 8* creates a right for employees to have privacy in the workplace in a general sense, the *Halford* case suggests that the right can be asserted only where the employee reasonably expects their communications to remain private. Thus if an employee has been expressly informed that their calls are to be monitored, then an expectation of privacy cannot be argued. It is interesting to note that this expectation of privacy is also a key feature of American case-law on the subject.

It should be noted also that the since the implementation of the *Telecommunications (Lawful Business Practice) (Interception of Communications) Regulations 2000* (see **6.13**), interception of employees' telephone calls (or emails) will be lawful provided employees are properly informed that monitoring is to take place (and provided such interception is carried out for one of the purposes expressly defined in the Regulations).

In summary therefore, in the context of workplace communications and their possible interception, *Article 8* means that where employees are permitted to use the telephone, email or the internet for private purposes during working hours, they are entitled to privacy in respect of those communications, i.e. such private communications should not be intercepted by the employer. There are, however, two key aspects to employees' rights in this context:

Express permission [7.38]

The right to privacy will normally only apply where an employee has express permission to use the particular means of communication for private purposes. Employees are not entitled to privacy when carrying out activities that are contrary to their contracts of employment, or contrary to an employer's policies (provided these policies have been agreed and properly communicated). Thus where an employer's policy states that telephone and email facilities are provided for business use only, an employee would find it difficult to build a human rights argument that there had been an invasion of their privacy as a result of their private calls or email being intercepted. However, employers should also bear in mind the provisions of the Data Protection Code of Practice on Monitoring at Work (see **4.47** and **7.35** above) in which it is suggested that employers should not intercept emails that are clearly personal or private even where the employer has banned personal use of the email system.

Consent to interception [7.39]

Similarly, the right to privacy will apply only where the employee in question has an expectation of privacy (i.e. they have not consented to interception). As stated earlier, it is permissible under the *Human Rights Act 1998* for employees to agree contractually to waive their rights, for example by signing a contractual document in which it is clearly stated that the employee has agreed to have their workplace communications monitored. If the employee has no expectation of privacy, then the employer may be free to monitor their communications. This is of course subject to the overriding principle (see above) that any monitoring that is carried out must be for a legitimate business purpose and be proportionate to that purpose.

It is therefore the employer's responsibility to make sure that employees are properly informed about any monitoring activities that take place within the organisation. This is in any event required by the *Telecommunications (Lawful Business Practice) (Interception of Communications) Regulations 2000* which state that in order for monitoring to be lawful, the employer must have taken all reasonable steps to inform potential users that interceptions may be made (see **6.14** above).

The implied duty of trust and confidence [7.40]

If an employer was to blatantly breach an employee's right to respect for their privacy or correspondence, this could provide grounds for the employee to argue that the conduct in question was a breach of the implied duty of trust and confidence, giving them the right to resign and bring a claim for constructive dismissal to an employment tribunal. In order to succeed in this course of action, the employee would have to show that:

- there had actually been a breach of the right to respect to privacy or correspondence;

- the conduct complained of was fundamental to the notion of trust and confidence in the working relationship;

- it was this breach (and not some other reason) that had caused them to resign;

- they had resigned promptly following the breach.

The implied duty of trust and confidence is inherent in every employment contract. In essence it means that employees have a contractual right not to suffer any kind of treatment that would have the effect of making it intolerable for them to continue in the employment relationship. Common law dictates that there has to be a continuing bond of trust between the employer and the employee. Serious bullying is a good example of a breach of trust and confidence, and there is a great deal of case law supporting this principle.

In the leading case of *Courtaulds Northern Textiles Ltd v Andrew* [*1979*] *IRLR 84*, the EAT defined the duty of trust and confidence by stating that it would be a fundamental breach of contract for an employer, without reasonable cause, to behave in a way that was 'calculated or likely to destroy or seriously damage the relationship of confidence and trust between the parties'. In another major case (*Woods v. W M Car Services* [*Peterborough*] *Ltd* [*1981*] *ICR 666),* the EAT said:

> 'To constitute a breach of this implied term it is not necessary to show that the employer intended any repudiation of the contract: the tribunal's function is to look at the employer's conduct as a whole and determine whether it is such that its effect, judged reasonably and

sensibly is such that the employee cannot be expected to put up with it'.

The scope of the implied duty of trust and confidence is limitless, but a breach will only be judged to have occurred if the conduct of the employer is unreasonable to the extent that it makes continuing in the working relationship impossible or intolerable for the employee.

In the case of *Stewart v Texas Homecare IT Case No 29209/91*, a tribunal held that there had been a fundamental breach of trust and confidence when a letter containing serious and false allegations against an employee (made by his supervisor) was left visible on a computer screen and was subsequently seen by both the employee and his colleagues. The tribunal ruled that the employee, who had resigned on account of the incident, had been unfairly constructively dismissed.

Examples of when a breach of an employee's privacy could amount to a breach of the implied duty of trust and confidence [7.41]

Other possible examples of a breach of the implied duty of trust and confidence relating to the right to privacy could include:

- deliberate and covert 'listening in' to an employee's private or personal telephone conversations made on a workplace telephone where the employee had no knowledge that this was happening;

- monitoring telephone calls or email communications out of sheer curiosity without there being any legitimate business purpose, without authority under the *Lawful Business Practice Regulations 2000* and without the employee's consent;

- deliberately opening an employee's incoming mail (i.e. letters) which are clearly marked 'private' or 'personal' for no good reason;

- leaving confidential information about a particular employee visible on a computer screen in an open-plan office (which would also be in breach of the *Data Protection Act 1998*);

- forwarding an email containing personal or private information about a colleague to another colleague, perhaps out of spite, or as part of office gossip;

- the hasty introduction of a new policy purporting to authorise the employer to conduct monitoring of employees' communications without consultation with employees or their representatives and without agreement having been reached.

If the incident in question is serious enough to constitute a breach of the duty of trust and confidence, the individual whose privacy has been breached in this way could argue that it amounted to a fundamental breach of contract on the part of the employer. Equally, a series of relatively minor incidents could collectively be viewed as breach of trust and confidence even if no single incident on its own would amount to a breach.

Dealing with complaints of a breach of the right to privacy [7.42]

A failure on the part of management to deal promptly and adequately with a genuine complaint of a breach of an employee's right to privacy or correspondence could also constitute a breach of trust and confidence provided the breach could be regarded as fundamental in all the circumstances of the case. It follows that managers should treat any complaint raised by an employee concerning an alleged breach of their right to privacy in the workplace seriously and ensure it is properly investigated and dealt with.

The right to claim constructive dismissal on account of a breach of the implied duty of trust and confidence [7.43]

If an employee believes that their right to respect for privacy or correspondence under *Article 8* of the *Human Rights Act* has been fundamentally infringed by their employer to the extent that the employer's conduct constitutes a breach of the duty of trust and confidence, they would have the option of resigning and bringing a claim for constructive dismissal to an employment tribunal. This is subject to the employee having a minimum of one year's continuous service.

Such action must, however, be taken promptly by the employee otherwise it can be argued later that the treatment about which they were complaining was not sufficient to make working life intolerable and that there was therefore no fundamental breach of contract.

Limitations and restrictions on the rights contained in Article 8 [7.44]

Article 8 (like most of the other Articles in the *Human Rights Act)* is subject to certain defined exceptions. The privacy rights of individuals can lawfully be interfered with in the following circumstances:

- in the interests of national security;

- in the interests of public safety;

- in the interests of the economic well-being of the country;

- for the prevention of disorder or crime;

- for the protection of health or morals;

- for the protection of the rights and freedoms of others.

The phrase 'the protection of the rights and freedoms of others' would include the rights of the employer, and of course the rights of other employees. Thus it may be legitimate under this provision for an employer to monitor a particular employee's telephone calls, email messages and internet access in a way that constitutes an infringement of a their right to privacy or correspondence if the reason for doing so is to:

- check whether the person is spending an inordinate amount of working time making personal telephone calls, sending personal email messages or surfing the net for personal purposes – which would be an infringement of the employer's right to expect its employees to fulfil the job for which they have been employed. In this case, the monitoring should be restricted to a review of the time spent on personal activities and an inspection of the subject headers/address lines of emails and the titles of internet sites visited. Monitoring in these circumstances should not include reading the employee's emails;

- identify and deal with offensive messages sent from one employee to another if, for example, there is reason to believe that the content of the messages might amount to sexual harassment. Such messages would infringe the rights of others not to suffer sex discrimination. Given the seriousness of the employee's suspected misconduct, the employer may be justified in these circumstances in reading the employee's emails.

It is clearly much better for an employer to have a policy in place defining what is and is not acceptable use of the employer's communication systems, and a policy allowing monitoring to take place. Employees should also be informed before any monitoring takes place.

The Oftel Guidance [7.45]

In late 1999, Oftel, the regulator for the UK telecommunications industry, issued guidance for employers on telephone monitoring. The guidance recommends that employers should:

- clearly inform their employees about any monitoring or recording of telephone communications that is to take place; *and*

- provide employees with access to a separate and secure telephone line in the workplace where they can make and receive personal and private calls. This secure line should not be subject to any kind of interception or monitoring.

The Oftel guidance was issued at the request of the Home Office in anticipation of the implementation of the *Human Rights Act 1998*. It is not a legally binding document, but nevertheless may act as a useful guide as to how employers might strike a reasonable balance between the needs of the business to operate efficiently and the rights of employees to enjoy privacy when using workplace telephones.

The 'right' to make private calls at work [7.46]

Although the Oftel guidance seemed to imply that employees have an inherent right to make and receive personal calls whilst at work, this is not a legal requirement. Oftel's recommendation (which in any event is not legally binding) was that separate provision should be made in the workplace for employees' private calls. They suggested specifically that employers could install a payphone in the workplace for this purpose. Where employers adopt a policy of banning personal calls on their business network, the installation of one or more payphones (depending on the size of the business and number of employees) would therefore be a sound course of action.

The inference that employees have a right to make personal telephone calls whilst at work in any event extends beyond the provisions in *Article 8* of the *Human Rights Act 1998* that employees have the right to respect for privacy and correspondence. Furthermore, there is no legal obligation contained in the *Telecommunications (Lawful Business Practice) (Interception of Communications) Regulations 2000* compelling employers to provide employees with any kind of facility to make and receive personal calls whilst at work. There is certainly no authority for the argument that employers must allow employees unfettered use of their business telephone system to make private calls.

Employees should be granted privacy [7.47]

Essentially Oftel has interpreted Article 8 and the *Halford* case (see **7.36** above) to mean that it is reasonable for employees to expect privacy in relation to personal or private telephone calls made (or received) whilst they are at work, and to have a telephone provided by their employer for this purpose.

The Oftel guidance also stipulates that the interception of an employee's telephone calls without their knowledge will amount to an unacceptable breach of their privacy. This ties in with the *Halford* decision and the subsequent *Telecommunications (Lawful Business Practice) (Interception of Communications) Regulations 2000* which require employers to inform their employees if their calls are to be intercepted (see **6.13** above).

Conclusion [7.48]

The *Human Rights Act 1998* has had a major impact on employers' right to monitor employees' communications, including use of email and the internet. The Act confers rights on individuals to sue a public authority if they believe that one of their rights under the Act has been breached. This in effect gives public authority employees the right to sue their own employer if they have grounds to believe that their right to respect for privacy in relation to correspondence has been breached (under *Article 8*). Private sector employees have no similar right, but there is a provision in the Act that compels courts and tribunals (as public authorities themselves) to interpret all existing legislation (including employment law) in such a way as is compatible with the rights contained in the Act insofar as it is possible to do so. Thus private sector employees have rights under the Act too, albeit indirectly.

It is advisable, in light of the impact of *Article 8*, for employers to seek employees' consent to all and any monitoring of communications that the employer may wish to carry out. Where an employee has consented to their communications being monitored, they cannot argue when monitoring actually takes place at a later date that their right to privacy has been breached. By consenting to monitoring, the employee has in effect waived their right to privacy in respect of correspondence in the workplace.

Questions and Answers [7.49]

Question

How does the *Human Rights Act 1998* affect employees' rights in an employment context?

Answer

The *Human Rights Act* confers the right on individuals to take a public authority to court where they believe that one of their rights, as defined in the Act, has been infringed by that authority. This means that employees of public authorities can take a direct claim against their employer in court or tribunal if any of their rights under the Act is infringed by the employer.

Question

How does the *Human Rights Act 1998* impact upon employees who work in the private sector?

Answer

The *Human Rights Act* imposes a duty on courts and tribunals to interpret legislation in line with the rights contained in the European Convention on Human Rights insofar as this is possible. This is the underlying ingredient that allows private sector employees who believe their rights are being infringed by their employer to enforce their rights, albeit indirectly. Private sector employees can therefore use the human rights argument to support any existing legal claim they may have.

Question

Can an employer ask its employees to sign contractual agreements the terms of which appear to limit their rights under the *Human Rights Act 1998?*

Answer

Yes, it is feasible for employees to agree contractually to waive their rights under the *Human Rights Act* in an employment context. For example, an express statement in an employment contract giving the employer contractual authority to monitor an employee's email messages and internet access would have the result of debarring the employee from claiming later that their right to privacy had been infringed when the employer carried out reasonable monitoring.

Question

What types of organisations are regarded as 'public authorities' for the purposes of the *Human Rights Act?*
Answer

'Public authority' is defined only very broadly in the *Human Rights Act* as including 'a court or tribunal, and any person certain of whose functions are functions of a public nature'. Thus an organisation does not need to carry out public functions exclusively in order to qualify as a 'public authority' for the purposes of the Act. A private organisation that provided a public function could be caught in the definition.

Question

Can it ever be justifiable for an employer knowingly to infringe an employee's right to privacy as defined in the *Human Rights Act 1998?*

Answer

The majority of the rights contained in the *Human Rights Act*, including *Article 8*, are subject to certain qualifications. This means that individuals' rights can be limited or restricted by their employer provided the employer can show that there is proper justification for such limitations based on the 'principle of proportionality' contained in the Convention. Thus if an employer applies a policy or procedure that in practice restricts the privacy rights of employees, this may be justifiable provided the policy or procedure is designed to achieve a legitimate business aim, and is proportionate to the achievement of that aim (i.e. not excessive).

Question

Is it not fair to assume that when an employee is at work, their right to privacy is suspended?

Answer

This view is unsupportable in light of the *Human Rights Act 1998* and the *Data Protection Act 1998*. Even though people are (to one degree or another) under the control of their employer whilst at work, it is not possible for the intrinsic human need for privacy to be completely relinquished during working hours. Although it is fair and reasonable for an employer to seek to exercise a reasonable degree of supervision and control over what their employees do in the workplace, this will not entitle them to expect employees to put up with arbitrary or intrusive monitoring that breaches their right to privacy.

Question

How do the provisions of the *Telecommunications (Lawful Business Practice) (Interception of Communications) Regulations 2000* interrelate with the right to privacy contained in *Article 8* of the *Human Rights Act 1998?*

Answer

The *Telecommunications (Lawful Business Practice) (Interception of Communications) Regulations 2000* provide for a number of defined circumstances in which it is lawful for employers to intercept, monitor and record communications on their own business network without the consent of sender, recipient or caller. The underlying principle of the Regulations is that, for interception to be lawful, it must be for a purpose relevant to the business. Provided therefore that interception falls within one of the purposes defined by the Regulations, provided employees are informed that interception is to take place and provided the measures taken are not excessive, then such interception should not breach employees' rights to privacy.

Question

Can it ever be lawful for an employer to intercept an employee's email messages where these are clearly personal or private in nature?

Answer

The interception of email messages that are personal or private in nature and unrelated to the employer's business will generally fall outside the scope of the *Telecommunications (Lawful Business Practice) (Interception of Communications) Regulations 2000* unless the sending of personal messages by email is in clear breach of company policy. In this case it could be argued that the interception of personal emails would fall within the scope of the provision in the Regulations that allows employers to monitor communications for the purpose of investigating or detecting unauthorised use of their system. It should be noted, however, that the monitoring of personal or private email messages could still be regarded as a breach of *Article 8* of the *Human Rights Act 1998* and as unfair under the data protection principles. The Data Protection Code of Practice on Monitoring at Work recommends that employers should avoid intercepting emails that are clearly personal or private even where personal use of the email system is banned. The supplementary guidance to the Code suggest that the employer would have to be able to justify taking action to read a personal email by weighing up the intrusion into the employee's private life with the employer's need to know the content of the email.

Question

If an employer has informed all their employees that their email messages and internet access may be monitored, to what extent can monitoring still be regarded as an infringement of the right to privacy?

Answer

Case law suggests that the right to privacy can be asserted only where the employee reasonably expects their communications to remain private. If employees have been expressly informed that their email messages and internet access are to be monitored, there can be no expectation of privacy. Provided the employer carries out monitoring only for stated purposes that are relevant to the business and provided the monitoring is proportionate to those purposes, there should therefore be no infringement of employees' right to privacy.

Question

What can the employer do in terms of monitoring if there is a suspicion that an employee is misusing email or internet facilities, for example if personal use is contrary to the company's rules?

Answer

The right to privacy will only apply where an employee has express permission to use the particular means of communication for personal purposes. Employees are not entitled to privacy when carrying out activities that are contrary to their employer's rules, provided these rules have been agreed and properly communicated. Thus if an employer's rules state that email and internet facilities are provided to employees strictly for business use only, an employee would find it difficult to build a legal argument that there had been an invasion of their privacy as a result of their employer's interceptions. This principle would only hold good, however, if the monitoring carried out by the employer to investigate the employee's alleged misuse of the facilities was no more intrusive than was absolutely necessary.

Question

If an employer was to blatantly breach an employee's right to respect for their privacy or correspondence, could this provide grounds for the employee to resign and bring a claim for constructive dismissal to an employment tribunal?

Answer

Yes, a case of constructive dismissal in these circumstances could succeed provided the employee could show that there had actually been a breach of their right to respect to privacy, that this breach was fundamental to the notion of trust and confidence in the working relationship and that they had resigned promptly on account of the conduct in question (and not for some other reason).

Question

If an employer has grounds to believe that a particular employee is spending an inordinate amount of working time sending personal email messages or surfing the net for personal purposes, could they take steps to monitor the employee's use of these facilities in the absence of a company policy or rules on the subject?

Answer

Under the *Human Rights Act 1998*, the privacy rights of individuals can lawfully be interfered with in certain defined circumstances, including the purpose of protecting the rights and freedoms of others. 'Others' in this context includes the employer who has a right to expect its employees to fulfil the job for which they have been employed. However, it is much better for the employer to have a policy defining what is and is not acceptable use of email and the internet, and a policy allowing monitoring to take place. Employees should also be informed before any monitoring takes place.

8 Email and Internet Policies and Guidance Notes

Introduction [8.1]

Because of widespread access to email and the internet in today's high-tech workplaces, and because of the wide range of potential legal liabilities that can be created for employers as a result of misuse of these facilities, it is essential for employers to devise and implement comprehensive policies, procedures, rules and guidance notes for employees who have access to email and the internet in the course of their work. Technology has developed very rapidly in recent years and it is only now that the legal liabilities involved in using it are catching up with businesses.

Until relatively recently, access to the internet would have been limited in most organisations to IT specialists, whereas nowadays it would be unusual for an office-based employee not to have a computer on their desk. Many employees will have a very limited understanding of the potential problems and liabilities that can be created through accidental, or deliberate, misuse of computer facilities, in particular email and the internet. The internet is largely unregulated and provides limitless opportunities for employees to access information on an infinite variety of topics, but many dangers lurk in cyberspace and employers need to make employees aware of what these dangers are and how to avoid them.

What policies and rules should cover [8.2]

Clearly every employer's needs are different, and there is no one policy or set of rules that will be appropriate for all businesses. In some larger organisations, it may even be desirable to have different sets of rules for different groups of employees, depending on the requirements of their jobs and the degree to which they need to use email or the internet in the course of their work. For example employees who, because of the nature of their jobs, need to use the internet to research information in their specialist areas will need to be granted more 'freedom' than employees whose only requirement is the occasional use of email for the purpose of providing a monthly report to their colleagues.

Employees' expectations **[8.3]**

The content of a policy and any rules to be introduced will also flow from employees' expectations and from past practice. For example, if employees have been permitted (expressly or impliedly) over a period of years to use the office telephone for reasonable personal purposes, they may have understandably developed an expectation that they may use email and the internet for similar purposes. Other influencing factors will be the size and resources of the organisation, the company culture and the degree to which confidential information and commercially sensitive data may be put at risk as a result of any misuse.

Tailoring the policy and rules **[8.4]**

It follows that the nature and scope of policies and rules will need to be tailored to suit the size and type of the employer's business, and take into account both the extent to which employees have access to email and internet facilities in the course of their work and the degree to which regulation is felt to be appropriate.

In general, an employer may wish to consider introducing some or all of the following:

- a policy governing access to email and the internet, together with security and confidentiality measures that employees must adhere to;

- guidelines on the extent to which employees may use email and the internet for personal or private purposes (if at all);

- rules on how email should be used, the content of emails and email etiquette;

- rules governing how the internet should be used, whether and to what extent surfing is permitted, together with an indication of what uses are prohibited, for example the viewing or downloading of pornography;

- a policy on whistle-blowing to allow employees to bring a colleague's computer misdemeanours to the attention of management without fear of repercussion;

- a policy on monitoring.

As a minimum, every employer should formulate an 'acceptable use policy' which will set out the uses of email and the internet that are permissible in the workplace, and also any prohibited uses and the consequences (i.e. disciplinary action) of any breach of the policy.

Consistency with other company documentation [8.5]

Where policies and rules governing how employees may use email and the internet are introduced or modified, it is essential to review other relevant company documentation to ensure that the email/internet policy is compatible with any existing policies and rules.

In particular, it is important that a clear indication is given of the disciplinary penalties that will be imposed for unauthorised use of email and the internet, and an unambiguous statement outlining the sorts of activities that will be regarded by the company as gross misconduct leading to summary dismissal. Amendments may therefore need to be made to the list of offences classed as gross misconduct in the disciplinary procedure. The topic of introducing new procedures or amending existing procedures is examined in **CHAPTER 9** and disciplinary procedures and dismissal are dealt with fully in **CHAPTER 11**.

A further aspect of email policy is that employees should be informed that any pre-existing rules concerning confidentiality of company information apply when using email and the internet (see **8.62** below).

The status of policies and rules [8.6]

It is advisable for any policy and rules governing how employees may use email and the internet to be incorporated into contracts of employment. In this way there will be no doubt that all employees are subject to the terms contained in the policy and rules. The subject of introducing new policies, rules and procedures is dealt with in **CHAPTER 9**.

The Purpose of Having Clear Policies Governing Use of Email and the Internet and on Monitoring [8.7]

Main objectives of a policy [8.8]

The prime objectives of a policy setting out the employer's attitude to email and internet use will be to:

- communicate and explain why policies are necessary (i.e. in the light of legislation and the potential for legal liability);

- shield the organisation against potential legal liability occurring as a result of computer misuse;

- ensure that all employees understand the purposes for which email and the internet should be used and any restrictions on their use, in particular whether personal use is to be limited or banned;

- regulate employees' conduct insofar as their use of email and the internet is concerned;

- inform employees of the likely penalties for misuse of email or the internet, and ensure consistency of application of any disciplinary penalties following misuse;

- encourage effective and positive use of the company's computer resources;

- create awareness amongst employees both about the potential benefits to be gained from using email and the internet for work purposes, and about the potential hazards and legal liabilities;

- explain any monitoring which the employer conducts, the form monitoring will take, and the reasons why it is necessary (see **8.9** below).

The underlying aim of introducing policies and rules governing employees' uses of email and the internet will be to maximise the advantages which access to email and the internet can confer on the employer, whilst at the same time minimising the associated legal risks and practical hazards. Thus both the employer and their employees will gain the best out of technology.

Thus a well-drafted policy, combined with rules and guidelines tailored to the organisation's needs, will enable both the organisation and the employees who work for it to gain the maximum benefit from email and the internet, and will alert employees to the dangers inherent in the use of these facilities and the legal liabilities that can accrue to the employer through misuse.

A policy document should include or be accompanied by a clear statement setting out the penalties that will apply to any employee who breaches its provisions.

A basic policy statement should therefore be designed to:

- create awareness;

- communicate management commitment to the policy;

- explain the rationale behind any rules (e.g. to comply with legislation and/or ensure efficient running of the business);

- set out the standards expected from employees and other workers;

- indicate what information employees are and are not allowed to transmit, paying particular attention to the clarification of any prohibited uses;

- explain any principles of etiquette that should be born in mind when communicating by email.

Policy on monitoring **[8.9]**

Furthermore, it is important, in light of the laws governing the monitoring of employees' communications (see Chapter 6) and the privacy provisions in the Human Rights Act 1998 (see Chapter 7), to consider devising and implementing a clear policy and procedure on the monitoring of employees' use of email and the internet at work. Provided such policies and rules are clearly drafted, are in line with the legitimate business interests of the employer, and are properly communicated to all employees, they should not fall foul of Article 8 of the Human Rights Act 1998.

Rules on acceptable use **[8.10]**

Over and above a policy statement, employers should devise clear rules governing email and internet use. Such rules should define clearly what sorts of activities are, and are not, acceptable. Examples of appropriate and inappropriate uses should be given and restrictions clearly spelled out. This will clarify for all employees what type of conduct and behaviour is, and is not, acceptable to the employer and encourage consistent and professional behaviour throughout the organisation. Rules help to prevent and deter abuse and so often prevent problems arising. Provided any restrictions introduced are not any more severe that is necessary for the efficiency of the business, and provided the reasons for their introduction are properly explained, most employees will accept the need for them.

If personal use of email and the internet is to be banned, this should be spelled out clearly in the policy and rules. Banning all personal use is, however a radical measure and should not be imposed without a full process of consultation with either a recognised trade union or employee representatives (see chapter 9 for a full discussion of this topic). Even then, perhaps the rules could permit personal use of email and the internet during employees' own time, for example during lunch-breaks. Otherwise employee morale and motivation could be seriously damaged. Alternatively, the policy may state simply that occasional and reasonable' personal use of computer facilities is permitted, provided that email and internet usage does not interfere with work, nor take up more than a defined amount of time (see 8.32 below).

The aim should be to introduce policies and rules that will protect the employer's interests whilst at the same time avoiding the imposition of an over-strict regime which could lead to disharmony in the workplace. In other words, there will be a delicate balance to be struck.

The Advantages of Clear Policies and Rules [8.11]

The establishment of clear policies and rules governing how employees may use email and the internet in the course of their employment will be of significant benefit to both employer and employees alike.

Although no policy can provide comprehensive protection against misuse, the establishment of a policy will:

- act as a deterrent to employees who may otherwise may tempted to use email or the internet for inappropriate purposes;

- increase the likelihood that the employer will not be held vicariously liable for any illegal or other inappropriate activities carried on by an employee during the course of their using email or the internet, whether accidentally or deliberately;

- provide a basis for gaining employee consent to monitoring which will be necessary to comply with the provisions of the *Data Protection Act 1998* (see **4.35** above);

- enable employers to dismiss staff who fundamentally breach the policy without falling foul of unfair dismissal legislation.

From the perspective of employees, the establishment of a policy will:

- set consistent standards for everyone;

- improve employees' knowledge and understanding of the potential risks and hazards that use of email and the internet can create;

- provide clear guidelines on how they should use email and the internet, thus reducing any doubt, concerns or misunderstandings – employees will, put simply – know where they stand;

- reduce the likelihood of distraction as a result of colleagues spending excessive amounts of time using email or the internet for inappropriate purposes.

The Risks and Pitfalls of not Having Policies, Procedures and Rules in Place [8.12]

The internet, although largely unregulated, is not a law-free zone and legal actions such as copyright infringement, defamation or breaches of the laws on obscenity and child pornography may be brought against employers on account of their employees' on-line activities. Similarly, inappropriate statements or remarks written in an email message can give rise to legal liability for defamation or unlawful discrimination on grounds of sex, race, religion, disability or sexual orientation.

Essentially an employers is responsible and will be vicariously liable for their employees' activities when they are using email or the internet in the course of their employment, irrespective of whether or not the employer is aware of each individual's specific activities. Employers may be liable in a number of ways because the laws of contract, defamation, copyright, harassment, obscenity and confidentiality apply to email and internet communications in the same way as they apply to traditional methods of communication. Employers without proper policies and rules in place thus risk being held vicariously liable for the misdeeds of their employees committed whilst using email or the internet (see **CHAPTER** 2 for an in-depth discussion of these topics).

Reducing employer liability [8.13]

The likelihood of being held liable in law for employees' email or internet wrongdoings can be reduced if the employer introduces a rigorous policy governing employees' use of these facilities, and takes positive steps to communicate and apply the policy in practice. By taking such actions, the employer may be able to show that an employee who commits an act which is in clear breach of the policy was not acting 'in the course of employment' (a key criterion for the employer to be held vicariously liable for an employee's actions).

Risk of virus transmission [8.14]

Another aspect of email and internet use is the risk of the transmission of a virus to the employer's computer system through email attachments being opened, or through software being brought in by employees to the workplace and loaded on to the employer's system without proper virus-checking. A policy banning such activities can reduce the likelihood of a virus destroying the entire contents of the employer's computer system.

Risk of unfair dismissal claims [8.15]

Without a policy and rules governing employees' use of email and the internet, it is also possible that a dismissal for inappropriate use of email or the internet at work will be unfair. In the case of *Humphries v VH Barnett & Co* [*1998*], the employment tribunal chairman stated that if an employer does not make it clear what sort(s) of conduct constitutes gross misconduct, then it cannot be justifiable to dismiss an employee simply on account of the fact that he has used the internet for unauthorised purposes. In the case of *Dunn v IBM UK Ltd* [*1998*], the employee, who had been dismissed for accessing and downloading pornography and other inappropriate material via the internet, won his complaint of unfair dismissal simply because he had not been told that such behaviour could result in dismissal. **CHAPTER** 11 describes the law on unfair dismissal and how it applies to email and internet misuse.

Risk of sexual harassment claims [8.16]

If there is no policy in place governing employees' use of email and the internet, there may also be an increased risk of sexual harassment claims against the company on account of employees transmitting sexually explicit or sexist material by email or accessing similar material on the internet. This topic is dealt with fully in CHAPTER 3.

Risk of damage to reputation [8.17]

Finally, an employer who does not impose minimum standards of professionalism on their employees in terms of the content and tone of their emails risks damaging their business reputation in the eyes of the outside world. A curt or ill-thought-out email message sent in haste may create a very negative impression on its recipient and may lead to the loss of business.

What to Include Within Policies, Rules and Guidance Notes [8.18]

The following sections are aimed at providing guidelines for employers who are considering formulating an email and internet policy, rules and/or guidance notes for employees who use these facilities. Similarly, the advice given below may be useful for employers who are seeking to revise, update or extend existing policies and rules. Clearly not every point will be relevant or necessary for every employer, and the actual content of the policy document and any accompanying rules should be tailored to the needs of the organisation. The suggested content for a policy is split up into the following headings:

- the scope of the policy;
- access;
- acceptable use;
- personal and private use;
- the content of emails;
- flamemail;
- surfing the net;
- pornography;
- defamation;
- security and confidentiality;
- monitoring;
- whistle-blowing.

The scope of the policy [8.19]

It is important that any policy, procedure, rules or guidelines governing uses and abuses of email and the internet should be made applicable to all workers within the organisation who have access to the company's computer systems. Often company policies and procedures apply only to employees and not to other categories of worker whose services may be provided (for example) on a self-employed basis or through an employment agency. Equally, temporary employees, or those engaged through an employment agency are often overlooked. These workers may be just as capable as permanent employees of bringing chaos and mayhem into the organisation through computer misuse, and the employer is just as likely to be vicariously liable for any misdeeds they commit in the course of their work.

Teleworkers [8.20]

Another policy decision will be whether any rules or guidelines should be devised and implemented for tele-workers and other employees who perform all or some of their work from home. Such workers may have acquired their own computer and software or may have had their computer equipment and systems supplied by the employer. One key issue would be whether or not there should be a rule prohibiting members of the employee's family from accessing the computer systems. The perceived fairness of this will depend in part on whether or not the employer is paying for the cost of the telephone line that links the system to the internet, and to what extent the actual cost of calls is reimbursed.

The policy should also be made applicable, where appropriate, to any laptop computers used by employees who work remotely.

Model general policy statement [8.21]

A suggested general policy statement covering its scope could read:

> 'This policy applies to all company employees and other workers, and to all company desktop and portable computers, whether they are located on company premises or situated at other locations'.

All workers who will have access to computers during the course of their work should be given a copy of the company's email and internet policy and any accompanying rules, and asked to sign a document along the following lines:

> 'I have read, understood and accept the company's policy document on email and internet use [and the accompanying rules]. I understand

that the policy and rules form part of my contract with the company and that I am required to comply fully with them at all times.

Signed Name'

A suggested statement for employees (as opposed to workers engaged indirectly by the organisation) incorporating the company's email and internet policy into their contracts of employment is given in **CHAPTER 5** at **5.4**.

Access [8.22]

The company policy should make a broad statement about who within the organisation has the authority to use email and access the internet and any general restrictions that apply to everyone. The former will require a policy decision to be made as to whether as many employees as possible should have open access to the organisation's computer facilities or whether email and the internet access should be provided only to employees who need these facilities for the performance of their duties. Since access to the internet can be an extremely valuable learning tool, it may be counter-productive to deliberately restrict access.

Over and above the policy, every employee should be made aware individually whether and to what extent they are authorised to use email and/or the internet, and the broad purposes for which they may use these facilities. A system of passwords can of course be used to regulate access.

Sample statement on access [8.23]

A sample statement in the policy could read:

'All employees in the A, B and C departments of the company have full access to company computer facilities for business purposes including email and the internet. Such employees will be issued with a password which must be kept confidential at all times. In addition, workers in the X, Y and Z departments are granted the use of email for internal communications purposes only, but they are not permitted access to the internet in the course of their work. The purposes for which these facilities may and may not be used are explained fully in the Company's Employee Handbook, a copy of which has been supplied to you. You should check carefully with your line manager as to the uses of email and the internet which are permitted within your job.'

Access for trade union representatives [8.24]

Where a company recognises a trade union for bargaining purposes, the policy should also document whether and to what extent union representatives may use email and the company's intranet for union purposes, for example for communicating union matters to the workforce. Consideration should also be given to whether the union should be permitted to set up their own web-site on the company's intranet.

Disclosure of email addresses [8.25]

It may also be prudent for a policy statement to specify who may or may not disclose details of the company's email address, and to whom employees may or may not reveal their own or their colleagues' individual workplace email addresses.

Banning use of a colleague's computer [8.26]

It may also be advisable for employers to introduce a rule that bans employees from sending messages from other employee's computers in their colleague's name. Exceptions could, of course, be made in the event of an employee being absent from work on holiday or for some other reason, provided the line manager's consent is first obtained.

Such fundamental matters should be in writing and should form part of each employee's terms and conditions of employment.

Specifying the purpose for which the internet may be used [8.27]

For employees who are allowed access to the internet in particular, it is essential to specify clearly the purposes for which the internet may be used, and whether browsing is permitted. Browsing can be a very unfocussed and time-consuming activity, and one which all employers should seek to regulate and, where appropriate, restrict or even ban.

Sample statement regarding using the internet [8.28]

A sample statement might read:

'You are permitted to use the internet in the course of your job duties in order to conduct research into matters that are relevant to your job, or obtain specific information on [job–related matters]. This will include web-sites on topics such as ...

However, since browsing can be a very unfocussed and time-consuming activity, you should aim to limit the amount of time you spend browsing to no more than [half an hour, 1 hour, 2 hours] in any one [day / week]. If you believe that you need permission to spend more time surfing the net for work-related purposes, you should discuss the reasons for this with your manager. Using the internet for any purpose other than in connection with your job is strictly forbidden.'

Sensible and workable policy [8.29]

The question of access to email and internet facilities should be given careful thought and rational policy decisions should be made. The aim should not be to impose arbitrary or rigid restrictions on the use of the company's computer facilities, but rather to introduce a sensible and workable policy that provides access to those who need it for the effective performance of their duties, whilst at the same time disallowing inappropriate usage.

How to gain access [8.30]

One approach is to introduce an internet policy which defines certain job holders as essential users, but requires other workers to justify their need to use the internet in the course of their work before they are granted access. An accompanying procedure or guiding document can be put in place defining how employees who believe access to the internet would help them in their job can apply for access.

Sample application form [8.31]

A simple application form could be devised along the following lines:

Access to email and the internet – Application form

Name:Job title:

Date:Department:

I wish to apply for access to *email / the internet for use within my job.

The purposes for which I wish to use *email / the internet are as follows:

....

Access to email and the internet must be justifiable if it is to be granted. Please explain below why you think access to email or the internet would help you in your job.

Access to *email / the internet would help me to perform my job more effectively because:

....

I understand that if I am granted access to email and/or the internet, then I may use these facilities for the above work-related purposes only.

Signed:

Delete where applicable

This form should be passed to your line manager for approval.

Access to *email / the internet is recommended for the above employee.

Signed:

Name of employee's manager

The manager should pass the form to the IT Manager / General Manager for approval.

Acceptable use [8.32]

One of the key features of any email and internet policy will be to define what is and is not acceptable use of these facilities. This will mean deciding at the outset whether and to what extent personal use is to be granted (see para [8.34] below). Other matters for the employer to consider for inclusion in an acceptable use policy are whether to:

- ban the use of unauthorised software, and explain why, i.e. to avoid possible liability for copyright infringement and prevent viruses from entering the employer's computer system;

- ban the downloading of any software from the internet without express permission from, for example, the IT manager (because this may lead to an infringement of the law on copyright);

- specify whether certain types of confidential information should *not* be communicated by email;

- set down clear rules for making contracts by email or over the internet, whether orders can be accepted in this way and if so any restrictions on the acceptance of orders (see **2.47** above);

- make it clear that employees must not, when writing emails, present any views and opinions that they personally hold as the views of the organisation;

- ban pornography, material that could be perceived as sexually explicit, messages that could be offensive or provocative on grounds related to race, religion or sexual orientation and flamemail (see **8.59** below);

- permit access to the internet only at certain defined times of the day;

- prohibit the sending or forwarding of chain email messages;

- specify clearly what the penalties will be for breach of the acceptable use rules, especially if misuse is to be regarded as gross misconduct leading to summary dismissal.

The policy should also provide guidelines for employees as to what to do if they receive an email from outside the organisation that is inappropriate, for example if it is a chain letter or a message with sexually explicit content. In most cases it will be enough for the employee to send a polite reply stating that it is the Company's policy not to permit employees to respond to personal email messages of this kind, and asking the sender not to transmit any further similar material. A standard clause along the following lines could be provided in the policy:

'It is (Company name's) policy that its employees are not permitted to send certain types of personal email messages, nor to respond to incoming emails of the type that you sent to this email address. It would be appreciated therefore if you would kindly refrain from sending any further similar non work-related email messages to this Company. The Company appreciates your cooperation in this regard'.

There could also be a clause in the policy advising employees who may be concerned about inappropriate email messages sent to their computer to declare any such emails that they have received to a named person in the organisation. In this way, the employee cannot be accused at a later date if the email message is detected on the company's computer system.

The policy should also state that if an employee is unsure of the propriety of any email or any document attached to an email or file downloaded from the internet, they should seek advice from a named individual, for example the organisation's IT manager.

Housekeeping   **[8.33]**

A policy document could usefully contain guidelines for email use covering:

- how emails should be stored;

- how they should be dealt with in the employee's absence;

- in what circumstances emails should be deleted;

- recommended time-frames within which employees should check their in-boxes and respond to incoming emails;

- any general principles such as double-checking email addresses and restricting the number of copies;

- restrictions on the length of emails and on the sending and opening of attachments;

- an instruction that incoming attachments that need to be retained should be saved on the hard disk and not left on the email system;

- restrictions on the number of people to whom the same email can be sent;

- restrictions on the forwarding on of emails to other people.

Further information on housekeeping is given in **1.24** above.

Personal and private use [8.34]

One of the most important and controversial policy decisions that an employer will have to take is whether to adopt a strict 'business use only' policy for employees who use email and the internet, or whether to permit a degree of personal use.

Any rules and restrictions on personal and private use of email and the internet should be formulated in conjunction with pre-existing rules on telephone use for personal purposes. If no previous guidelines on telephone use have been in place, then it would be sensible for the policy and any restrictions to be introduced to cover all three methods of communication.

Choice of approaches [8.35]

Essentially, an employer has the choice of four approaches:

1. To introduce a complete ban on all personal and private use of computer facilities.

2. To implement a ban on personal and private use during working hours, but allow employees to use email and the internet for limited personal purposes during their own time, for example lunch breaks.

3. To permit reasonable personal use with guidelines in place to clarify the extent and type of private use that is permitted and prohibit certain types of use, thus minimising the likelihood of abuse.

4. Unlimited use of email and the internet – which is not recommended.

The option of a total ban [8.36]

If a total ban on personal use is introduced, this should of course be spelled out clearly, but such a restrictive policy may cause resentment amongst workers, especially if they were previously permitted to use company telephones for personal use, or even if such use was silently condoned. If this is the case, the introduction of a complete ban on sending personal messages by email may technically be in breach of contract if it can be argued that using the telephone for reasonable private purposes had evolved into an implied contractual entitlement as a result of custom and practice. In any event, it is likely that an over-restrictive policy will be breached regularly.

Sample policy statement imposing a total ban on personal use [8.37]

A sample policy statement making it clear that email and the internet may be used for business purposes only could read:

> 'The majority of employees in the company have access to company telephones, email and the internet in the course of their work. It is the company's policy that these facilities should be used strictly for work-related purposes only, and not for personal or private use. In the event of a family or personal problem, however, you may seek permission from your line manager to use a company telephone or email for personal purposes and in these circumstances such use will not be unreasonably refused.

> You should advise your friends, relatives and others who may wish to make contact with you that the Company does not permit personal telephone calls or email messages except in emergency circumstances.

> The company has provided pay-phones in [location] [and computers with on-line access are also provided for personal use in [location]. All workers are invited to use these facilities during their break periods [or before the start and after the end of their shifts]. Exceptionally, employees may seek their line manager's permission to use the pay-phones during normal working hours. It should be noted that the pay-phones will not accept incoming calls.

> Any employee who is found to have been using company telephones, email or the internet for personal or private purposes will be subject to disciplinary action, up to and including summary dismissal.'

Possible effects of a total ban on morale **[8.38]**

In many workplaces, employees work long, irregular or unsocial hours whilst at the same time their employer expects total cooperation, commitment and dedication from them at all times. Arguably cooperation, commitment and dedication can only be realistically expected of employees where they are shown some consideration, respect and trust in return. Imposing a complete ban on all personal or private use of email and the internet is unlikely to achieve the levels of commitment the employer may seek and more likely to cause untold damage to employees' levels of motivation and commitment.

Considering employees' needs **[8.39]**

A key point to consider is that many employees work long hours and dedicate large chunks of their lives to their employer, perhaps assenting to considerable flexibility over when they work and how long they work. In these circumstances it would – arguably – be unrealistic to expect an employee not to engage in some private communications during the course of their working time. Realistically it will be necessary sometimes for employees to deal with private business or personal matters during the course of their working day. Doctors' and dentists' appointments may have to be made or altered, a call may need to be made to a child-minder if an employee has to work late, and an employee may only be able to speak to their lawyer or accountant during normal office hours. It is therefore desirable as a matter of good employment practice to permit limited private and personal use.

The option of limited personal and private use **[8.40]**

A better approach may therefore be to state that limited personal and private use will be permitted, provided such use is reasonable and does not interfere with work, nor take up more than a defined amount of time. The policy should state that this arrangement is based on trust and that employees are expected to apply common sense and use the system responsibly. The policy statement should also provide clear guidance, and a list of examples, on the timing (i.e. times of day), amount of time and the type of personal use that is to be permitted.

The Data Protection Code of Practice on Monitoring at Work (see **4.47**) provides some useful suggestions for employers in relation to personal communications at work, including the following two options:

- to set up a system whereby private emails can be marked 'personal and private' and adopt a policy of not monitoring such emails unless the employee is genuinely suspected of serious wrongdoing;

234

- to review whether it is feasible to provide employees with two different passwords or methods of logging on depending on whether their web access is work-related or personal.

Sample clause on limited personal use [8.41]

A sample clause follows:

> 'The company provides access to email and the internet to most employees for use during the course of their work. Since the company owns these systems, the policy is that these facilities are provided for work-related purposes. However, it is understood that employees sometimes need to deal with private business or personal matters during the course of their working day. Limited personal and private use of telephones and email is therefore permitted, provided such use is reasonable and does not interfere with work, nor take up more than [five minutes at a time; ten minutes out of the working day; a short time]. This arrangement is based on trust and employees are expected to apply common sense and use the privilege responsibly.
>
> Any breach of trust concerning use of telephone or computer facilities, or excessive or unreasonable personal use, will be regarded as a disciplinary offence.'

Other alternatives [8.42]

Another approach would be to state that any specific incidences of personal or private use must be sanctioned by the employee's line manager.
Another alternative is to permit personal use of email and the internet during employees' own time, for example during break times.

Which approach is more straightforward and/or workable? [8.43]

It could be argued that enforcing a 'business use only' policy would be more straightforward from the employer's perspective than adopting a 'reasonable personal use' policy. In organisations where employees work regular or flexible hours, or where colleagues share email addresses, a complete ban on personal use may be workable, although even in those circumstances consideration should be given to granting access for reasonable personal use during employees' own time on the condition that this privilege is not abused. If the policy is to ban all personal use, a further helpful gesture might be for the employer to include within the policy some advice on how employees can obtain internet access at home at low cost.

Examples of appropriate and inappropriate uses [8.44]

If reasonable personal use is to be permitted, it can be beneficial for the policy to state some examples of appropriate and inappropriate uses. These would to an extent mirror permitted uses of company telephones for personal or private purposes. For example:

- It may be permissible to make a phone-call or send an email to make a dentist's appointment, but unacceptable to use email to send jokes to a friend.

- An employee may legitimately need to make a telephone call or send a brief email to a friend or relative in connection with social arrangements, for example if they have been asked to work late at short notice. On the other hand a lengthy, chatty telephone call to discuss the day's activities would not be permissible.

- It may be acceptable to spend five minutes accessing the internet to conduct personal banking, but unacceptable to spend an hour browsing the web for the purpose of deciding where to go on holiday.

- It may be constructive to permit employees to use the internet for the purpose of job-related education, but not for an employee to surf for in-depth information about a personal hobby that has no connection with their job.

Sample list of acceptable and unacceptable uses [8.45]

A suggested list of acceptable and unacceptable personal uses could read as follows:

'Although the company's policy is that telephones, email and the internet should be used for work-related purposes only, it is understood that employees sometimes need to deal with private business or personal matters during the course of the working day. The following represents guidance on the types of matters that are accepted as reasonable personal use of the telephone, email or the internet, provided that these activities do not take up an excessive amount of time:

- making or altering appointments with a doctor, dentist, hospital, optician, etc;

- communicating with a child-minder or carer where this is necessary in relation to the welfare of the child or the arrangements made with the child-minder or carer;

- telephoning relatives, or receiving incoming calls from relatives, in the event of a family illness, accident or other emergency;

- making a telephone call to a child's school in the event of a problem;

- altering personal or social arrangements in the event of being asked to work late;

- limited personal banking transactions;

- telephone calls in relation to matters relating to work being done to the employee's property, e.g. to builders;

- job-related education or training (permission should first be sought from the employee's line manager).

This list is not exhaustive, but all personal or private use should be reasonable and not excessive.

> Employees may not use workplace telephones, email or the internet for purposes such as chatting to friends, sending jokes by email or surfing the net for personal purposes.'

For employees who were still left in doubt, the policy could state that borderline cases should be cleared with their line manager before the email is sent or a web-site accessed.

Case study [8.46]

The following case demonstrates the dangers of not having a clear company statement governing personal use of email and the internet.

Case study

Donna, a 23-year old single parent, was engaged as a computer operator. As part of her job duties, she had to use both email and the internet, for which she was provided with a password to allow her access. The company had no policy, rules, or guidelines on the use of computer facilities in the workplace.

Donna's line manager, Donald, was not satisfied with Donna's conduct over the fifteen months she was employed and on several occasions told her off for using email to send private messages and jokes to her friends, and also for using the internet for personal purposes such as personal banking. No record was kept of these informal warnings. Following further instances of

---

use of internal emails for personal purposes, Donna was interviewed about the continuing problem and subsequently received a formal written warning stating:

> 'Following your interview on Tuesday 21st August, the company is issuing you with a formal written warning in relation to your misuse of email and the internet. Further instances of misuse may lead to further disciplinary action against you'.

The company's disciplinary procedure followed the usual structure with provision for a verbal warning, a written warning and a final written warning prior to dismissal for misconduct. It stated that:

> 'In the event of unsatisfactory conduct, the company will follow its disciplinary procedure. You will be entitled at all stages, except at the verbal warning stage, to have the opportunity to put forward your version of events at an interview, and to be accompanied, if you wish, by a fellow worker or trade union representative of your choice. You will thus be given full opportunity to answer any complaints against you prior to any decision being taken as to the penalty to be imposed'.

Three months after the written warning, Donald discovered a file on Donna's desk containing a large amount of material which had obviously been down-loaded from the internet. The material consisted of extensive information about Thailand as a holiday destination, and Donald recalled that Donna had been chatting about the possibility of going to Thailand on holiday later that year.

Reacting angrily, Donald called Donna into his office. He reminded her that she had already received a warning for similar misconduct, and asked her what she had to say for herself. Donna, surprised by this unexpected accusation, burst into tears, and was unable to offer an explanation. In reality, however, she realised in retrospect that she should not have downloaded such a large file of information about Thailand, but did not have the opportunity to tell Donald that she was on her lunch-break when she did so.

Donald took the view that Donna's behaviour constituted serious misconduct, and, having considered the matter, dismissed her with one month's notice. Donna, for her part, subsequently brought a claim for unfair dismissal to an employment tribunal.

What would an employment tribunal decide in these circumstances? Why?

In determining a claim for unfair dismissal, an employment tribunal will first require the employer to demonstrate the reason for dismissal, and that the reason given was sufficient to justify the penalty of dismissal. The tribunal will then go on to consider whether or not the employer acted reasonably in the manner in which they treated the employee prior to the dismissal, and whether a fair procedure was followed.

As regards the reason for the dismissal, Donald did not have proper grounds to dismiss Donna because her final act of misconduct was not serious enough to justify the penalty of dismissal. This is because there was no company policy or rules stipulating that personal use of email and the internet would be regarded as gross misconduct. In any event, unless a single instance of misconduct is serious enough on its own to constitute gross misconduct justifying summary dismissal, a dismissal without the appropriate previous warnings will be unfair.

Donald also failed to follow the company's disciplinary procedure in several key ways:

- he missed out one of the stages in the procedure – i.e. there had been no final written warning;

- Donna was not told specifically in what way her conduct was unsatisfactory, nor what was expected from her by way of improvement;

- Donna was not given a proper opportunity to explain her side of events to Donald prior to her dismissal. This is a serious breach of procedure, which will almost always render a dismissal unfair;

- Donna was interviewed without prior warning and was not given the opportunity to bring a companion with her to the interview – another key procedural flaw;

- there was no right of appeal offered to Donna in relation to her dismissal.

The absence of a policy and guidelines on the use of email and the internet meant that Donna could not be expected to have reasonably known that downloading material about a holiday destination during her lunch-hour would be regarded as misconduct. Thus her dismissal would be unfair both in terms of the reason for it and because of the breaches of procedure.

The subjects of disciplinary procedures and dismissal are dealt with fully in **CHAPTER 11**.

As stated earlier in this chapter, the aim should be to introduce policies that will protect the employer's interests whilst at the same time avoiding the imposition of an over-strict regime which could lead to disharmony in the workplace.

Charging employees for personal use [8.47]

One further issue connected with employees' personal use of email and the internet at work is whether the employer wishes to charge the employee for any personal use. Clearly a decision to charge will necessitate a system of record-keeping for each employee and a degree of trust on both sides.

Providing facilities expressly for employees' personal use [8.48]

For employers who take the stance that the their computer should be used strictly for business purposes only, one approach to deal with the conundrum of employees' need to attend to personal matters during the working day would be to provide computers and telephone lines expressly for employees to use for personal purposes during their own time, for example tea breaks and lunch breaks. The creation of an 'internet café' would have the added advantage of allowing employees to gain useful experience in the use of technology.

The content of emails [8.49]

In relation to content, email policies should seek to set down fundamental guidelines on the content of email messages. The guidelines should clarify three key areas:

- the type of information which employees are permitted to transmit and/or prohibited from transmitting;
- security, confidentiality and efficiency measures to protect the system;
- the tone and style of email communication (etiquette – see **1.23** above).

The policy should also state categorically that the sending of rude or offensive email messages, whether to colleagues or outsiders, is expressly forbidden (see **8.53** below). In particular any material that could be construed as sexually explicit, racist or likely to cause offence on grounds related to religion, sexual orientation or disability, should be expressly banned. A further rule could state that the practice of sending lists of jokes to friends and colleagues is prohibited.

Sample statement providing guidance on the use of email　　　**[8.50]**

A sample statement providing informal guidelines on the use of email could read as follows:

> 'Employees should treat email communication with the same degree of care and professionalism as they would treat a letter sent out on company-headed notepaper.
>
> Email is not a suitable medium for the communication of confidential, personal or other sensitive information, nor for communication on any matter which requires dialogue or discussion. Email should not be used as a substitute for face-to-face communication between colleagues.
>
> Employees should take great care to ensure that all data sent or received by email is virus-free.
>
> The sending of emails (or email attachments) that might be perceived as curt, rude, sexually explicit, racially biased or that might cause offence on grounds related to disability, religion or sexual orientation is strictly prohibited. Equally, employees are advised not to send emails in the heat of the moment.
>
> Employees should not send unsolicited, irrelevant or inappropriate email messages to outside parties, nor should they participate in chain or pyramid letters by email. Furthermore personal opinions should not be presented as if they were those of the organisation.
>
> Email messages should be courteous and written in a style appropriate to a business communication, and not in a casual or flippant tone. Careless or casual use of humour should be avoided because it can easily be misinterpreted. The sending of jokes by email or as an attachment to an email is strictly prohibited.'

List of purposes for which email should not be used　　　**[8.51]**

It can also be useful to produce a list of purposes for which email should not be used. In general email is not suitable for communication on any topic where dialogue or negotiation is required, or in a situation where differences of opinion need to be aired. The policy should state that email should not be viewed as an alternative to face-to-face communication.

Further matters that should be committed to writing include any rules or restrictions on disclosing email addresses to outsiders, and any rules for the forwarding and distribution of emails either internally or externally.

Email and supervisory functions [8.52]

In particular, managers and supervisors should be advised **not** to use email for certain supervisory functions, which would include:

- Staff appraisal or any kind of feedback to staff on their job performance.

- Advice or guidance to employees on work-related or conduct matters.

- Criticism of work or conduct.

- Disciplinary matters.

These types of issues should be dealt with only on a private face-to-face basis.

Flamemail [8.53]

Clearly any policy on email use should ban the sending of 'flamemail'. 'Flamemail' has been defined as an abusive, aggressive or deliberately anti-social email message. Emails that may be viewed as rude, upsetting, unduly sarcastic or sexually or racially unacceptable would fall under the heading of flamemail. Even those that are curt or badly worded may give rise to offence and the policy should provide guidance on the tone and style of email communication. It is helpful also if the policy advises employees not to send emails when they are angry or have a complaint, and to resist the temptation to reply to an incoming flamemail in the heat of the moment.

Remedies for an employees who receives flamemail [8.54]

An employee who repeatedly receives flamemail from their supervisor or manager could, depending on the content of the email messages and the degree of bullying involved, argue that such conduct was in fundamental breach of the implied duty of trust and confidence and hence their contract of employment. This could give the employee the right to resign and bring a claim for constructive dismissal to an employment tribunal, subject to a minimum period of continuous service of one year. This in turn could lead to the employer having to pay out a substantial sum in compensation to the employee.

In addition to a claim for constructive dismissal, an employee who was being seriously harassed by email (or by other methods) might be able to invoke the *Protection from Harassment Act 1997*. This law makes it a criminal offence to pursue a course of conduct on at least two occasions that amounts to harassment, or to cause a person to fear that violence will be used against them. Even though the Act is not specifically designed for the employer-employee relationship, it could in practice be used by an employee who becomes the victim of email harassment at work, provided the content of the emails could reasonably be described as harassment. Apart from the possibility of a complaint to the police, the individual who was the victim of the harassment could pursue a civil action to claim damages against the harasser. It may be helpful for a policy governing email use to contain a section advising employees what to do if they receive flamemail, particularly in light of evidence that the incidence of flamemails appears now to be widespread in the UK. In the first instance, employees could be encouraged to speak directly to the individual who has sent the offensive message to make them aware that the content and/or tone of the email was unacceptable, and to ask them not to send further offensive messages. There should, however, also be a formal channel for employees to raise instances of this type of email abuse in the event that an informal approach has failed, where the employee feels unable to speak to the sender directly or where the content of the flamemail is so offensive that informal action would be inappropriate.

Sample statement for employees who receive or send flamemail   **[8.55]**

A sample statement could read:

> 'Any employee who believes that they are the victim of flamemail may choose either to speak directly to the person who sent the offensive message, or to raise a complaint with their line manager or with [name of senior manager, HR professional or trade union official]. Any formal complaint raised with management will be promptly investigated and appropriate steps taken to put a stop to this type of behaviour.
>
> Any employee who is found to have been sending flamemail to a colleague (or to someone outside the organisation) will be subject to disciplinary action up to summary dismissal. Complaints will of course be dealt with in a manner which respects the rights of both parties, and will also be dealt with in confidence in so far as possible.'

The advantages and disadvantages of setting up a formal channel to deal with flamemail   **[8.56]**

The provision of a formal channel to deal with problems and complaints of this nature should act to:

- deter flamemail;

- provide reassurance to employees;

- provide a means for anyone who is being bullied in this way to seek redress;

- enable the employer to deal fairly and consistently with employees who are guilty of this type of unacceptable conduct.

Without such a policy statement, employees may come to believe that the company condones flamemail behaviour, and those who are guilty of flaming can plead ignorance to conduct which is essentially destructive, damaging and unfair.

Many employees who are the victims of flamemail (or other forms of bullying) will not come forward to complain about it unless there is a policy in place expressly banning flamemail and providing a proper means to raise a grievance. This is because often an employee who is the victim of flamemail will feel embarrassed or intimidated and will fear that if they complain, they will be penalised in some way, or viewed as weak, or as a trouble-maker. In addition, since much of the flamemail sent in the UK emanates (according to research) from employees' immediate line managers, there may be no obvious route for an employee to deal with the problem unless there are guidelines in place explaining to employees how they may raise this type of grievance.

Surfing the net [8.57]

Clearly the internet can provide employees with a valuable way of accessing information relevant to their jobs, including research and keeping up to date with the latest initiatives and legislation.

Internet policies should include guidance for users on matters such as:

- specific web-sites for which access is authorised;

- prohibition on use of the internet for certain purposes, for example to carry out any freelance work, buy or sell goods unrelated to the employer's business, gamble, contribute to internet newsgroups, play games or conduct political activities;

- a ban on the viewing, accessing or downloading of pornography or any kind of offensive or illegal material such as hate speech, information on illegal drugs, criminal activities or terrorism

- to what extent, if at all, surfing is permitted;

- if surfing is permitted, a limit on the amount of time employees should spend searching for information;

- whether there are any restrictions on downloading material from the internet, for example whether the employee's line manager's permission should first be sought;

- a limit on the size of file that can be downloaded;

- restrictions on the placing of the company name or any company-related material on to any web-site accessible to the public, or on to the company's own web-site, without express authority;

- an instruction that employees should not add their names to any mailing lists;

- information on the implications of the law of copyright (see **2.53** above);

- a reminder to employees that, because the internet is largely unregulated, the information available on it may not necessarily be accurate, up-to-date or reliable.

Access to the employer's own web-site [8.58]

Employees should be told via a policy document who in the organisation has the authority to make amendments to the company's own web-site, add information to it or delete information from it.

A full discussion on the setting up and operation of a company web-site is outside the scope of this book.

Pornography [8.59]

Clearly any policy on email and internet use should expressly ban the accessing, downloading, displaying or distributing of pornography or sexually explicit material and make it clear that any employee who is found to have been engaging in such activities will be dismissed for gross misconduct.

Sample statement banning pornography [8.60]

The policy might, for example, include the following statements:

'Use of email and the internet

Access to the internet is provided for employees so that they may use it in the course of their work. However, it is well known that pornographic material is widely available on the internet.

Employees are expressly forbidden to access, view, download, display or distribute any material that constitutes pornography or which is sexually explicit, sexist, homophobic, racist or otherwise offensive. This will include transmitting any such material by email or email attachment, whether to colleagues or people outside the organisation.

If an employee accidentally accesses a website they consider to be pornographic or offensive, the employee should report the matter immediately to their line manager or the IT manager. Similarly, if the employee receives any such material by email or email attachment, the matter should be immediately reported to management. The offending material should be immediately deleted from the computer.

[All images displayed on employees' computers are electronically scanned for obscene or indecent material, and for racist or illegal remarks].

For the avoidance of doubt, the deliberate accessing, viewing, downloading or distributing of pornographic or otherwise offensive material is regarded as gross misconduct under the company's disciplinary procedure. Any employee found to have been engaging in such activities will be subject to summary dismissal.'

Defamation [8.61]

Written material will be defamatory if it involves the publication of an untrue statement which tends to lower a person in the estimation of right-thinking members of society generally. There is no distinction in the law of defamation between the content of an internal email and text contained in a printed letter or other written communication.

Company policy on email and internet use should therefore clearly state that it is forbidden for any worker to make any defamatory or derogatory statement about another person or organisation either in an email or in a message to be sent over the internet. Even statements that make or infer criticism of another person or organisation should be avoided.

It should be explained in the policy that anyone who sends a defamatory message by email or posts a defamatory statement on the internet may be held personally liable in law for any damage the libellous message causes to the reputation of the individual or company concerned, and that the employer may also be held vicariously liable.

Further guidance, and a sample statement on the law of defamation, is given in **2.18** above.

Security and confidentiality [8.62]

In order to promote security of the employer's system and confidentiality of information, it may also be prudent for the policy to ban:

- the downloading of software from the internet without implementing virus protection measures that have been approved by the employer or alternatively without expression permission from the organisation's IT Manager or the employee's line manager;

- the use of software belonging to the employee, and especially the use of pirated software;

- the opening of email attachments transmitted from outside the organisation, given the risk of viruses entering the system;

- the transmission of certain defined types of confidential information by email;

- the use or change of another person's password, user name, files, or output without express authorisation.

As stated earlier, the policy should make it quite clear that any pre-existing rules concerning confidentiality of company information apply when using email and the internet. It should also be made clear what types of emails, if any, require a disclaimer.

It will be useful also to include within the policy a statement that any message that is wrongly delivered should be promptly redirected to the right person, and that if the message received in error contains any confidential information (whether from within the organisation or from an outside source), the recipient should not use this information, nor disclose it to anyone else.

More detailed information on the subject of confidentiality is contained in chapter 4, and further information on security measures in CHAPTER 10.

Passwords [8.63]

The rules for choosing a password, and for changing a password should be clearly spelled out in the company policy governing email and internet usage. Employees should be advised not to select the name of their partner, house, dog, cat or favourite hobby as a password. as such obvious choices may be easily guessed by an unscrupulous colleague who wishes to create mischief.

There should also of course be a clear written warning that the disclosure of a password is strictly forbidden unless (for example) such disclosure has been authorised in writing.

Monitoring [8.64]

It is up to each employer to decide what, if any, type of telephone, email or internet monitoring they wish to conduct, and the purposes for which they wish to conduct monitoring. Given the inevitable intrusion monitoring will cause, it should be carried out only where it is necessary and relevant to the business. The type and degree of monitoring should be proportionate in relation to the needs of the business and should not be excessive.

What monitoring should consist of [8.65]

Employers who decide that it is prudent to carry out monitoring on their employees' use of the telephone, email and the internet will have to decide as a preliminary, but very important issue whether monitoring should consist of:

- occasional spot-checks on the telephone numbers, email addresses and internet sites that are being accessed by employees generally, without pinpointing which employees are responsible for accessing specific numbers and sites; *or*

- specific checks on individual employees' use of the communications network by reviewing each person's access to telephone numbers, email addresses and internet sites individually. Often this would be done following the identification of a problem as a result of a general spot check, or following a complaint about a particular worker's activities; or

- interception of employees' telephone calls and email messages, i.e. listening to the calls and reading the email messages; and/or

- creating records of the communications that have been monitored. This could, for example, involve recording telephone conversations, or creating a file on a particular employee's email and internet activities. Such records would be subject to the provisions of the *Data Protection Act 1998* (see **4.30**) and the Data Protection Code of Practice on Monitoring at Work (see **4.47**).

The Data Protection Code of Practice on Monitoring at Work (see **4.47**) recommends that if there is a less intrusive method for an employer to establish facts that they need to know, then they should pursue that less intrusive method rather than intercepting an employee's email communications. Clearly there is a major difference between carrying out spot checks and intercepting actual communications. This matter will need to be carefully thought through by management before any policy decisions are taken.

The purpose and content of a policy on monitoring [8.66]

Although the *Telecommunications (Lawful Business Practice) (Interception of Communications) Regulations 2000 (SI 2000 No 2699)* authorise the interception of employee communications in a wide range of circumstances relevant to the business (see **6.13**), it is nevertheless important to have a clear policy in place regarding any monitoring that takes place in the organisation. It is also necessary to obtain employees' consent to any monitoring that does not fall within the ambit of the *Telecommunications (Lawful Business Practice) (Interception of Communications) Regulations 2000.*

A policy on monitoring should:

- explain what monitoring activities the employer carries out;

- explain the purposes for which monitoring is carried out;

- make it clear that employees' telephone calls, email messages and internet access cannot be regarded as private;

- nominate a senior person within the organisation whom employees may approach if they have any questions or concerns about monitoring.

Check-list [8.67]

A check-list for employers considering the introduction of monitoring is as follows:

- Should monitoring be designed primarily to highlight access rates, as a spot check on possible problem areas, or to monitor actual content?

- Should monitoring be restricted to workers about whom complaints have been made, or about whom there are reasonable grounds to suspect misconduct?

- Should monitoring be targeted only at employees who work in jobs which pose a particularly high risk to the employer?

- In the event of a problem being identified as a result of monitoring (for example if an employee is found to have accessed an inappropriate website), should the employee's line manager be notified?

- What action will be taken against an employee who, as a result of monitoring, is found to have been misusing email or internet access?

- Who within the organisation will have the overall responsibility for carrying out monitoring?

- Who will be given the authority to carry out the monitoring and what training will they require?

- What steps will be taken to ensure that monitoring is carried out fairly and lawfully and only for the purposes defined in the Company's policy?

- What steps will be taken to ensure the confidentiality of the results of monitoring?

- How will the policy be kept under review in the light of the results of monitoring?

The subject of monitoring is dealt with fully in CHAPTER 6.

Whistle-blowing [8.68]

It is advisable to structure any email and internet policy to include a specific facility for employees to disclose to management any abuse of email and internet facilities perpetrated by others in the organisation. The normal grievance procedure is not a suitable medium for employees to disclose technology malpractice on the part of their colleagues. This is because grievance procedures are designed to permit employees to raise work-related matters that are related to them personally, and the onus is on the worker to prove their case at a grievance hearing convened for that specific purpose. A whistle-blowing policy on the other hand allows workers to disclose wrongdoings on the part of others, which would represent a matter of interest to the business, rather than to the worker personally. The onus would then be on management to investigate the allegations and act upon them accordingly.

The advantages of a introducing a whistle-blowing policy [8.69]

Essentially, If a problem exists, it is much better for management to know about it than to remain ignorant. A whistle-blowing clause inserted into the email/internet policy will have the following advantages:

- it will provide employees with a route to raise genuine concerns about computer malpractice without fear of retribution;

- it will increase the chances of management being alerted at an early stage to any illegal or other inappropriate activities on the part of employees who are using email and the internet;

- it will help to ensure that disclosures are made internally rather than to an outside party such as a regulatory body, thus keeping such maters confidential;

- it will provide some protection to employers against the likelihood of legal claims against them.

Clearly it is important for managers to give very serious consideration to a complaint from an employee about pornography on a workplace computer, or any other type of abuse of email and internet facilities. It is equally important that the manager to whom a genuine complaint is brought should make sure that the employee who raised it is not victimised or penalised in any way for having made such a disclosure.

The topic of disclosures about computer malpractice is examined further in **2.39** above and a model procedure for complaints is given in **2.46** above.

Sample Policies, Rules and Guidance Notes on Acceptable Use [8.70]

The first step in devising a policy governing the acceptable use of the company's communications systems will be for management to decide whether to have one policy covering the use of telephones, email and the internet, or separate policies for each. Normally one policy is preferable provided that discrete sections are constructed to cover aspects of usage specific to each of the three modes of communication, for example rules on what can and cannot be downloaded from the internet. The creation of separate policies could lead to substantial quantities of unnecessary duplication. Devising one comprehensive policy is to be recommended because it will minimise duplication whilst at the same time ensuring consistency between the rules on the different modes of communication that the employer wishes to regulate.

Design of the policy [8.71]

Clearly the length, format, degree of formality and content of any policy will depend on what the organisation wishes to achieve by implementing an email and internet policy, and the level of restriction on employees' activities which is deemed to be appropriate. The emphasis will vary from company to company. One company may wish to focus on legal compliance and the avoidance of legal liability, whereas another may consider system security to be the main priority. Other organisations may prefer to keep their policy brief and informal so that employees are not made to feel they are being overburdened with rules.

The remainder of this section provides various model policies which employers may wish to adopt as they stand, or adapt or combine them to suit their own specific business needs.

Model policy one – Simple and informal policy statement on acceptable use for the small business – Reasonable personal use permitted [8.72]

This document sets down the Company's policy on use of the Company's telephones, email system and the internet during the course of your work. It is important that you read the policy carefully as the Company requires compliance from all employees at all times.

The policy has been devised in order to enable both the Company and its employees to gain the maximum benefit from email and the internet, to protect the Company from potential legal liabilities and to inform employees about how they may and may not use computer facilities.

The Company has provided access to email and the internet for work-related purposes. However, because it is accepted that employees may sometimes need to attend to personal matters during working hours, limited personal use is permitted provided this does not interfere with your work nor take up more than a very short time. You may also, if you wish, make reasonable use of the company's telephones, email and internet access during break times. The Company will not make a charge for this provided you do not abuse the privilege.

It is important to note that you may *not* at any time use email or the internet for any of the following purposes:

- to communicate information that is confidential to the Company;

- to access, view or download pornography, or any other type of offensive material on the internet;

- to communicate anything by email that could be interpreted as defamatory, derogatory or offensive, whether internally or externally.

The above activities will be regarded as gross misconduct which is likely to lead to your summary dismissal.

If are unsure about your use of email and the internet, you should seek permission from your line manager.

Model policy two– Wider policy statement on acceptable use to form part of employees' contracts of employment –Reasonable personal use permitted   **[8.73]**

Introduction

This policy governs the Company's stance on how employees and other workers may use the Company's telephones, email system and the internet during the course of their work. It is important that you read the policy carefully as the Company requires compliance from all employees at all times.

Purpose and scope

The policy has been devised in order to enable both the Company and its employees to:

- gain the maximum benefit from email and the internet;

- comply with legislation;

- minimise the threat of the Company being legally exposed;

- ensure the effective running of the business;

- prevent disruption caused by computer viruses;

- inform employees about how they may and may not use computer facilities.

This policy applies to all employees of the Company and also to other workers who may work for the Company on a temporary or contract basis. It also applies to employees who have access to the Company's computer systems from home or whilst travelling on Company business.

This policy forms part of the terms and conditions of your contract of employment and any breach of the policy will be regarded as misconduct, leading to disciplinary action up to summary dismissal.

Personal and private use

The Company provides its employees with access to email and the internet for work-related purposes. However, because it is accepted that employees may sometimes need to attend to personal matters during working hours, limited personal use is permitted provided this does not interfere with your work nor take up more than a few minutes at a time. You may also, if you wish, make reasonable use of the company's telephones, email and internet access during break times. The Company will not charge for this so long as the privilege is not abused.

Acceptable use of email

Email provides employees and the Company with a speedy, convenient and efficient means to communicate information to colleagues and to the Company's customers and suppliers. Like all systems, however, it is capable of being overused or used for inappropriate purposes.

To avoid email overload, you should refrain from sending vast quantities of material via email or email attachments. As a general rule, email messages should not be sent to a distribution list of more than ten people, and email attachments should not be longer than thirty pages or approximately 0.5 megabytes, unless you have first obtained permission for a wider distribution from your line manager.

To ensure efficiency you should:

- aim to read and respond to all emails within two days;

- double-check all email addresses and distribution lists before sending an email;

- set up distributions lists for people to whom you regularly transmit email messages;

- organise and file email messages logically and efficiently on your hard disk;

- delete email messages regularly once they have been actioned or when they are no longer current or relevant;

- make proper use of the feature on your computer that highlights when you are absent from the office for more than two days.

To ensure professionalism, you should refrain from using a casual or careless style or tone in your email messages. Email communication should be treated with the same degree of care and professionalism as you would treat a letter sent out on company-headed notepaper. Email messages should also be courteous and written in a style appropriate to a business communication.

If are unsure about your use of email and the internet, you should seek advice from your line manager.

Acceptable use of the internet

When you use the internet in the course of your work, it is advisable to bear in mind that, because the internet is largely unregulated, the information available on it may not necessarily be accurate, up-to-date or reliable.

You may use the internet for the following purposes:

- to seek information on matters that are relevant to your job;

- for the purpose of job-related education, provided you have first obtained your line manager's permission;

- for limited personal purposes during break times, subject to the prohibited uses stated below.

Whilst the Company recognises the value of the internet as a resource for information, it is easy to spend inordinate amounts of time searching and easy to become distracted. Excessive surfing or browsing should therefore not be undertaken. If you cannot locate the information you are seeking within ten minutes, you should stop surfing and, if necessary, seek advice from your line manager.

Unacceptable uses

It is important to note that you may *not* at any time use the Company's computers for any of the following purposes:

- to load unauthorised software on to the system – because this creates a risk of viruses entering the computer system and may also lead to liability for copyright infringement;

- to download software from the internet (including screen-savers) without express permission from your line manager;

- to load files or other material from a floppy disk that has been brought into the Company from an external source without first sending the disk for virus-checking;

- to communicate information that is confidential to the Company;

- to access, view or download pornography, or any type of offensive or illegal material on the internet;

- to use the internet to carry out any freelance work unrelated to the Company's business, gamble, contribute to internet newsgroups, play games or conduct political activities;

- to use the internet to search for vacant jobs or post your own CV;

- to use the internet to purchase goods unless expressly authorised to do so;

- to communicate anything by email that could be interpreted as defamatory, derogatory, rude or offensive, whether internally or externally;

- to send or forward chain or junk email messages;

- to send lengthy lists of jokes to friends and colleagues.

Any of the above activities will be regarded as gross misconduct and is likely to lead to your summary dismissal.

In addition to the above prohibited uses, employees should not use email for communication on any matter which requires dialogue, discussion or negotiation. Email should never be used as a substitute for face-to-face communication between colleagues.

Acceptance

I have read, understood and accept this policy. I understand that the policy forms part of my contract with the Company and that I am required to comply fully with it at all times.

Signed

Name

*Model policy three: Rules on use of email and the
internet – strictly business use only*   **[8.74]**

This document sets out the Company's rules on how employees and other workers should use email and the internet during the course of their work. It is important that you read these rules carefully as the Company requires compliance from all employees at all times.

The policy has been devised in order to enable both the Company and its employees to gain the maximum benefit from email and the internet, to protect the Company from potential legal liabilities and to inform employees about how they may and may not use computer facilities.

The Company's computer systems are Company property and It is the Company's policy that email and internet access provided to employees should be for work-related purposes only, and not for personal or private use, except in the event of a family or personal emergency.

Rules for use of email

When using email, employees should:

- recognise that email is not a secure form of communication and therefore refrain from sending any confidential information by email;

- aim to limit the distribution list for email messages to those for whom the information is relevant and necessary in the course of their work;

- refrain from sending lengthy email attachments – any attachment that is larger than 1.5 megabytes is not suitable for sending by email;

- refrain from forwarding incoming email messages on to other people unless the sender's permission is first obtained;

- double-check with the sender before opening any email attachment from outside the company to make sure the attachment is genuine and that it is virus-free;

- do not open any email attachments from unknown senders;

- refrain from disclosing your own or your colleagues' email addresses unless there is a valid business reason for doing so;

- destroy any email received in error without reading it and inform the sender that you have done so;

- double-check all email addresses before sending an email;

- refrain from sending email messages in the heat of the moment and avoid writing anything that could be interpreted as defamatory, derogatory, rude or offensive;

- make sure all email messages are clear, concise and courteous;

- use a business-like style of writing, rather than a casual style, and pay proper attention to spelling, grammar and sentence structure.

Rules for internet access and use

When using the internet, employees should:

- use only software provided by the Company – loading unauthorised software (including screen-savers) on to the system is strictly prohibited;

- obtain permission from your line manager before downloading software from the internet;

- refrain from spending lengthy periods of time surfing the net as this can be a time-wasting activity.

The accessing, viewing, downloading or distributing of pornography or any other type of offensive or illegal material from the internet will be regarded as gross misconduct leading to your summary dismissal from the Company.

Model policy four – Formal detailed policy and rules on internet use [8.75]

This document sets out the Company's internet policy. It seeks to provide advice and assistance for employees who need to use the internet during the course of their work. A further aim of this document is to set down rules which all employees must follow when using the internet. Thus both the Company and its employees will be able to gain the maximum benefit from the internet.

The internet is an extremely valuable tool for obtaining information on an infinitely wide range of topics. Employees who are provided with internet access should use the facility sensibly and only in relation to the needs of their job. Examples of uses to which internet access may be put include the checking of information, research and keeping up to date with the latest initiatives or legislation relevant to the employee's job.

Employees should be aware that because the internet is largely unregulated, information accessed may not be accurate, complete or up-to-date. Where there is any doubt about the accuracy of information accessed, the employee should take steps to verify it. If this is not possible, the information obtained should not be relied on.

Access to the internet is provided for work-related purposes only and employees are not permitted to use the internet for personal or private purposes during working hours. The Company reserves the right to remove internet access from any employee.

As a privilege to employees, the Company may, at its discretion, permit access to the internet during break times for limited personal purposes. Such access is, however, subject to the employee obtaining prior written permission from their line manager, and such permission is not automatic or guaranteed. Even when permission is granted, employees may not use the internet for extensive surfing or expensive searches. Certain uses are also strictly prohibited – see below under 'prohibited uses'.

Prohibited uses

The following represents a list of prohibited uses of the internet. Any employee who breaches these rules will be subject to disciplinary action up to summary dismissal.

- downloading software from the internet (including screen-savers) without express permission from your line manager. Where permission for downloading is obtained, you should download only on to a computer that has been loaded with appropriate virus-checking software;

- loading files or other material from a disk that has been brought into the Company from an external source without first sending the disk to IT department for virus-checking;

- accessing, viewing or downloading pornography, or any type of offensive or illegal material on the internet;

- using the internet to carry out any freelance work unrelated to the Company's business, to buy or sell goods, gamble, contribute to internet newsgroups, play games or conduct political activities;

- using the internet to search for vacant jobs or post a CV;

- creating or transmitting defamatory material over the internet, whether on the Company's own web-site or externally;

- disseminating material that may bring the Company's name or the name of any of its employees into disrepute;

- copying or transmitting materials accessed on the internet in infringement of copyright.

Model policy five – Detailed policy and rules on email use   **[8.76]**

This document sets out the Company's email policy. It seeks to provide advice and assistance for employees who use email during the course of their work. A further aim of this document is to set down rules which all employees must follow when using the Company's email system. Thus both the Company and its employees will be able to gain the maximum benefit from the use of email. The policy applies to all company staff whatever their employment status.

Email is provided for work-related purposes only and employees are not permitted to use it for personal or private purposes during working hours except in an urgent or emergency situation.

As a privilege to employees, the Company may, at its discretion, permit use of email for limited personal purposes during break times. Such use is, however, subject to the employee obtaining prior written permission from their line manager, and such permission is not automatic or guaranteed. Even when permission is granted, employees may not use email indiscriminately and personal incoming emails are not permitted. Certain uses are also strictly prohibited – see below under 'prohibited uses'.

Rules for confidentiality

Email is not a secure method of communication. Employees should not transmit any information that is confidential, personal or otherwise sensitive unless it has first been encrypted by IT department.

Rules for efficiency

Email communication should be treated with the same degree of professionalism as a letter sent out on company-headed notepaper. A formal business style should be adopted.

The following general rules apply to all employees:

Incoming emails

- double-check with the sender before opening any email attachment from outside the company to make sure the attachment is genuine and that it is virus-free;

- do not open any email attachments from unknown senders;

- refrain from disclosing your own or your colleagues' email address unless there is a valid business reason for doing so;

- destroy any email received in error without reading it and inform the sender that you have done so.

Outgoing emails

- aim to limit the distribution list for email messages to those for whom the information is relevant and necessary in the course of their work;
- refrain from sending lengthy emails or email attachments, especially photographs and graphics – any attachment that is larger than 1.5 megabytes is not suitable for sending by email;
- refrain from forwarding incoming email messages on to other people unless the sender's permission is first obtained;
- double-check all email addresses before sending an email;
- ensure that all emails contain the Company's standard header and footer and your own name and job title.

Organising and filing

- aim to read and respond to all emails within two days;
- organise and file email messages logically and efficiently on the computer hard disk;
- delete email messages regularly once they have been actioned or when they are no longer current or relevant;
- make proper use of the 'out-of-office' computer feature that automatically informs the sender of an email when you are absent from the office for more than two days.

Rules on etiquette

- refrain from sending email messages in the heat of the moment and avoid writing anything that could be interpreted as defamatory, derogatory, rude or offensive;
- make sure all email messages are clear, concise and courteous;
- use a business-like style of writing, rather than a casual style, and pay proper attention to spelling, grammar and sentence structure.

If are unsure about your use of email and the internet, you should seek advice from your line manager.

Prohibited uses

The following represents a list of prohibited uses of email. Any employee who breaches these rules will be subject to disciplinary action up to summary dismissal:

- sending obscene or defamatory emails whether internally or to an external party;

- sending derogatory, malicious, rude or offensive messages (known as 'flamemail') whether internally or externally;

- communicating confidential or sensitive information by email;

- sending or forwarding junk or chain email messages;

- sending unsolicited information to newsgroups or mailing lists;

- sending lengthy lists of jokes to colleagues or friends.

Model policy six – Comprehensive policy on email and internet use [8.77]

Introduction

This document sets down the Company's policy on employees' use of the Company's telephones, email system and the internet. It is important that all employees read the policy carefully, and all users are required to sign at the bottom to indicate acceptance.

This policy forms part of the terms and conditions of every employee's contract of employment and any breach of the policy will be regarded as misconduct, leading to disciplinary action up to and including summary dismissal.

Scope

This policy applies to all employees of the Company and also to temporary and contract staff, external consultants, those working through an employment agency and tele-workers. It also applies to employees who have access to the Company's computer systems from home or whilst travelling on Company business, and to use of Company-owned laptop computers.

Purpose

The policy has been devised in order to enable both the Company and its employees to gain the maximum benefit from its communications systems. The policy also aims to:

- protect the Company from potential legal liabilities;

- ensure the effective running of the business;

- prevent disruption caused by computer viruses;

- safeguard confidential and sensitive information;

- increase employees' awareness of the legal, security and productivity issues relating to use of email and the internet;

- inform employees about how they may and may not use computer facilities;

- encourage best practice.

Personal use

The telecommunications systems operating within the Company are a business resource provided to employees for work-related purposes. It is accepted, however, that employees may sometimes need to attend to personal matters during working hours, and limited personal use is therefore permitted provided this does not interfere with work, nor take up too much time. Employees may also make reasonable use of the company's telephones, email and internet access during break times. The Company will not make a charge for this, provided the privilege is not abused.

Security and confidentiality

Employees are accountable for their own PC's and their operation. Employees should not leave their workstation logged on and unattended.

Passwords must be kept confidential at all times and should not be disclosed to anyone else unless prior written authority to do so is obtained from the relevant line manager. The line manager should be notified immediately if there is a suspicion that an employee is using a colleague's password. As a further precaution, employees should change their passwords regularly and no less frequently than once a month.

Employees should be aware that email is not a secure or confidential method of communication. Confidential or sensitive Company information should not therefore be transmitted by email or email attachment unless the file has been encrypted by IT department and a disclaimer attached.

Virus protection

In order to minimise the risk of viruses entering the Company's computer system, employees are expressly forbidden to load unauthorised software on to the system or download software from the internet. For the same reason, files or other material should not be loaded from a floppy disk that has been brought into the Company from an external source, unless the disk has first been virus-checked by IT department and the employee's line manager's permission obtained.

A further precaution is that employees should not open any email attachment from an unknown sender. If there is any doubt whatsoever about the security of an incoming email attachment, the employee should double-check with the sender before opening it to make sure the attachment is genuine and that it is virus-free.

Telephone guidelines

Limited personal use of Company telephones is permitted provided the privilege is not abused. Employees should not, however, make or receive lengthy personal telephone calls, and outgoing overseas calls are prohibited.

Email guidelines

Email provides employees and the Company with a speedy, convenient and efficient means to communicate information to colleagues and to the Company's customers and suppliers. Like all systems, however, it is capable of being overused or used for inappropriate purposes.

Email should be used prudently and only where it is the most appropriate method of communication. Email should not be used where there is a need for two-way discussion or where differences of opinion need to be aired and resolved. Email should never be used as a substitute for face-to-face communication between colleagues, nor between supervisors and their staff for matters involving advice, guidance, appraisal, feedback, criticism or discipline.

Avoiding overload

The efficiency of the computer network is of paramount importance and any overuse that slows the system down must be avoided. To avoid email overload, employees should:

- refrain from sending vast quantities of material via email;

- refrain from distributing or copying email messages to large numbers of people unless wide distribution is necessary for business purposes;

- refrain from transmitting large file attachments as these can be slow to download and may clog up the system;

- store incoming attachments on the computer's hard disk if there is a need to retain them at all;
- take care to remove incoming attachments when sending a reply to an incoming email message.

Housekeeping

To ensure efficiency all employees should:

- check emails at the start of the day and once during the afternoon rather than random checking throughout the day;
- aim to respond to all emails within two days;
- set up distributions lists for people to whom email messages are regularly transmitted;
- limit the distribution list for email messages to those for whom the information is relevant and necessary in the course of their work;
- refrain from forwarding incoming email messages on to other people unless the sender's permission is first obtained;
- double-check all email addresses and distribution lists before sending an email;
- always complete the 'subject' field in an outgoing email message in a way that is meaningful so that the recipient can identify what the email is about quickly and correctly;
- organise and file email messages logically and efficiently;
- delete email messages regularly once they have been actioned;
- create an 'out-of-office message on the computer whenever the employee expects to be absent for more than two days.

Etiquette

Email communication should be treated with the same degree of care and professionalism as a letter sent out on company-headed notepaper. Email messages should be courteous and written in a style appropriate to a business communication with due attention being paid to sentence structure, grammar and spelling. All email messages must be clear, concise (but not curt) and courteous.

Anyone who is unsure about use of email should seek advice from their line manager.

Prohibited uses

It is important to note that employees may not at any time use email for any of the following purposes:

- to communicate information that is confidential to the Company (unless express authority to do so has first been obtained);

- to transmit text or other material that may be regarded as sexually explicit, racially biased, sexist, homophobic, racist, religiously offensive or harassing;

- to communicate anything by email that is illegal, or that could be interpreted as defamatory, derogatory, intimidating, rude or offensive, whether internally or externally;

- to compile, send or forward chain or junk email messages whether internally or externally;

- to send unsolicited information to newsgroups or mailing lists;

- to send lengthy lists of jokes to friends and colleagues.

The Company has a separate policy covering bullying and harassment, including the prohibition on the sending of flamemail. Employees should make sure they read and comply with this policy at all times.

The internet

Employees should bear in mind that, because the internet is largely unregulated, information available from it may not necessarily be accurate, up-to-date or reliable.

Employees who are granted access to the internet may use it for the following purposes:

- to seek information on matters that are relevant to the employee's job;

- for the purpose of job-related education, provided permission is first obtained from the line manager;

- for limited personal purposes during break times, subject to the prohibited uses stated below.

Surfing

Whilst the Company recognises the value of the internet as a resource for information, it is easy to spend inordinate amounts of time searching for information and very easy to become distracted. Excessive surfing or browsing should therefore not be undertaken. If the information being sought cannot be located within ten minutes, the employee should stop surfing and, if necessary, seek advice from the line manager or the Company's IT manager.

Downloading from the internet

The law of copyright applies to electronic communication in the same way as it does to printed material and other forms of communication. Information posted on the internet, although available to the general public, may nevertheless be subject to copyright restrictions. Employees should not therefore download, copy or distribute software, graphics, screen-savers or documents without first gaining permission from their line manager or the Company's IT manager.

Prohibited uses

It is important to note that employees may not at any time use the internet for any of the following purposes:

- to create or transmit defamatory material, whether on the Company's own web-site or externally;
- to disseminate material that may bring the Company's name or the name of any of its employees into disrepute;
- to access, view or download pornography, or any type of offensive or illegal material;
- to carry out any freelance work unrelated to the Company's business, gamble, contribute to internet newsgroups, play games or conduct political activities;
- to search for vacant jobs or post a CV;
- to enter into a contractual agreement with any outside party, unless expressly authorised to do so by the Company;
- to buy or sell goods unless expressly authorised to do so by the relevant line manager.

Breaches of the policy

Any employee who is found to have breached this policy will be subject to disciplinary action, and may, depending on the seriousness of the breach, be summarily dismissed. In the event that an employee knowingly engages in any of the 'prohibited uses' of email or the internet defined in this policy, they will be summarily dismissed.

Whistle-blowing

Any employee who is concerned that a colleague is abusing the Company's communications systems or acting in any way contrary to this policy is encouraged to disclose the abuse in confidence to either their line manager or [named senior manager]. Any genuine complaint of email or internet abuse will be treated seriously by management and promptly investigated and dealt with. No employee will be penalised for raising genuine concerns about instances of email or internet abuse.

Acceptance

I have read, understood and accept this policy. I understand that the policy forms part of my contract with the Company and that I am required to comply fully with it at all times.

Signed

Name

Sample Policies on Monitoring [8.78]

Before devising a policy on monitoring, it will be necessary for the employer to make a broad policy decision on whether monitoring should consist only of checks on the telephone numbers, email addresses and internet sites that are being accessed by employees, or whether they wish to carry out interception and (possibly) recording of actual calls and email messages. Of the two model policies below, the first is designed to allow spot-checking of telephone numbers, email addresses and internet sites, whilst the second is written to permit interception and recording.

Model policy one – Spot-checking on numbers and addresses accessed [8.79]

The Company has adopted a policy of monitoring employees' use of telephones, email and internet access. The Company's telecommunications system is company property and it follows that telephone calls made and received, email messages sent and received and internet sites accessed should not be regarded as private.

This policy applies to all staff, including temporary and contract workers, consultants and those engaged through an employment agency.

The specific reasons for monitoring are:

- to uphold the Company's email / internet policy and guard against misuse of the telecommunications systems;

- to guard against excessive personal use of the Company's telecommunications systems;

Monitoring will consist of random checks being carried out on the telephone numbers, email addresses and internet sites being accessed by workers in all departments of the Company. Spot-checks may also be carried out on the telephone numbers, email addresses and internet sites being accessed by individual employees where there is reason to suspect that there may be a problem or where a complaint has been received about a particular employee's activities. Employees who have internet access during the course of their work should be aware that the Company may track the history of the internet sites they have visited.

In the event of a problem being identified as a result of monitoring (for example if an employee is found to have accessed an inappropriate web-site), the employee's line manager will be notified. The line manager will then speak to the employee and if it is established that the employee has breached the Company's email / internet policy, the outcome may be disciplinary action ranging from an informal warning through to summary dismissal, depending on the circumstances of the individual case.

The Company will take all possible steps to ensure that monitoring is carried out as unobtrusively as possible and will treat the results of monitoring in strictest confidence.

Full details of the policy and the rules are available [in the employee handbook / Company policy manual], a copy of which has been [provided to you / is available from HR department]. If you have any queries or concerns regarding the policy, you may either raise the matter with your line manager or alternatively contact [named manager].

Model policy two – Interception and recording of telephone calls and email messages and monitoring of internet access　　　**[8.80]**

Introduction

The Company has adopted a policy of monitoring employees' use of telephones, email communication and internet access.

Although the Company permits limited use of the telephone, email and the internet for personal and private purposes, such use should not be excessive and should not interfere with employees' work. The Company's telecommunications system is company property and it follows that telephone calls made and received, email messages sent and received and internet sites accessed should not be regarded as private.

Scope

This policy applies to all staff, including temporary and contract workers, consultants and those engaged through an employment agency. All workers are required to sign at the end of this policy to indicate that they have read the policy and have agreed to interception.

Purpose

The overall purpose of monitoring is to ensure the efficient running of the Company's business and to prevent abuse of the Company's computer facilities and telecommunications systems.

Specific reasons for monitoring (which are in line with the provisions of the *Telecommunications (Lawful Business Practice) (Interception of Communications) Regulations 2000 (SI 2000 No 2699)* include:

- to protect the Company against legal liabilities;

- to make sure that employees are not using the Company's computer facilities for purposes that are expressly prohibited in the Company's email / internet policy or rules;

- to check emails and email attachments for offensive material for the protection of all workers;

- to guard against excessive personal use of the Company's telecommunications systems;

- to provide a record of transactions that may form part of contractual agreements;

- to monitor whether employees who deal with customers on the telephone conduct themselves in line with the quality standards of the Company;

- to gain access to telephone or email messages relevant to the business whilst an employee is absent from work, for example on holiday or off sick;

- to guard against computer viruses.

Monitoring

Employees should be aware that the telephone calls they make or receive, their incoming and outgoing email messages (whether internal or external), and the internet sites they access during the course of their work may be intercepted by the Company. No-one should make telephone calls that they would object to management hearing, nor send emails they would object to the Company reading. Over and above interception, telephone calls may be recorded for the purpose of monitoring quality standards and training.

Employees who have internet access during the course of their work should also be aware that the Company may track the history of the internet sites they have visited.

[Software has also been installed on to the Company's computer systems to monitor and record the details of any network activity in which employees transmit or receive any kind of file. There is also software to check for viruses and limit the size of files].

All monitoring and recording will conform with the provisions of the *Telecommunications (Lawful Business Practice) (Interception of Communications) Regulations 2000 (SI 2000 No 2699*, the *Human Rights Act 1998* and the *Data Protection Act 1998.*

Breaches of Company policy

In the event of a problem being identified as a result of monitoring, for example if an employee is found to have accessed an inappropriate web-site, the employee's line manager will be notified. The line manager will then speak to the employee and if it is established that the employee has breached the Company's email / internet policy, the outcome may be disciplinary action ranging from an informal warning through to summary dismissal, depending on the circumstances of the individual case. Hard copies of inappropriate email messages may be used as evidence in disciplinary proceedings.

The Company will take all possible steps to ensure that monitoring is carried out as unobtrusively as possible and will treat the results of monitoring in strictest confidence. Personal messages will not knowingly be intercepted.

Further information

Full details of the policy and the rules are available [in the employee handbook / Company policy manual], a copy of which has been [provided to you / is available from HR department]. If you have any queries or concerns regarding the policy, you may either raise the matter with your line manager or alternatively contact [named manager].

Acceptance

I have read and understood this policy and agree that the Company may monitor, intercept and / or record my telephone calls, email messages and monitor the internet sites I access during the course of my work.

Signed

Name

Conclusion [8.81]

Comprehensive policies, procedures and rules for employees who have access to email and the internet in the course of their work are essential elements in the modern workplace. There is, however, no single policy or set of rules that will be suitable or appropriate for all businesses, but instead each employer should design and implement policies and rules appropriate for their business, depending on its size, industry sector, the extent to which employees have access to email and internet facilities in the course of their work and the degree of potential risk created by their use of communications systems.

The prime objective of any policy and rules governing employee's use of email and the internet will be to maximise the advantages which access to email and the internet can confer on the employer, whilst at the same time minimising the associated legal risks and practical hazards. The policy and rules should also be designed to ensure that employees understand the purposes for which email and the internet should be used and any restrictions on their use. Employers also need to make policy decisions on whether to monitor employees' use of email and the internet, and if so, to devise and implement an appropriate policy to meet their business needs. The extent to which monitoring is to be carried out, and the type of monitoring that is appropriate will require careful consideration. The type and degree of monitoring should be proportionate in relation to the needs of the business and should not be excessive.

Questions and Answers [8.82]

Question

Why is it important for employers to devise and implement policies regulating their employees' use of email and the internet?

Answer

It is essential to devise and implement a comprehensive policy and rules for employees who have access to email and the internet in the course of their work primarily because of the wide range of potential legal liabilities that can be created for employers, both accidentally and deliberately, as a result of misuse of these facilities. Employees need to be informed about the dangers of misuse and provided with a set of guidelines on acceptable use so that both the employer and their employees can gain the most out of technology.

Question

To what degree should policies and rules act to restrict employees in their use of email and the internet?

Answer

Clearly every employer's needs are different, and there is no one policy or set of rules that will be appropriate for all businesses. The degree to which employees should be restricted will depend on the level of access they have to email and the internet, the company's size and resources and the degree to which confidential information and commercially sensitive data could be put at risk as a result of any misuse.

Question

Should the organisation's disciplinary procedure make specific reference to any email or internet policy?

Answer

Yes, it is important that a clear indication is given of the disciplinary penalties that will be imposed for unauthorised use of email and the internet, and an unambiguous statement outlining the sorts of activities that will be regarded by the company as gross misconduct leading to summary dismissal. It follows that, upon the introduction of an email / internet policy, amendments may need to be made to the list of offences classed as gross misconduct in the disciplinary procedure. This will ensure consistency.

Question

What would be the main aims of introducing an email and internet policy?

Answer

The underlying aim of introducing policies and rules governing employees' uses of email and the internet will be to maximise the advantages which access to email and the internet can confer on the employer, whilst at the same time minimising the associated legal risks and practical hazards. A policy will ensure that all employees understand the purposes for which email and the internet should be used and any restrictions on their use, regulate employees' conduct insofar as their use of email and the internet is concerned and create awareness both about the potential benefits to be gained from using email and the internet for work purposes, and about the potential hazards.

Question

Is it really a good idea to impose strict rules on employees who need to use email and the internet in the course of their work?

Answer

Rules are of benefit to employees because they clarify what type of conduct and behaviour is, and is not, acceptable and encourage consistent and professional behaviour throughout the organisation. Written rules will reduce any doubt, concerns or misunderstandings and make it clear to employees where they stand in relation to computer use. Rules also help to prevent and deter abuse and so often prevent problems arising in the first place. Provided any restrictions introduced are not any more severe that is necessary for the efficiency of the business, and provided the reasons for their introduction are properly explained, it is likely that most employees will accept the need for them.

Question

What are the risks and disadvantages of not implementing an email / internet policy?

Answer

The main risk is that the employer may be legally liable for misdeeds such as defamation, copyright infringement and the inadvertent formation of contracts. The likelihood of being held vicariously liable for the computer misdeeds of employees can be reduced if the employer introduces a policy governing employees' use of email and the internet, and takes positive steps to communicate and apply the policy in practice. Without a policy, there is also an increased risk of virus infection, and the increased possibility of claims for sexual harassment and unfair dismissal against the employer succeeding at tribunal.

Question

Who should the policy cover?

Answer

Any policy, procedure, rules or guidelines governing uses and abuses of email and the internet should be made applicable to all workers within the organisation who have access to the company's computer systems. This should include temporary and contract staff, those engaged through employment agencies and teleworkers. These workers may be just as capable as permanent employees of bringing chaos and mayhem into the organisation through computer misuse, and the employer is just as likely to be vicariously liable for any misdeeds they commit in the course of their work.

Question

How should an employer decide which workers should be granted access to the internet?

Answer

The question of access to the internet should be given careful thought and rational policy decisions should be made. The aim should not be to impose arbitrary or rigid restrictions on the use of the company's computer facilities, but rather to introduce a sensible and workable policy that provides access to those who need it for the effective performance of their duties, whilst at the same time introducing rules to disallow inappropriate usage, such as excessive browsing. Access to the internet can bring many benefits to employees, including, for example, the opportunity for job-related learning.

Question

Is it advisable to introduce a complete ban on personal and private use of email and the internet?

Answer

Whether to adopt a strict 'business use only' policy or introduce a 'reasonable personal use' approach will depend on a number of factors, including to what extent personal use of company telephones has been permitted or condoned in the past. Imposing a complete ban on all personal or private use of email and the internet is straightforward from the employer's perspective, but such a strict regime may damage employees' motivation and commitment and be more likely to be breached. Realistically it will be necessary sometimes for employees to deal with private business or personal matters during the course of their working day and a reasonable personal use policy may therefore be more appropriate. The policy should of course state clearly that personal use must not interfere with work, nor take up more than a limited amount of time. An alternative approach is to permit personal use of email and the internet during employees' own time, for example during lunch breaks.

Question

What issues should an employer's email policy address?

Answer

Email guidelines should clarify three key areas, namely the type of information which employees are permitted to transmit and/or prohibited from transmitting, security, confidentiality and efficiency measures to protect the system and etiquette, i.e. the tone and style of email communication. The policy should of course state categorically that the sending of rude or offensive email messages, or messages containing sexually explicit, homophobic, racially biased or religiously offensive material is expressly forbidden.

Question

Should the employer introduce a special policy to deter flamemail?

Answer

The banning of flamemail should form part of the employer's overall policy on email use. It may be helpful for the policy also to contain a section advising employees what to do if they receive flamemail, particularly in light of evidence that the incidence of flamemails appears now to be widespread in the UK. There should be a formal channel for employees to raise instances of this type of email abuse in the event that an informal approach has failed, where the employee feels unable to speak to the sender directly or where the content of the flamemail is so offensive that informal action would be inappropriate.

Question

What sorts of issues should an internet policy cover?

Answer

The company's policy should ban use of the internet for certain purposes, for example to carry out any freelance work, buy or sell goods unrelated to the employer's business, gamble, contribute to internet newsgroups, play games, conduct political activities or access pornography. The policy could also include guidance for users on matters such as whether there are any restrictions on downloading material, whether and to what extent surfing is permitted, the implications of the law of copyright and a reminder to employees that, because the internet is largely unregulated, the information available on it may not necessarily be accurate, up-to-date or reliable.

Question

Is it necessary for an email / internet policy to specifically address the law on defamation?

Answer

It is advisable that any company policy on email and internet use should clearly state that it is forbidden for any worker to make any defamatory or derogatory statement about another person or organisation either in an email or in a message to be sent over the internet. This will reduce the likelihood of the employer (and the employee) being sued for defamation.

Question

What type of monitoring policy is appropriate to protect employers' interests whilst at the same time avoiding the imposition of an over-intrusive regime?

Answer

Each employer should make a broad policy decision on whether monitoring should consist only of checks on the telephone numbers, email addresses and internet sites that are being accessed by employees, or whether they wish to carry out interception and (possibly) recording of actual calls and email messages. Given the inevitable intrusion that interception will cause, it should be carried out only where it is necessary and relevant to the business. The aim should therefore be to introduce monitoring that is proportionate in relation to the needs of the business and not excessive.

Question

What are the key elements that a policy on monitoring should cover?

Answer

A policy on monitoring should explain what monitoring activities the employer carries out and the purposes for which they are carried out, make it clear that employees' telephone calls, email messages and internet access cannot be regarded as private and specify a senior person within the organisation whom employees may approach if they have any questions or concerns about monitoring.

Question

Should an employer's email and internet policy include a whistle-blowing clause to allow employees to inform management of any computer abuse on the part of their colleagues?

Answer

Yes, it is advisable to structure any email and internet policy to include a specific facility for employees to disclose to management any abuse of email and internet facilities they believe are being perpetrated by someone in the organisation. This will provide employees with a route to raise genuine concerns about computer malpractice without fear of retribution, increase the chances of management being alerted at an early stage to any illegal or other inappropriate activities on the part of employees who are using email and the internet and help to ensure that disclosures are made internally rather than to an outside party such as a regulatory body. It will also provide some protection to employers against the likelihood of legal claims against them.

Question

Should the employer have one policy covering all aspects of company communications or separate policies covering use of telephones, email and the internet?

Answer

Normally one policy is preferable provided that discrete sections are constructed to cover aspects of usage specific to each of the three modes of communication, for example rules on what can and cannot be downloaded from the internet. The creation of separate policies could lead to substantial quantities of unnecessary duplication. Devising one comprehensive policy is to be recommended because it will minimise duplication whilst at the same time ensuring consistency between the rules on the different modes of communication that the employer wishes to regulate.

9 Introducing New Policies, Rules and Procedures

Introduction [9.1]

The introduction and implementation of policies, rules and procedures governing employees' use of email and the internet will be a major step for any employer. Equally, if an existing policy is to be substantially changed, or the rules strengthened as regards what employees can and cannot do when working with the employer's computer systems, this will require an organised and fair approach by management. If monitoring is to be introduced, employees will have to be informed and consulted (see **CHAPTER 6** for a full discussion of monitoring).

There are four separate stages involved in the introduction of policies and rules:

- reviewing the needs of the business and formulating proposals;
- consultation with employees prior to introduction;
- implementation, including publicising the new rules and procedures and training;
- policing and enforcement.

Responsibility for creation of the policy [9.2]

A decision will have to be taken at an early stage as to who should take the overall responsibility for the creation of the policy. Usually, this would be the joint responsibility of the HR and IT departments. IT specialists are well placed to provide the technical knowledge which will be essential for the practical implementation of the policy (especially if monitoring is to be introduced) whilst HR professionals will have the underlying knowledge and skills to deal with the process of consultation, and the enforcement of the rules through the company's disciplinary procedure. It can, however, be advantageous to involve representatives from every department as this will increase the likelihood of cooperation with the policy once it is implemented.

Larger companies may consider setting up a working party or committee comprising senior managers from various departments to plan and implement the policy, whilst smaller organisations may prefer to nominate one senior manager to oversee the introduction of policies and rules.

Whatever approach is taken, it is vital that any new or revised policy on email and internet use should have a strong commitment from senior management. Without such a commitment, employees will be unlikely to feel motivated to adhere to the policy or appreciate why it is important to observe the rules.

Whether Policies and Rules Should be Contractual   [9.3]

The decision as to the status of any new policy, procedure or rules must be considered carefully and defined clearly. Generally, a company policy or procedure may either have contractual force, i.e. be incorporated into all employees' contracts of employment, or alternatively be regarded simply as a management guideline indicating the employer's overall approach to the subject covered by the policy. In the latter case, the policy will not have contractual force. The status of rules, and the consequences of breaching them must also be spelled out unambiguously so that all employees know categorically what type of conduct is and is not acceptable, and what the penalties will be for breach of the rules (see **9.30** below).

Given the potentially serious consequences of employees misuse of email and internet facilities, it is normally advisable for employers to elect to make their email and internet policy and any accompanying procedures part of employees' contracts of employment. In this way there will be no doubt that all employees are subject to the terms contained in the policy and rules. If the policy is not given contractual force, an employee who fails to adhere to it will technically not be in breach of contract, thus making it more difficult for the employer to deal with problem conduct through their disciplinary procedure.

Advantages of making the policy contractual   [9.4]

There is, however, one key advantage of not making a policy or procedure part of employees' contracts, at least in the short term. Put simply, management guidelines can be introduced without employees' involvement or consent, whilst changes to any of the terms or conditions of employees' contracts must have employee agreement if they are to be enforceable. Equally, if an employer wishes to change the policy at a future date, the express agreement of all affected employees will be required if it has been introduced as a contractual document. On the other hand, a policy document which consists only of a set of management guidelines can be changed without the consent of the workforce.

One way to deal with this conundrum is to introduce a policy on email and internet use as part of employees' contracts of employment, but include a clause within the policy stating that the employer may vary the content of the policy from time to time at the discretion of management. By doing this, the employer will not need to repeat the process of obtaining employees' agreement each time a minor change to the policy is needed after its implementation.

It is important therefore that management weigh up the advantages and disadvantages of making their email and internet policy and rules contractual, and make it clear through the documentation itself whether or not any policy and rules on email and internet use form part of employees' contracts. Given the degree of exposure that employees' use of email and the internet can create for employers, it is, as stated above, strongly advisable to give contractual force to the policy.

Sample clause incorporating the policy into contracts of employment [9.5]

The policy itself may be contained in an employee handbook or manual, and can be incorporated into employment contracts by means of a clause in the contract itself along the lines of:

> 'The company's policy on email and internet use is contained in the Employee Handbook, a copy of which has been supplied to you. This policy and the rules contained within it form part of the terms and conditions of your contract of employment with the Company. Any breach of the policy or the rules will be regarded as a disciplinary offence and may lead to your dismissal'.

Clearly there will be a requirement for employees to sign to confirm that they have received a copy of the policy document, and preferably a statement that they have read, understood and accepted its terms.

Custom and practice [9.6]

If a ban on all personal use of email and the internet is to form part of the employer's acceptable use policy, this could technically constitute a change to employees' contractual terms in circumstances where they had previously been permitted to use these facilities for personal purposes, or even if such use had been silently condoned in the past.

Equally, if over a period of time managers have openly condoned personal use of company telephones, an argument could be put forward that using the company telecommunications system for reasonable personal purposes had evolved into an implied contractual entitlement as a result of custom and practice.

For a term to be implied into employees' contracts as a result of custom and practice, it must be:

- reasonable, i.e. fair and not arbitrary or capricious;

- certain, i.e. precisely defined;

- notorious, i.e. well known and established over a long period of time.

A term will only be implied into a contract on the basis of custom and practice if the practice has been regularly adopted in the company or in the particular industry over a period of years. The notion is that, because the term or practice has regularly applied and employees have come to expect it, it has evolved into a contractual right. The law does not define any minimum period of time necessary for a custom or practice to mutate into a contractual entitlement, but normally the custom or practice would have to be one which had applied consistently during a number of years.

In circumstances such as these, it is advisable for management to view the introduction of a ban on personal use of email and the internet as a change to the existing terms of employees' contracts, rather than a simple change to the attitude of management. This means that employees' agreement to the change is required (see **9.7** below).

Introducing new Policies, Procedures and Rules Without Breaching Employees' Contracts [9.7]

The prime issue in the introduction of new policies, procedures and rules which are to have contractual effect is that the policy, procedures and rules must be agreed to by all employees who will be affected by them. The same principle applies to changes to existing policies and procedures if these already have contractual force, or of they are to be given contractual force in the future. In most cases, this should not present an insurmountable barrier to employers, but it will require a fair, unhurried and reasonable approach. The key to success is consultation (see **9.8** below).

If a major new policy or set of rules is introduced without proper consultation, and without employee consent, then managers are likely to run into serious difficulties as soon as they try to implement the policy in practical terms or enforce the rules. An employee forced to submit to a policy or rule to which they have not agreed could resign and argue that the employer had acted in breach of their contract of employment through the unilateral imposition of new terms of employment. This could give rise to claims of constructive dismissal from employees with a minimum of one year's continuous service (see **9.22** below).

Provided employers adopt a reasoned and reasonable approach towards the introduction of an email and internet policy, and provided the objectives of the policy are fully communicated at an early stage, the majority of employees is likely to support it. It is up to management to communicate to employees that an email and internet policy is necessary for the efficient running of the business and for protection against computer misuse and potential legal liabilities. Provided the policy is proportionate to the needs of the business and not excessively restrictive, employees should be capable of understanding that it is in everyone's interests. Clearly, effective two-way communication will be an essential ingredient in the effective introduction of the policy.

It is important that the policy and any associated procedures are promoted as business policies necessary for the efficient and successful running of the business, rather than as IT or HR initiatives. Employees need to be encouraged to understand why the policy is necessary and the link between the policy and the protection of the company's business interests. Strong management commitment will be essential.

Consultation [9.8]

The key to the successful implementation of any new policy, procedure or rules is consultation. This of course means seeking employees' views, ideas and advice – and taking employee feedback into account. Consultation should be genuine and not a sham exercise. It is important to remember that any fundamental change to an employee's contract of employment must be agreed by the employee.

Sound business reasons [9.9]

The first principle underlying the introduction of any change to employees' terms and conditions is that the change must be based on sound business reasons. It will not be difficult for management to justify a new or revised email/internet policy on business grounds. The initial proposals (which should at this stage be proposals and not firm decisions that have already been taken) should spell out:

● the reasons why management wishes to introduce a policy;

● the potential consequences for the business of computer misuse;

● the areas in which the employer and employees could be held legally liable for misuse; *and*

● the intention of management to adopt a fair and reasonable approach.

The structure of the consultation [9.10]

The structure of any consultations will depend on the number of people employed in the organisation and whether any trade unions are recognised. Where one or more trade unions is recognised, the employer should consult the appropriate union representatives. Where there is no recognised trade union, then the employer may elect to consult either the entire workforce (if numbers are not too great) or else ask the workers to elect employee representatives for the purposes of consultation. The number of representatives should be sufficient to represent all the workers and every department in the organisation.

The employer should keep records of the various stages of the consultation process, for example minutes of all meetings held.

Statutory consultation provisions [9.11]

In setting up consultations with a view to introducing a major new policy that will affect all staff, it is advisable to adhere to the consultation periods laid down in law for the purposes of redundancy consultations. This will be the case whenever it is envisaged that one or more employees may either resign or be dismissed on account of a refusal to agree to the policy. In the case of *GMB V. Man Truck & Bus UK Ltd [2000] IRLR 636*, the EAT held that the wide definition of redundancy that is used for the purposes of collective consultation should also apply to situations where an employer proposes to alter employees' terms of employment by terminating their existing employment contracts and re-engaging them on revised terms and conditions.

Dismissal on the grounds of a refusal to accept a new policy [9.12]

Although employers planning new policies on email and internet use will not wish to envisage dismissals as a result of the introduction of a new policy, it is advisable to prepare for every contingency. In the event that one or more employees is ultimately dismissed for refusing to agree to the new policy, the employer may face unfair dismissal claims. In this eventuality, the employer will wish to be in a position to persuade an employment tribunal that they acted reasonably in the manner in which they treated the employee in question. Evidence that a policy had been hastily introduced without proper consultation and without any genuine concern for the employee's views or needs is unlikely to be perceived as reasonable by a tribunal. Conversely a reasoned approach, following the legal guidelines for consultation laid down in the *Trade Union and Labour Relations (Consolidation) Act 1992* will make a much more favourable impression on a tribunal (and make it much less likely that the need for dismissal will arise).

In the case of *Scotch Premier Meat Ltd v Burns & ors [2000] IRLR 639*, the EAT accepted the assertion that the wording of the *Trade Union and Labour Relations (Consolidation) Act 1992* can include situations in which the employer **may** dismiss employees as a consequence of changed terms of employment. In other words, it is not necessary for there to be a definite intention to dismiss anyone before the duty to consult is triggered. Arguably, the possibility of dismissal for those who refuse to accept the change to their contract will always be in the background. It follows that employees and their representatives will be able to contend that there was a 'proposal' to dismiss and that consultation should therefore have taken place.

The relevant definition of 'redundancy' (which applies only for the purposes of consultation, and not for redundancy pay) states that dismissal for redundancy is 'dismissal for a reason not related to the individual concerned'. This definition, contained in *s 195(1)* of the *Trade Union and Labour Relations (Consolidation) Act 1992*, is very broad. *Section 195(2)* of the Act further states that 'where an employee is or is proposed to be dismissed, it shall be presumed, unless the contrary is proved, that he is or is proposed to be dismissed as redundant'.

The consultation provisions in *section 188* of the Act stipulate that, where an employer is proposing to dismiss as redundant 20 or more employees at one establishment within a period of 90 days or less, the employer must consult all the appropriate representatives of any of the employees who may be affected by the proposed dismissals, or by measures taken in connection with those dismissals. Where the employer is proposing to dismiss 100 or more employees as redundant, the consultation period must be at least 90 days. The section also stipulates that consultation must begin 'in good time'.

Combining the effects of statute and case law, the safest course of action for employers planning to introduce a major new contractual policy that will affect 20 or more employees is to put arrangements in place for consultation as soon as the proposals are formulated. The consultation must be either with trade union representatives (if a trade union is recognised) or with elected employee representatives.

The process of consultation [9.13]

Once the appropriate representatives are identified, consultation should begin with preliminary discussions to put forward the employer's initial proposals. It should be made clear at this stage, that what is on the table is a set of proposals, and not a non-negotiable statement of intent. The aim should be to try to reach agreement with the representatives on the key aspects of the proposed policy and rules.

Once the representatives have had a reasonable amount of time to communicate with the employees whom they represent about the proposals, another meeting should be set up to receive their feedback. If employees have put forward any objections to the proposals or suggestions for modification, management should listen to these and take steps to incorporate any reasonable points raised into the draft policy and rules. The aim should be to overcome any problems or objections raised by employees in connection with the proposals and also to incorporate any constructive ideas and suggestions.

Finalising the proposals [9.14]

Following the period of consultation, the proposals can be finalised and a copy issued to every employee, along with a full explanation of the consultation process and any modifications made to the proposals as a result of their feedback. Reasons for not incorporating any ideas put forward should also be explained. At the same time, a target date for implementation should be indicated. Reasonable notice should be given of the date for introduction, ideally not less than three months. Each employee should be asked to sign to indicate their agreement to the new policy and rules within a specified time scale, for example two weeks.

Employees who refuse to agree to the new policy/rules [9.15]

Individual employees who refuse to sign to indicate their acceptance of the new policy should be interviewed with a view to ascertaining any objections they may have, and overcoming those objections. It may be that the employee simply needs reassurance about the new policy, and wishes to resolve some outstanding concerns. A further period of time (for example a week) should be given for the individual to signify their acceptance of the new policy and rules.

Failing agreement after this process of individual consultation, the employee should be interviewed again, and informed that a failure to agree to the policy and rules could lead to the termination of their existing contract of employment, and an offer of re-employment on the revised terms (i.e. revised to include the new policy and rules as part of the contract). Employees should be given one final opportunity to reconsider their decision.

Dismissing employees who refuse to agree to the new policy/rules [9.16]

Ultimately, if an employee still refuses or fails to agree to the policy and rules, the employer can proceed to terminate the contract of employment (with proper notice according to the terms of the contract) and at the same time offer re-employment on the revised terms. It should be made clear that the new contract will run consecutively with the old, and that continuity of service and all statutory rights will be preserved. It is important to note that the notice given must be to **terminate** the contract because notice to **vary** the contract (without agreement having been reached) is likely to amount to a breach of contract.

The easiest way to implement this course of action is to include within the offer to re-engage a statement explaining that if the employee turns up for work as usual on the specified date, they will be deemed to have accepted the new contract.

Model letters for termination and re-engagement [9.17]

Model letters for termination and re-engagement follow:

Termination letter [9.18]

Dear [employee name]

This letter is to inform you that [Company name] is terminating your contract of employment, however it should be read in conjunction with the attached letter which offers you new employment on revised terms.

Your current contract will terminate on [date], i.e. the Company is giving you [x weeks/months] notice in accordance with the terms of your contract.

The reason for the termination is that, following a full period of consultation, you have not signified your agreement to the Company's [new/revised] email and internet [policy/procedure/rules] which the Company wishes to implement as part of all employees' contracts of employment. This [policy/procedure/rules] is necessary for the Company in order to protect itself from legal liability and ensure business efficiency.

We hope that you will accept the new contract as per the attached letter.

Yours sincerely

Re-employment letter **[9.19]**

> Dear [employee name]
>
> [Company name] wishes to offer you employment as [job title] commencing on [date should be the calendar day after the date of termination defined in the termination letter].
>
> The terms of this contract of employment are the same as your previous contract with [Company name] with the exception of the terms contained in the email/internet policy, procedure and rules appended to this letter. The policy, procedure and the rules form part of the terms and conditions of this contract of employment with [Company name].
>
> We would appreciate it if you would inform the undersigned as soon as possible whether you wish to accept this contract. In any event, provided you turn up for work on [date] and continue to perform the duties that were part of your previous contract of employment, you will be deemed to have accepted this contract of employment and all the terms within it, including the email/internet policy, procedure and rules.
>
> [Company name] hopes that you will accept this contract. If you do accept, the contract will run consecutively with your previous contract and your continuity of service and all statutory rights will be preserved.
>
> Yours sincerely

This approach will remove the need for the employer to chase around after employees who have still not signified their acceptance to the change in writing.

Clearly this approach will only become necessary for employees who have failed or refused to confirm their agreement to the introduction of the new policy and rules. Where employees have signed a document to indicate their consent to the introduction of the new policy, there will be no need to proceed to take action to terminate the contract and offer re-engagement.

Weighing up the risks **[9.20]**

This process of dismissal and re-engagement is not risk-free, as employees who feel disinclined to accept the offer of revised terms will (if they have a minimum of one year's service) have the right to bring a claim for unfair dismissal to an employment tribunal. The reason for dismissal will be 'some other substantial reason', a category permitted under the *Employment Rights Act 1996, s 98(1)(b)*. Provided there has been reasonable consultation and proper consideration of the impact on the employee of the new policy and rules, and of any genuine objections raised, a refusal to accept an offer of changed terms will generally amount to a fair reason for dismissal. This will be so especially where the majority of employees has accepted the change. Proceeding in this manner is therefore less risky than imposing a contractual change without employees' agreement, which could lead to claims for breach of contract and constructive dismissal (see **9.22** below). Such a course of action would also lead the employer into difficulties when attempting at a later date to enforce the policy or rules, or administer disciplinary action against an employee who had failed to adhere to the rules.

Changes to contractual terms and conditions following a TUPE transfer [9.21]

It should be noted that where the proposal to change employees' terms and conditions of employment is related to the fact there has been (or is about to be) a transfer of a business under TUPE (*Transfer of Undertakings (Protection of Employment) Regulations 1981 (SI 1981 No 1794)*), such changes will be void and unenforceable – *even if the employee agrees to them* (for example by signing a new contract). Furthermore, if employees' contracts are terminated for a reason connected with the transfer of a business, the dismissals will be automatically unfair, unless the reasons for the dismissals are an 'economic, technical or organisational reason entailing changes in the workforce' – known as an ETO reason. There are no time limits on these restrictions.

At the time of writing, proposals are underway which (when enacted) will introduce revisions to the TUPE Regulations, probably during 2004. One proposal (which, at the time of writing is not confirmed) is to amend the Regulations so that changes to employees' terms and conditions of employment related to a TUPE transfer will be permissible provided they are for an ETO reason. Employers therefore need to take great care in this area of law which, unfortunately, is outside the scope of this book.

The Right For an Employee to Claim Constructive Dismissal on Account of a Breach of Contract [9.22]

It is well established in law that if an employer imposes new terms of employment on an employee without the individual's agreement, such action will constitute a breach of contract. If the breach is fundamental, this could give the employee the right to resign and claim that they had been constructively dismissed because of the unilateral imposition of the new terms.

Case study [9.23]

Victoria is a long-serving, hard-working member of the support staff in an oil-related company. All employees in the office have access to email in the course of their work, and the company has increasingly made internet access available to employees to the extent that most are now on-line. The company has never had a policy regulating employees' use of these facilities, although it has been their practice for some time to carry out regular reviews of the telephone numbers, email addresses and internet sites accessed by employees.

Recently IT department has done a study for management on employees' use of email and the internet. The results of the study have indicated that on average, employees are spending between five and six hours a week using email and the internet for non-business purposes. The detailed report has come before the senior management group and has caused anger and consternation amongst them.

As a consequence of the information provided by IT department, and with a view to increasing efficiency, the management has taken a decision to introduce a 'no personal use' policy in relation to email and the internet. A letter has been drawn up and sent out to all employees notifying them that this policy will be implemented on the first day of the following month (some ten days away). The letter indicates that any breach of the policy after the beginning of the following month will be viewed seriously and will result in disciplinary action. The letter also states that the company's disciplinary rules, which form part of every employee's contract of employment, have been amended to include 'using email and the internet for non work-related purposes' as a disciplinary offence.

Shortly after the implementation of the policy, Victoria is requested to come to a disciplinary meeting with her manager (Victor), bringing a colleague along if she wishes. At the meeting, Victor produces evidence that a particular email address to which Victoria has recently been sending messages is unconnected with work. Victoria explains that it is the address of a travel agency through whom she had been communicating (prior to the introduction of the new policy) in relation to flight bookings for herself and her family for a forthcoming holiday. There had been some problems with the flights, with the result that several emails had gone back and forward before the matter had been finally resolved. Victoria explains to Victor that she needed to sort out the flights fairly urgently and continuing to use her workplace email address was the only way to achieve this. Although she was aware of the introduction of the new policy, she did not believe that a few more emails to the travel agent would be regarded as misconduct. She assures Victor that, since the matter is now resolved, there will be no further communication with the travel agent from her workplace computer.

Victor, however, takes the view that Victoria has blatantly breached the new policy on email use, and, following the interview with her, issues her with a written warning. Victoria is very upset.

What, if any, employee relations and legal implications might there be relating to the management's actions in general and to Victor's actions in particular?

From an employee morale point of view, it is highly likely that the sudden unilateral introduction of such a radical policy will cause serious disgruntlement amongst the staff. There has been no consultation, no consideration of employees' views or needs, and very little notice of the introduction of the new policy. Since it has been the practice for some time for employees to use the company's email system for personal purposes, the new policy will represent a severe curtailment in a benefit that they have to date enjoyed. Furthermore, it is hardly surprising that Victoria is upset at having received a written warning for something which had previously been condoned, and which, arguably, was a one-off situation which had in any event come to a natural conclusion.

It may not have been obvious to Victoria from the wording of the company letter accompanying the new policy that a first breach of the policy would be regarded as sufficiently serious to justify a written warning. Victor has acted very harshly, particularly since Victoria has no previous disciplinary record, and it would not be surprising if she decided to raise a formal grievance on account of her treatment.

From a legal standpoint, it could be argued that, since the disciplinary rules are contractual, management had no authority to change them without the consent of the workforce (or their representatives). In the event that anyone should be dismissed on account of a first breach of the policy, the absence of any consultation and the speedy manner in which the policy was implemented would in all likelihood be perceived as unreasonable by an employment tribunal, thus rendering the dismissal unfair.

Although Victoria has not been dismissed, the issuing of a written warning in the particular circumstances could potentially be regarded as a fundamental breach of contract, giving her the right to resign and claim constructive dismissal. This could be argued on two counts, firstly that because Victoria had not expressly or impliedly consented to the

introduction of the new policy or the change to the disciplinary rules, the
written warning for personal use of email constituted a fundamental breach
of contract, and secondly that her manager's actions in issuing her with a
written warning amounted to a breach of the implied duty of trust and
confidence.

What constitutes a constructive dismissal? [9.24]

Constructive dismissal occurs in the following circumstances:

- where the employer takes some action which breaches the employee's
  contract of employment; *and*

- the breach if fundamental; *and*

- the employee resigns (with or without notice) as a direct result of the
  breach; *and*

- the employee resigns immediately or very soon after the employer's
  breach of contract.

The employer's action must constitute a breach which is significant enough to
go the root of the contract, and typically would involve some major change
to one of the key terms of employment introduced without the employee's
agreement. Depending on the circumstances, an employee might be able to
argue that the unilateral introduction of a new policy governing employees'
use of email and the internet constituted a breach of the implied term of trust
and confidence (see **5.11** above). The practical effect would be that the
employee felt the situation was intolerable to the extent that they had no
alternative but to resign. In *Morrow v Safeway Stores plc EAT 275/00*, the EAT
held that where there has been a breach of the implied term of trust and
confidence, this will always amount to a breach of the employee's contract.

It is important to note that a breach of contract does not of itself terminate a
contract. To claim constructive dismissal, the employee must actually have
resigned from employment. Furthermore, employees require to have a minimum
of one year's continuous service to be eligible to bring a complaint of
constructive dismissal to an employment tribunal. The complaint must be
brought within three calendar months of the date of termination of employment.

Determining the fairness of a constructive dismissal [9.25]

Once it is established to the tribunal's satisfaction that an employee has
resigned on account of a fundamental breach of contract on the part of the

employer, the tribunal will proceed in the usual way to address the question of whether the dismissal was fair (see **11.41** below). In most cases where constructive dismissal is proven, the dismissal will be unfair and the employee awarded compensation (see **11.53** below).

Where the employee agrees to the change to contractual terms [9.26]

Clearly no employee will be able to succeed in a claim for constructive dismissal if they have indicated their agreement to the change to the terms of their contract. Agreement can be argued in any of the following circumstances:

- where the employee has signed a document to signify their express agreement;

- where the employee has impliedly agreed to the change through their actions, e.g. by continuing to work normally.

If the employee continues to work normally for any length of time after the policy is introduced, this will in most circumstances be capable of being viewed as an acceptance of the new policy and rules, provided that the policy and rules have an immediate impact on the employee's day-to-day activities and duties. Thus an employer may be able to take some comfort following the introduction of a new email and internet policy if everything carries on as normal. It is, however, definitely preferable to have the express (and written) agreement of individual employees. The consultation procedure outlined above will have the additional advantage that any worries, grudges, concerns or complaints that employees may have about the notion of an email/internet policy will have been addressed and hopefully ironed out, thus preventing any residual resentment or resistance.

Avoiding breach of contract claims [9.27]

Provided the employer has consulted employees properly prior to the implementation of the policy and acted reasonably in an overall sense, there will be no need to fear constructive dismissal claims from employees on account of the introduction of an email and internet policy. If the process outlined above in **9.8** above is followed through, there will be no risk of constructive dismissal claims simply because there will have been no breach of contract.

Implementing the New Policy, Rules and Procedures [9.28]

The implementation of a new policy, procedure and/or rules on email and internet use is a major step for any employer and should be regarded as a management issue rather than an IT responsibility.

Decisions will have to be made as to who will take responsibility for the implementation and enforcement of the policy. Normally, HR department would assume the role of advisor to line managers in implementing the policy, whilst IT department would be the source of support and information regarding any technical aspects of implementation or monitoring. Line managers for their part should hold the main responsibility for implementing the policy for the staff within their departments. This will mean dealing with breaches of the policy or rules should they occur, whether informally or formally through the organisation's disciplinary procedure.

Where monitoring is carried out, a system should be in place for line managers to be notified of any relevant matter that comes to the attention of IT department (or whoever is responsible for the process of monitoring). For example, if monitoring shows that a particular employee has accessed an internet site that contains pornography, it should be the employee's line manager (and not IT department) who takes the responsibility for raising the matter with the employee. This may be done informally (and of course confidentially) in the first instance in order to establish whether or not a disciplinary offence has been committed. Thereafter the line manager should follow the organisation's disciplinary procedure (see **CHAPTER 11**) if appropriate.

The need for consistency [9.29]

Where policies and rules governing how employees may use email and the internet are introduced or modified, it is essential to review other relevant company documentation to ensure that the email/internet policy is compatible with any existing policies and rules. For example, the company's disciplinary procedure and any policies related to termination of employment should be reviewed to ensure that their contents are consistent with any statements made in the email/internet policy. The same is true for any anti-harassment or anti-bullying policy and also any company statements on data protection. There will need to be clear cross-references between different procedures.

Consistency with disciplinary procedures [9.30]

In particular, it is important that a clear indication is given of the disciplinary penalties that will be imposed for unauthorised use of email and the internet, and an unambiguous statement outlining the sorts of activities that will be regarded by the company as gross misconduct leading to summary dismissal. It is essential that employees understand fully not only what the rules are on use of computer facilities at work, but also what the outcome will be if they choose to break the rules.

Amendments may therefore need to be made to the company's disciplinary procedure to incorporate specific references to prohibited computer activities, in particular the list of offences classed as gross misconduct. At the very least, a phrase along the lines of 'deliberate or serious abuse of the company's email and internet policy' should be inserted as an item in the list of offences that the organisation regards as gross misconduct leading to the employee's summary dismissal. Disciplinary procedures and dismissal are dealt with fully in CHAPTER 11.

Consistency with any anti-bullying/harassment policy [9.31]

The company's anti-bullying/harassment policy may also have to be adjusted to ensure consistency with the email and internet policy. For example a special email clause could be introduced into the anti-bullying/harassment policy covering a prohibition on flame mail (see 2.33 above) and the anti-bullying/harassment policy should also expressly prohibit harassment of any kind by email and the downloading of sexually explicit, homophobic, racist or religiously offensive material from the internet. The topic of harassment is dealt with fully in CHAPTER 3.

Publicising the policy [9.32]

The effective communication of an email/internet policy is essential in order to create employee awareness and raise the profile of the whole issue of cyberliability. In publicising the policy, the employer should aim to:

* confirm the reasons why the policy is necessary, i.e. to protect the employer's business interests and ensure business efficiency;

* explain the potential consequences for the business of computer misuse, for example legal liability for copyright infringement, claims of sexual harassment, defamation, etc (see CHAPTER 2);

* provide details of the content of the policy and rules, and how these will affect employees in their jobs;

* explain any policy on monitoring and how monitoring will be carried out (see CHAPTER 6);

* inform employees how the rules will be enforced;

* allow employees the opportunity to ask questions;

Methods of promotion [9.33]

There are a number of ways of promoting the new policy and rules, for example:

- sending a hard-copy to all employees, together with an explanatory letter signed (preferably) by the most senior person in the organisation;

- transmission by email to every employee;

- publishing the new policy and an explanation of why it is being introduced on the organisation's intranet;

- presenting the same information in an in-house magazine;

- holding team briefings throughout the organisation to provide more detail of the policy and its rationale on a face-to-face basis;

- placing posters on notice-boards;

- communication by video, possibly with some filmed role-play scenarios to give real-life examples of computer misuse and their consequences.

Whatever method or methods are chosen, the emphasis should be on two-way face-to-face communication between management and staff. There will be far greater understanding and acceptance of the new policy and rules if management provides the opportunity for employees to discuss them openly and ask questions, both upon initial implementation of the policy and on an ongoing basis thereafter. This will facilitate acceptance and cooperation by employees.

Induction [9.34]

Once the policy and rules have been implemented, arrangements should also be put in place for all newly recruited staff to be fully informed about the company's computer policies as part of their induction training. Ideally training in the company's email/internet policy should be a prerequisite for the employee to be granted internet access.

Ongoing communication of the policy [9.35]

Communication of the policy and rules should not be viewed as a once-only initiative. There will be a need for regular reminders to employees (for example once very three months) so that the issue of proper use of email and the internet is reinforced on a regular basis. One idea is to have IT department set up an electronic message to appear on all employees' computer screens every so often to remind them of the email/internet policy and ask them to signify their understanding of it by clicking a box on the screen.

Follow-up meetings are also useful to allow employees to discuss any aspects of the policy or rules which are causing concern or confusion. This will facilitate understanding and acceptance of the new policy and rules.

Training [9.36]

Training will be a major consideration when the new policy and rules are being implemented. There are two main aspects to training:

- training in how to use the equipment and systems; *and*

- training in the new policy.

It will be advantageous to the employer to conduct an in-house training needs analysis with regard to employees' existing skills levels in computer use, for example how to search the internet, making efficient use of email, etc. Training of this type will reduce the likelihood of employees accidentally accessing inappropriate web-sites or wasting inordinate amounts of time copying colleagues in on emails that they do not need.

Training in the policy itself should be designed to familiarise employees with every aspect of the policy, the specific nature of the rules, and how any procedures will be applied. This training should include information about the dangers posed by careless or unauthorised computer use. Training should also be designed to explain clearly what the penalties will be for various types of breaches (see **9.30** above). If the employer is to be able to assert at a later date that an employee has breached the policy in a way that merits disciplinary action, it is essential to be able to show that the employee had been made properly aware of the rules governing use of email and the internet.

Communication and effective education of all employees in the organisation is the key to the successful implementation of any new email and internet policy. This will minimise the risk of breaches of the policy occurring and at the same time ensure that managers can deal effectively with any breaches that do nevertheless occur.

Maintaining the policy [9.37]

Like many aspects of business, the success of an email/internet policy will depend on whether the policy is kept up to date with changes in the company's business practices, management expectations, legislation and computer technology. There will be a need to review and update the policy regularly, preferably at least once a year, and possibly more often if the organisation is undergoing a period of rapid change, or if any specific problems have been encountered.

When carrying out a review of the policy and its effectiveness, it is useful to:

- seek feedback from employees on how they view the policy, and on any positive suggestions for change;

- review whether refresher training is required;

- analyse whether the policy is placing unnecessary or overly onerous restrictions on employees, or whether any of the restrictions are having a detrimental impact on employees' work;

- review whether any new or different restrictions may have to be imposed, for example in response to new web-sites, new viruses, new legislation or new trends;

- check to make sure that regular updates are being obtained for any anti-virus and filtering software;

- check whether there have been any breaches of security or confidentiality, and review what steps might be needed to prevent further breaches;

- review whether there have been any specific incidents that indicate that a change of policy might be desirable, or that more in-depth monitoring might be needed.

Policing and Enforcing Policies, Procedures and Rules [9.38]

Following the implementation of the policy, management should not be tempted to sit back and relax, assuming that all will run smoothly. There will be a need for follow-up training, and of course for enforcement measures to be taken from time to time. There is little point in expending a great deal of time and effort devising, tailoring, implementing and publicising an email and internet policy if action is not taken to ensure it is enforced effectively and consistently. The employer will gain limited protection from having put a policy in place, but maximum protection will be obtained only through effective policing and enforcing.

Enforcement of the policy is a line management responsibility, rather than being the sole territory of HR department. The role of HR professionals will be to provide information, advice and support to line managers. Thus line managers will be responsible for making sure that employees comply with the rules and that any computer misuse is dealt with promptly and effectively.

Initial period [9.39]

Where the new policy and rules have brought about major changes to employees' working practices, or have introduced restrictions such as a ban on personal use of email and the internet, it may be useful to agree an initial period, for example a month, during which a 'data amnesty' is declared. This would allow employees to delete or surrender inappropriate material on their computer, clear out their email files and/or declare to their manager or IT department (without fear of disciplinary action) that unauthorised material (for example pirated software) is held on their computer. During this initial period, employees should also be encouraged to discuss any areas of individual concern with their line manager, HR department or a specially appointed person from IT department. This will help the new policy and rules to bed down and provide reassurance to employees that any minor computer misdemeanours committed in the past will not be cast up against them in the future.

Enforcement – informal action and disciplinary sanctions [9.40]

A key element of any new email and internet policy will be how the policy is to be supported by disciplinary action. Clearly no employer will wish to be perceived as heavy-handed, but at the same time if the policy is not enforced by appropriate disciplinary measures, it will have no clout and will quickly fall into disrepute.

In most cases of minor breach of the policy, the issue can be dealt with informally by means of a private discussion between the employee who has transgressed and their line manager. This may take the form of a gentle reminder by the manager, for example if the tone of an employee's emails is found to be antagonistic, or conversely may involve a more detailed consultation or individual coaching where an employee has clearly failed to grasp one of the key elements of the new policy.

If this type of informal approach does not have the desired effect and the employee repeats the same type of policy breach, formal disciplinary action will be needed. Equally, if the employee commits a deliberate or serious breach of the new policy, formal action will be appropriate.

Level of disciplinary action [9.41]

The type of disciplinary action that will be appropriate for a breach of the email/internet policy will depend on the seriousness of the breach, and the consequences of the breach (if any) for the organisation.

In determining the level of disciplinary action appropriate to an employee's breach of the new rules, managers should be reasonably flexible in their approach, particularly during the first two or three months following the implementation of the policy. Nevertheless managers should bear in mind that if an employee who has patently breached the rules is allowed to 'get away with it', the policy could be severely undermined. Thus common sense, patience and reasonableness should be applied to the application of the policy and rules, particularly in the early days after its introduction.

It should be borne in mind at all times that, irrespective of the potential seriousness of an employee's misconduct, and irrespective of the degree to which it is in breach of company policy, proper procedures should be followed. If they are not, any dismissal on account of a breach of the email/internet policy may be judged to be unfair by an employment tribunal (see **CHAPTER 11** for a full discussion of disciplinary procedures and dismissal).

Once the manager has completed the appropriate disciplinary procedure, including carrying out any relevant investigation and interviewing the employee to hear their version of events, it will be necessary to decide on the appropriate penalty. This will depend on a number of factors, including:

- the extent to which the employee had been properly informed about the new policy and rules;

- whether the employee's use of email or the internet involved dishonesty or any unlawful activity;

- the reasons put forward by the employee for their misuse of email or internet access, and any mitigating factors;

- whether the employee has had previous warnings for misconduct, and whether these warnings are still 'in date'.

Another key element will be whether there were any negative consequences following the employee's computer misuse, for example:

- damage or disruption to the computer network;

- a reduction in productivity;

- a breach of confidentiality or security;

- damage to the organisation's reputation;

- adverse press publicity;

- the creation of a hostile working environment;

- the risk of legal action against the company.

The manager should therefore aim to treat similar offences in the same way, thus ensuring consistency and fairness, whilst at the same time applying a reasonable degree of flexibility (within the parameters of the policy and the disciplinary procedure) depending on the individual circumstances of the specific instance of misuse and any mitigating factors.

In general, most instances of a first offence will not warrant dismissal, (unless the employee's breach of the policy constitutes gross misconduct – see **11.33** below) and will often be best handled by means of an informal discussion with the employee to raise their awareness of the policy and encourage adherence to it in the future. If this approach fails, formal disciplinary action can be taken following any further breach.

It is not advisable to take formal disciplinary action against an employee on account of a breach of policy for the sole purpose of setting an example to others, especially if the misdemeanour in question has occurred very soon after the introduction of the new policy or rules. If such action constitutes dismissal, it may be viewed as unreasonable by an employment tribunal.

Conclusion [9.42]

The introduction and implementation of a new or revised email and internet policy is a vital stage in the process of achieving protection for the business against computer misuse. The process needs time and full management commitment if it is to be successful.

It is essential that all employees who will be affected by the new policy and rules are properly consulted before the proposals are finalised, and that reasonable notice is given of the introduction of the policy and rules. If there is a unilateral imposition of new terms amending employees' contracts of employment, this could constitute a breach of contract leading potentially to claims for constructive dismissal. It is vital therefore that employees' agreement to the introduction of the new policy and rules is obtained. Communication (preferably including face-to-face briefings) and training will also play an important part.

Following implementation, the main responsibility will lie with line managers to ensure the rules are consistently enforced and that appropriate action is taken against any employee who is found to be in breach of the rules. This may be informal action in the first instance, but may ultimately involve the application of the organisation's disciplinary procedure.

If the various stages of implementation are properly thought through and sufficient time and commitment given to the processes of implementation, communication and enforcement, the introduction of the new policy, rules and any accompanying procedures governing employees' use of email and the internet will have a much greater chance of winning employee support and cooperation.

Questions and Answers [9.43]

Question

Who is the best person to be appointed to design a new email/internet policy?

Answer

The design of a new email/internet policy would normally be the joint responsibility of the HR and IT departments. IT specialists are well placed to provide the technical knowledge which will be essential for the practical implementation of the policy whilst HR professionals will have the underlying knowledge and skills to deal with the process of consultation, and the enforcement of the rules through the company's disciplinary procedure. Larger companies may consider setting up a working party or committee comprising senior managers from various departments to plan and implement the policy, whilst smaller organisations may prefer to nominate one senior manager to oversee the introduction of policies and rules. Whatever approach is taken, it is vital that any new policy on email and internet use should have a strong commitment from senior management.

Question

Should a new email/internet policy be introduced as part of employees' contracts of employment?

Answer

Given the potentially serious consequences of employees misuse of email and internet facilities, it is advisable for employers to elect to make their email and internet policy part of employees' contracts of employment. In this way there will be no doubt that all employees are subject to the terms contained in the policy and rules. If the policy is not given contractual force, an employee who fails to adhere to it will technically not be in breach of contract, thus making it more difficult for the employer to deal with problem conduct through their disciplinary procedure.

Question

Is it technically necessary to obtain employees' agreement to the introduction of an email/internet policy?

Answer

If the policy is to have contractual force, it is necessary to obtain employees' agreement to it, otherwise the employer will be acting in breach of contract the first time they try to enforce the policy, for example through disciplinary action. An employee forced to submit to a policy or rule to which they have not agreed could resign and argue that they had been constructively dismissed on account of the employer's unilateral imposition of new terms of employment.

Question

How should the employer go about obtaining employees' agreement to the new policy and rules, especially if it is felt that some employees may be reluctant to agree?

Answer

The key to the successful implementation of any new policy, procedure or rules is consultation, the structure of which will depend on the number of people employed in the organisation and whether any trade unions are recognised. Consultation must be genuine and not a sham exercise. Meetings with employees or their representatives should be held and employees' views, suggestions and objections taken on board. This should all take place before the content of the policy and rules are finalised.

Question

How much notice should the employer give the workforce of the introduction of the new email/internet policy?

Answer

Reasonable notice should be given of the introduction of the policy, ideally not less than three months. This notice should be given only on the conclusion of the process of consultation.

Question

How should the employer deal with any employees who, despite the process of consultation, have refused to agree to the new policy and rules?

Answer

Individual employees who refuse to agree to the new policy should be interviewed with a view to ascertaining any objections they may have, and overcoming those objections. Failing agreement, the employee should be interviewed again, and informed that a failure to agree to the policy and rules could lead to the termination of their existing contract of employment, and an offer of re-employment on the revised terms (i.e. revised to include the new policy and rules as part of the contract). If there is a continuing refusal to confirm agreement, the employer can proceed to take this course of action, giving appropriate notice of termination and offering a new contract on the revised terms, which, if accepted, will run consecutively with the old contract without any loss of continuity of service or statutory rights.

Question

What is constructive dismissal and could an employer's introduction of a restrictive email/internet policy lead to constructive dismissal claims from employees?

Answer

Constructive dismissal occurs where the employer takes some action which fundamentally breaches the employee's contract of employment and the employee resigns promptly as a direct result of the breach. The practical effect is that the employee feels the situation is intolerable to the extent that there is no alternative but to resign. The unilateral introduction of a major new policy and rules which restrict employees in their activities or take away a privilege they enjoyed previously could constitute a breach of contract. It is thus essential to obtain employees' agreement before the policy is introduced.

Question

Who should hold the responsibility for the implementation of the policy and rules on email and internet use?

Answer

Normally, HR department would assume the role of advisor to line managers in implementing the policy, whilst IT department would be the source of support and information regarding any technical aspects of implementation or monitoring. Line managers, however, should hold the main responsibility for implementing the policy for the staff within their departments.

Question

How should employers go about communicating the new policy and rules to employees?

Answer

The effective communication of an email/internet policy is essential in order to create employee awareness and raise the profile of the whole issue of cyberliability. There are a number of ways of promoting the new policy and rules, including sending a hard-copy to all employees together with an explanatory letter, transmission by email, publication on the organisation's intranet and/or in an in-house magazine and placing posters on notice-boards. Probably the most important aspect of communication is to set up team briefings throughout the organisation to provide employees with detail of the policy and its rationale on a face-to-face basis, and provide the opportunity for them to ask questions. There will also be a need for regular reminders to employees so that the issue of proper use of email and the internet is reinforced on an ongoing basis.

Question

What type of training will be necessary upon implementation of the new policy?

Answer

There will be a need for training in how to use the equipment and systems and in the new policy itself. Training in the policy should be designed to familiarise employees with every aspect of the policy, the specific nature of the rules, and how any procedures will be applied. This training should include information about the dangers posed by careless or unauthorised computer use. Training should also be designed to explain clearly what the penalties will be for various types of breaches. Induction training for new employees should also be adjusted to incorporate the new policy and rules.

Question

How should line managers approach the question of enforcement of the email and internet policy?

Answer

Enforcement of the policy is a line management responsibility, rather than being the sole territory of HR department whose role should be to provide advice and support. In cases of minor breaches, the issue can usually be dealt with informally by means of a private discussion between the employee and their line manager to point out the breach and remind the employee of the rules. If the employee subsequently repeats the same type of policy breach, formal disciplinary action will be needed. Equally, if the employee commits a deliberate or serious breach of the new policy, formal disciplinary action will be appropriate.

Question

Should line managers apply the new policy rigidly during the first few weeks or months following its implementation, or should some tolerance and leniency by applied?

Answer

Line managers should be reasonably flexible in their approach, particularly during the first two or three months following the implementation of the policy. Nevertheless it should be borne in mind that if an employee who has patently breached the rules is allowed to 'get away with it', the policy could be severely undermined. The manager should aim to treat similar offences in the same way, thus ensuring consistency and fairness, whilst at the same time applying a reasonable degree of flexibility (within the parameters of the policy and the disciplinary procedure) depending on the individual circumstances of the specific instance of misuse and any mitigating factors. In general, most instances of a first offence will not warrant dismissal, (unless the employee's breach of the policy clearly constitutes gross misconduct).

10 Security and Tackling Email and Internet Abuse

Introduction [10.1]

It has often been said that sending an email is like sending a postcard – anyone can read it. Certainly the issue of security of computer systems and company information is one that will concern employers who will wish to take various precautionary and preventative measures to deter (for example) hacking, inappropriate use of email and the internet by employees, breaches of confidentiality and virus infection.

Technical Security Systems [10.2]

Given the high level of investment in hardware, software and employee expertise and training to which many employers will have committed, the question of system security will inevitably be an important management priority.

Security of hardware [10.3]

Employers should have rules in place to ensure employees take proper care of all company property, including both office-based and laptop computers. A typical rule might read:

> 'All employees and other workers who use Company computers, including portable and laptop computers, must take adequate steps to protect the equipment from damage and theft. Upon leaving the Company's employment, all such equipment must be returned to the Company in good condition either before or on the employee's last working day. The Company reserves the right to remove any computer equipment from any worker at any time during their employment.'

Where expensive computer equipment is allocated to specific individuals and especially in organisations where equipment such as laptops is sometimes taken out of the workplace, it may be advisable to ask all users to sign a document indicating that they accept responsibility for the equipment.

Document assigning responsibility to employees   **[10.4]**

Such a document might take the following form:

'Name: Department:

Equipment type: Serial number:

[Software]:

I confirm that I am the authorised user of the equipment [and software] listed above. In signing this document I accept full responsibility for the above equipment [and software]. I undertake to take all reasonable steps to protect the equipment [and software] from damage and theft at all times, whether on the Company's premises or elsewhere.

Signed:

Date:'

Security of software   **[10.5]**

A similar provision should be implemented to protect the organisation's software. One important measure of protection would be to implement a strict rule that only software acquired by or approved by the organisation's IT manager (or other appropriate person) may be used on company computers. By banning all software belonging to employees from being loaded on to the company's computers, the risk of viruses entering the system can be reduced. There is the added advantage that the possibility of pirated software inadvertently (or deliberately!) being introduced to the employer's system can be limited, thereby decreasing the likelihood of a breach of copyright law (see **CHAPTER 2** for a full discussion of the dangers of copyright infringement).

It is advisable for employers to acquire software that will perform a check to detect any unlicensed software loaded on to any of the company's computers.

Sample rules on the security of software   **[10.6]**

Further rules relating to the security of software could read as follows:

'All employees of the Company who have access to company computers, including laptops, must comply with the following rules. Employees must ensure that:

- no unauthorised software or personally-owned software is loaded or run on any company computer;

- any disks to be used on a company computer are virus-checked by IT department before use;

- company-owned computers are not used by any unauthorised person;

- any computer entrusted to an employee's care is secured or locked away when not in use;

- back-up procedures are followed at all times;

- passwords are kept confidential and changed at regular intervals;

- work-stations are not left logged on and unattended at any time, even for a few minutes.'

Screening software [10.7]

Software is available commercially to carry out a number of useful security and screening functions. Employers may well consider the investment in such systems to be worthwhile, although no system should be introduced arbitrarily or until after proper thought has been given to the company's business needs and what type of software will best meet those needs.

Software applications have the ability to perform a variety of functions. In general, email monitoring software is used to check for viruses and monitor for inappropriate content.

More sophisticated software is available which records users' actual key strokes and which can, if required, capture everything displayed on an employee's computer monitor. Employers may, however, wish to consider carefully whether such intrusive surveillance is necessary for the efficient and effective running of their business. Employment relationships must be based to a considerable extent on trust if they are to be harmonious and productive, and any monitoring that invades an employee's privacy to the extent of recording their every movement may be perceived as excessive, unreasonable and unfair. There are also implications under the *Human Rights Act 1998* (see **CHAPTER 7**), the *Lawful Business Practice Regulations 2000 (SI 2000 No 2699)* (see **CHAPTER 6** and the *Data Protection Act 1998* (see **CHAPTER 4**).

Functions of software packages [10.8]

Instead of routinely recording the details of all computer users' activities, employers may prefer to consider software packages that achieve some of the following objectives:

- to block messages containing confidential information and thus prevent them from being sent outside the company;

- to examine the content of messages in order to pick up (for example) non-business email messages, junk email and C.V's;

- to highlight certain undesirable words ('trigger words') that may indicate sexually explicit, racially biased or otherwise offensive material;

- to identify images that may suggest a pornographic web-site has been accessed;

- to block access to certain defined internet sites, for example 'adult' sites and those belonging to recruitment agencies;

- to prevent material being downloaded from the internet such as unlicensed software;

- to monitor the size of files attached to emails and possibly block the downloading or uploading of files larger than a defined number of megabytes which could otherwise clog up the employer's system. Any file that is too large can be automatically removed from the system with an automatic message being forwarded to the sender.

Informing employees about software monitoring [10.9]

Employees should of course be made aware via the organisation's email/internet policy what software monitoring systems are installed, how they work and why they are necessary for the business. It should also be made clear what action management will take in circumstances where the monitoring software identifies a problem. This in turn creates the need for managers to be trained in how the software packages work, the types of problems they are designed to highlight and the appropriate courses of action to take following the identification of a possible problem.

A full discussion of software packages and their technical specifications is outside the scope of this book, and employers should seek advice from technical experts on the subject.

Preventing Unauthorised Access [10.10]

The *Computer Misuse Act 1990* makes it a criminal offence for an individual to secure unauthorised access to a computer system or to computer material in certain circumstances, or to modify the contents of a computer system without authority. 'Unauthorised modification' of computer material includes deliberate erasure or corruption of programmes or data, modifying or destroying a system file or another user's file or the addition of any programme or data to the computer's contents. It is also an offence under the *Computer Misuse Act 1990* to spread a computer virus (see **10.23** below).

'Unauthorised access' for the purposes of the Act is defined as:

'access of any kind by a person to any programme or data held on a computer when such a person is not him or herself entitled to control access to the programme or the data and does not have consent from any person who is so entitled.'

Employees who use the system for unauthorised purposes [10.11]

The Act was designed primarily to deal with the problems of external hacking, and therefore does not necessarily help employers to deal with employees who have permission to use their employer's computer network, but abuse their position and use the system for unauthorised purposes. For example, in the case of *Director of Public Prosecutions v Bignall (High Court Queen's Bench Division) 16.05.97*, police officers were prosecuted under the Act following their access for private reasons to data held on the Police National Computer. The prosecution failed, however, because the police officers had authority to access the data for legitimate police work, and their access to it could therefore not be described as 'unauthorised access'. This was the case even though the police officers did not have permission to access the data for private purposes.

The outcome might be different, however, if an employee gained access to information in a part of the employer's computer system which they were expressly prohibited from accessing. These were the circumstances in the case of *Denco Ltd v Joinson EAT [1991] ICR 172* in which the employee, who had been summarily dismissed for unauthorised computer access, brought a complaint of unfair dismissal to an employment tribunal. The employee had authority to gain access to certain files held on his employer's computer system, but was debarred from accessing other parts of the computer system. However, having learned the password for access to another part of the computer system from his daughter who worked for the same firm, he deliberately used it to gain access knowing that he was not entitled to see the sensitive information that was held there. When his activities were discovered, he was dismissed, even though his motive for accessing the data was one of curiosity and not malice. The EAT held that the dismissal was fair in all the circumstances and accepted that conduct involving deliberate access to computer data without authority amounted to gross misconduct justifying summary dismissal. The EAT also commented, however, that employers should take appropriate steps to make it clear to employees that any unauthorised access to information held on computer will be regarded as gross misconduct.

It is therefore very important for employers to have clear policies governing who is, and is not, authorised to gain access to computer data, and to modify the contents of files or programmes.

Firewalls [10.12]

Clearly the risk of theft, destruction or alteration of important company data is a very serious matter. However, would-be external hackers can be kept at bay to a great extent by using 'firewalls' and other security technology. The purpose of a firewall is to provide protection against unauthorised access to computer systems and receipt of unwanted correspondence. Technical advice should be sought from computer experts on this subject.

Internal security [10.13]

Realistically, employers are more likely to suffer the fate of computer information being tampered with by someone from within the organisation than from outside hackers. There are many reasons why an employee may wish to cause harm to their employer (or ex-employer) for example out of revenge for perceived unfair treatment such as dismissal or redundancy selection. This aspect of security calls for effective management rather than the introduction of complex technological systems. Sensible precautions include:

- careful reference checking at the recruitment stage for all employees, and in particular those who will have access in the course of their work to confidential or sensitive company data held on computer, and those who deal with customers and suppliers;

- sensible decisions on access to data and authority to use or amend data, based on the tangible needs of employees' jobs;

- disconnection of the floppy disk drives to prevent information from leaving the company;

- rigorous control of access to computer data through a system of passwords (see **10.15** below) and accompanying rules.

The British Standard for Information Security [10.14]

The British Standard for information security management, BS7799, originally published in 1995, has since been revised and is published in two parts:

BS7799–1:   1999Code of Practice for information security management

BS7799–2:   1999Specification for information security management systems

Part 1 is designed as a reference document for people who have responsibility for the development, implementation and maintenance of security within their organisation. Part 2 provides a framework for organisations that wish to achieve BS7799 certification and sets standards against which an employer's security management system would be measured in order to achieve certification.

Passwords [10.15]

One of the simplest and cheapest methods of ensuring the protection of confidential or sensitive company information is to formulate and implement a rigorous system of employee passwords.

Rules should be devised for employees governing the choosing of a password and for the regular changing of passwords. There should also be a clear written rule forbidding the disclosure of passwords to any unauthorised person which should be enforced consistently. Clearly those in managerial and supervisory positions need to set a good example with regard to the disclosure of passwords by adhering to the rule themselves and ensuring that no exceptions are made to the policy by others. Otherwise the password system will quickly become ineffective and fall into disrepute.

Company policy on passwords [10.16]

Specifically, company policy should include the following rules and guidelines for employees issued with passwords:

- passwords must not be disclosed to any person unless written authority is first obtained from the employee's line manager;

- passwords must be changed at least every [two weeks, four weeks, six weeks] and more often if necessary;

- passwords chosen must not be obvious, for example the name of a partner, house, dog or favourite hobby, etc.

Model clause on passwords [10.17]

A clause for insertion to the company's computer policy could read:

'Passwords must be kept confidential at all times and should not be disclosed to anyone else unless prior written authority to do so is obtained from the relevant line manager. The line manager should be notified immediately if there is a suspicion that an employee is using a colleague's password. As a further precaution, employees should change their passwords regularly and no less frequently than once a month.'

Making employees responsible [10.18]

Having password-protected each employee's email address, it may also be advantageous to make each individual employee responsible for all emails sent from that address. This will act as a disincentive for employees in terms of password disclosure. An employee who knows that they will be held responsible for all emails sent from their computer, including any 'ghost' emails, will be more likely to think twice before revealing their password.

Encryption [10.19]

Due to the fact that email is not a secure or confidential method of communicating information, it should not be used for the transmission of confidential information in the normal course of events. Instead messages can be encrypted. Encryption simply means the process of translating normal text into a series of letters and/or numbers which can be deciphered only by someone with the correct password or key. It is a useful tool to prevent outsiders from reading confidential, sensitive or private data which is sent over the internet or by email, or even for data stored on floppy disks.

Encryption software is available which can provide solid protection to companies that regularly use email and the internet to transmit or receive information.

Various organisations provide cryptography services. 'Cryptography' is the science of codes and ciphers and is an essential tool for organisations that engage in electronic commerce. Cryptography can be used as the basis for electronic signatures (see **10.21** below).

The Electronic Communications Act 2000 [10.20]

The *Electronic Communications Act 2000* was implemented to facilitate electronic commerce and in particular to permit businesses and individuals who wish to do so to communicate electronically with the Government rather than by conventional means. The Act introduced a voluntary 'approvals' scheme for providers of cryptography services who can apply to be included in the register of approved providers. Providers on the register will have been independently assessed against specified quality standards. Registration is voluntary, however, and there is nothing to prevent providers who are not on the register from providing cryptography services. Various organisations provide cryptography services

Electronic signatures [10.21]

An electronic signature (or e-signature) consists of data appended to other data that performs the same function as a hand-written signature, i.e. it indicates the source of a document or file. E-signatures can take many forms, for example a scanned in signature, the electronic representation of a hand-written signature, a unique sequence of characters or a signature created by cryptographic means.

The two key purposes of any e-signature are to:

- confirm that the communication comes from whom it purports to come from (this is known as 'authenticity'); *and*

- establish that the communication has not been tampered with (this is known as 'integrity').

Electronic signatures are admissible in evidence in legal proceedings in relation to both the authenticity of a communication and its integrity.

Public key cryptography [10.22]

A form of cryptography, known as 'public key cryptography', can be used to provide a secure electronic signature. Public key cryptography uses two distinct but related keys (known as a key pair). The keys are both large numbers with special mathematical properties. The first key, called the private key (i.e. it is known only to its owner) is used to 'lock' a document, and it does this by scrambling the information contained within the document. The other key, called the public key, is used to 'unlock' the document. Anyone with access to the public key can therefore check the signature and so verify whether the communication was signed by someone with access to the private key. Clearly if only one person has access to the private key, it can be proved that it was that individual who signed the message. It is also possible by this method to check that the content of the message has not been changed.

Public key cryptography can also be used the other way round in order to keep a communication secret. In this case, the sender of the message uses the intended recipient's public key to lock the message and the recipient can only unlock it by using the private key. No outside party would be able to read the message unless they had access to the private key.

Virus Protection [10.23]

One of the most common and most serious sources of potential damage to an employer's computer network and data is the introduction of a computer virus. A virus can be transmitted from software or other files downloaded from the internet, from attachments to email messages and from floppy disks. Viruses can spread frighteningly quickly from one computer to another, and can rapidly infect the whole network, damaging (and possibly destroying) both software and hardware. At worst a virus can destroy everything that is loaded on to the employer's computer system. Anti-virus software can provide considerable protection against virus protection provided it is used consistently and correctly. Firewalls can also be installed to provide protection against unauthorised access to the system and receipt of unwanted correspondence (see **10.12** above).

The deliberate spreading of viruses is an offence under the *Computer Misuse Act 1990*, but that will not stop the accidental introduction of a virus from an unsuspecting employee working in an organisation with no clear rules on email and internet use. Every employer has a responsibility to prevent viruses from spreading to other computer users. It follows that, in order to minimise the risk of virus transmission to customers and other contacts, employers should adopt a policy of virus checking everything that is to be sent out of the company by email. Otherwise the employer could find themselves liable for any damage caused to another company on account of negligent virus transmission.

Disclaimer statement for outgoing emails [10.24]

In addition, it is advisable to include a statement in relation to virus transmission in every outgoing email. Such a statement could read:

> 'Although [company name] has taken steps to ensure that this email and attachments are free from any virus, we advise that, in keeping with good computing practice, the recipient should run a check to ensure they are actually virus-free'.

Source of viruses [10.25]

The greatest risk of virus infection for employers lies in software and other files being downloaded from the internet by employees. By banning the downloading of software and other files on to individual computers and prohibiting personally-owned software from being loaded on to the company's computers, the risk of viruses entering the system can be substantially reduced.

Rules to prevent virus infection **[10.26]**

Employers should therefore implement strict rules stating that:

- only software acquired by or approved by the organisation's IT manager (or other appropriate person) may be used on company computers;

- no employee may download software [or other files] from the internet before first obtaining clearance from the IT manager;

- no employee may install a floppy disk on to their PC that has been used outside the organisation (including in the employee's home) unless the disk has first been virus-checked by IT department;

- employees should not open email attachments from unknown senders, and even where the sender is known, care should be taken.

Conclusion [10.27]

The security of computer systems and company information is inevitably an issue of major concern for employers. It is clearly in every employer's interests to take appropriate precautionary and preventative measures to deter (for example) hacking, inappropriate use of email and the internet by employees, breaches of confidentiality and virus infection.

Security measures will need incorporate rules for employees on taking care of hardware and rules banning unauthorised software. Screening software may be introduced to prevent or detect specific problem areas.

Other areas of protection will involve implementing an effective system of passwords and using encryption to protect sensitive or highly confidential information that is sent by email.

Questions and Answers [10.28]

Question

What steps can an employer take to protect its computer hardware from misuse?

Answer

Employers should introduce rules to ensure employees take proper care of all company property, including both office-based and laptop

---

computers. In addition, where expensive computer equipment is allocated to specific individuals and especially where equipment such as laptops is sometimes taken out of the workplace, it may be advisable to ask all users to sign a document indicating that they accept responsibility for the equipment.

Question

What measures can be taken to minimise the risk of unauthorised software causing problems for the organisation?

Answer

Rules on the use of software should be devised and communicated to all employees who have access to company computers, including laptops. Such rules should, for example, ban personal software from being loaded on to any company computer or downloaded from the internet, stipulate that any disks to be used on a company computers are virus-checked by IT department before use and advise employees that any computer entrusted to their care must not be used by any unauthorised person.

Question

What type of screening software might help the employer to prevent abuse of email and the internet?

Answer

Software applications have the ability to perform a variety of functions including (for example) checking for viruses and monitoring emails and internet sites for inappropriate content. Proper thought should be given to the company's business needs and the type of software that will best meet those needs, and advice sought from technical experts.

Question

What is the *Computer Misuse Act 1990* and how is it relevant to employers?

Answer

The *Computer Misuse Act 1990* makes it a criminal offence for an individual to secure unauthorised access to a computer in certain circumstances, or to modify the contents of a computer system without authority. It also makes the deliberate or negligent transmission of a computer virus an offence.

Employers should therefore ensure appropriate preventative measures are in place to prevent security breaches and virus infection.

Question

What steps can an employer take to prevent deliberate abuse of computer systems by employees?

Answer

Employers should always check references when recruiting employees whose jobs will involve access to confidential or sensitive company data, make sensible decisions on appropriate levels of access and authority and introduce a rigorously controlled system of passwords. This aspect of security calls for effective management rather than the introduction of complex technological systems.

Question

What specific rules are advisable in relation to the use of passwords?

Answer

Company policy should state that passwords must not be disclosed to any person without express authority, that they should be changed at least every month and that passwords chosen must not be obvious, for example the name of the employee's partner. Management should make sure that the rules are applied consistently throughout the organisation.

Question

What is 'encryption'?

Answer

Encryption is the process of translating normal text into a series of letters and/or numbers which can be deciphered only by someone with the correct password or key. It is a useful tool to prevent outsiders from reading confidential, sensitive or private data which is sent over the internet or by email, or for data stored on floppy disks.

Question

What is an electronic signature and what is it used for?

Answer

Electronic signatures (or e-signatures) can take many forms, for example a scanned in signature, the electronic representation of a hand-written signature, a unique sequence of characters or a signature created by cryptographic means. The two key purposes of any e-signature are to confirm the authenticity of the sender of the communication and establish that the message has not been tampered with.

Question

What can employers do to minimise the risk of viruses being imported into their computer system?

Answer

The greatest risk of virus infection lies in software and other files being downloaded from the internet. By banning the downloading of software and other files from the internet and prohibiting personally-owned software from being loaded on to the company's computers, the risk of viruses entering the system can be substantially reduced. Other precautions include a rule stipulating that floppy disks that have been used outside the organisation must not be installed on company PC's unless the disk has first been virus-checked by IT department and restrictions on the opening of email attachments.

11 Disciplinary Procedures and Dismissal

Introduction [11.1]

Where an employee is found to have been misusing their employer's telephones, email facilities or internet access, the matter should be dealt with under the employer's disciplinary procedure. This means appropriate warnings being given to the employee, with the possibility of eventual dismissal if the employee continues to misuse the employer's facilities. Dismissal for a first offence may also be appropriate but only if the employee's behaviour is of a very serious nature, amounting to gross misconduct (see **11.33** below).

It is essential in practical terms for employers to devise and implement clear disciplinary procedures, and to ensure that these cover potential misuses and abuses of the employer's communications systems, including the telephone network, email usage and internet facilities. Disciplinary rules and the disciplinary procedure would normally form part of employees' contracts of employment, and a copy should ideally be given to every employee, for example in a company handbook.

The ACAS Code of Practice on Disciplinary and Grievance Procedures, updated and re-issued in September 2000, provides excellent practical guidance on the handling of disciplinary matters. Paragraph 5 of section 1 suggests that disciplinary rules should cover (amongst other things) misuse of computer facilities such as email and the internet.

Provided therefore employers make it clear to employees what their rules are regarding access to email and the internet, and any limitations to be imposed on the extent and purpose for which they may use these facilities, the normal principles inherent in disciplinary procedures and fair dismissal can be applied.

Consistency between disciplinary rules and policies on acceptable use of email and internet facilities [11.2]

Where policies are in place governing what is and is not acceptable use of email and internet facilities, the employer should ensure that the content of their disciplinary rules and procedures is consistent with the provisions contained in the policy. It is of little use, for example, to state in a policy document that playing computer games during working time is not permitted, unless the sanctions for this type of conduct are clearly laid down in the disciplinary procedure. A policy will have little authority or effect if the penalties for disregarding it or acting in breach of it are not clearly specified and consistently imposed (whilst still taking into account the individual circumstances surrounding each case).

This may seem, at first glance, to be a very harsh approach. Nevertheless it is better for employers and employees alike that employees understand fully not only what the rules are on use of computer facilities at work, but also what the outcome will be if they choose to break the rules. In any event, knowledge of any relevant rules on the part of an employee is an essential ingredient if a dismissal for misuse of the employer's facilities is to be fair in law.

The Purpose of Disciplinary Rules and Procedures [11.3]

The key purposes of disciplinary rules and procedures should be to:

- set down a framework defining and (where appropriate) limiting employees' conduct at work;

- specify the consequences of different forms of misconduct for the employee;

- provide guidance for managers who may have to handle disciplinary matters so that they are able do so in a constructive, consistent and reasonable manner.

In light of the many complex and precarious issues surrounding employees' use of email and the internet at work, it may be advisable for employers to develop and implement a special sub-section to form part of their disciplinary procedure setting out the kinds of activity that are not permitted and the disciplinary penalties for breach of the rules. An example follows below in **11.36** below, and some sample policies, including examples of rules, is provided in **8.70** above.

Disciplinary rules [11.4]

Under the *Employment Rights Act 1996, s 3,* employers who have 20 or more employees are obliged to provide written details of their disciplinary rules to employees. This threshold of 20 is to be abolished in the future, probably in October 2004. Current provisions do not create a statutory obligation on employers to put disciplinary rules in place (although it is a sound idea to do so) but means that where rules exist, they must be given to employees in writing. This too will change as from October 2004.

Disciplinary rules should make it clear to employees what type of conduct is, and is not acceptable in the workplace, and in particular should specify the types of behaviour that will be regarded as misconduct leading to disciplinary action. The penalties that are likely to be imposed following a breach of the rules must be clearly specified, for example a disciplinary warning, suspension, demotion, dismissal etc.

Devising rules [11.5]

There is no law that defines the type of conduct which an employer may regard as misconduct. Every employer's business needs are different, and it is therefore up to each individual employer to devise and implement their own rules. Rules should, of course, cover all aspects of employees' conduct relevant to the business (for example absenteeism, safety, disobedience), and not only use of the company's communications systems.

It may be advisable, however, in light of the potentially serious consequences of employees' misuse of computer systems to devise a set of rules specifically to cover the use of telephones, email and the internet (see **8.70** above). These could cover not only the purposes for which these facilities may be used, but also the extent to which they should be used.

The ACAS Code of Practice on Disciplinary and Grievance Procedures recommends that:

- Rules should be set out in writing, and should be clear and concise.

- Rules should be made readily available to all workers, for example in handbooks or on company intranet sites, and ideally a copy should be given to every worker.

- Rules should also be explained orally and should form part of any induction programme for new employees.

- Management should take all possible steps to make sure that all workers know and understand the rules, and make suitable provision for any employees who have a disability or whose first language is not English.

- Rules should be checked regularly and updated where necessary.

Communicating the rules [11.6]

It is the responsibility of each employer to make sure that all rules, and any changes to the rules, are clearly communicated to all employees. It would be viewed as unfair and unreasonable for an employer to discipline an employee for breaking a rule governing, for example, internet access, if the rule in question had not been brought to the employee's attention through proper written documentation.

If new policies, procedures or rules are being introduced as part of employees' contracts, or if major changes are being made to existing rules which form part of employees' contracts, the employer should implement the new rules or the changes to the rules only after proper consultation with employees or their representatives. This is because changes to an employee's contract can only lawfully be made with the agreement of both parties, otherwise the employer may be acting in breach of contract when they attempt to enforce the policy or rules. The subject of introducing new policies, rules and procedures lawfully is covered fully in **CHAPTER 9**.

Flexibility in the application of the rules [11.7]

Although rules should be clear and specific, they should nevertheless be designed so as to incorporate a reasonable degree of flexibility and discretion for management so that individual circumstances can be taken into account in dealing with an employee who has in some way misused the organisation's email or internet facilities. This is preferable to a rigid application of the rules irrespective of the individual circumstances or any mitigating factors.

Furthermore, If management adopt an approach of rigidly applying a policy to dismiss staff for particular conduct without consideration of all the individual circumstances, this could result in dismissals being unfair. There is no rule in law that suggests it is fair to apply a policy rigidly to every single breach of an employer's policy without investigation of the individual circumstances and the application of a fair procedure.

In the case of *Dunn v. IBM United Kingdom Ltd [1998] Case No 2305087/97*, the employee succeeded in a claim for unfair dismissal at tribunal following his summary dismissal for accessing pornography and other non-business-related material on the internet and making printouts of downloaded pictures, activities which he had admitted to his manager when challenged.

Despite the fact that the employee's activities involved the viewing and downloading of pornographic material, the tribunal took the view that there was no indisputable breach of company policy which automatically warranted the employee's summary dismissal. It followed therefore that the dismissal did not fall within the range of reasonable responses open to the employer.

Managers should bear in mind therefore that, irrespective of the potential seriousness of an employee's misconduct, and irrespective of whether it is or is not in breach of company policy, proper procedures must be followed otherwise a dismissal may be judged to be unfair by an employment tribunal (unfair dismissal is dealt with below in **11.41**).

Although employers should not *automatically* dismiss an employee who is found to have breached a company policy, a policy could be severely undermined if an employee who has patently breached the rules is allowed to 'get away with it'. Thus common sense and reasonableness should be applied to the application of any policy.

One particular difficulty with applying disciplinary procedures to misconduct involving access to the internet is the ease with which it is possible to access a particular site accidentally. It is easy to make a mistake whilst performing an internet search and managers should not automatically assume that an employee has done anything wrong if it comes to light that they have viewed an inappropriate site.

A similar point in relation to email is that, whilst it is legitimate for employers to seek to control their employees' use of this facility, employees cannot realistically be expected to control what emails (or attachments) are sent to them by others, especially those from outside the organisation. No reasonable employer would penalise an employee for receiving unsolicited mail (otherwise every employee would have a disciplinary record!) and it follows that it would not be reasonable to discipline an employee just because they had received unsolicited email of an inappropriate character.

It would be beneficial for employers to introduce a specific mechanism for employees to declare or report (either to their line manager or to a nominated individual within the company) any inappropriate email messages sent to their computer. In this way, the employee need not fear disciplinary action at a later date if the email message is detected on the company's computer system.

Another approach that can be taken towards application of the rules is to take into account the amount of time and resources that are being used by employees who choose to use their employer's communications systems for personal or private purposes in contradiction of any laid down policies or rules. Clearly five minutes spent reading an email sent by a friend is a different matter from half an hour spent concocting three pages of jokes with a view to emailing these out to every employee in the workplace.

When devising disciplinary rules, it is particularly important to make sure that employees understand clearly what types of offences are regarded by the employer as sufficiently serious to constitute gross misconduct, leading potentially to summary dismissal (see **11.35** below).

Determining whether an employee's use of email and the internet constitutes misconduct [11.8]

Any deliberate or negligent misuse of an employer's property or facilities could legitimately be regarded as a disciplinary matter by the employer. This would be the case provided the employee was aware that such conduct could amount to a disciplinary offence.

Whether or not an employee's use of email and the internet constitutes misconduct (or gross misconduct – see **11.36** below) will depend on a number of factors.

- whether the employer has introduced a policy and rules covering uses and misuses of email and the internet;

- the terms of the employee's contract of employment;

- the extent to which the employee was aware of the policy and rules;

- how the employee's conduct is viewed in light of the rules, for example half an hour spent surfing the net during a lunch hour should not be viewed in the same manner as many hours spent surfing during working time;

- how other employees who have committed similar offences have been dealt with;

- whether the employee's use of email or the internet involved dishonesty or any unlawful activity;

- the reasons put forward by the employee for their misuse of email or internet access, and any mitigating factors;

- whether there is evidence to suggest that the employee was not to blame, for example, if sexually explicit pictures found on a computer were sent to the employee as an email attachment against their wishes;

- the context of the employee's conduct;

- whether the employee has previously breached the rules, whether or not warnings were given and whether these warnings are still 'in date';

- the employee's job and level of seniority;

- the employee's length of service and general record;

- the impact any misuse has had or might have on the organisation's reputation, for example if the press has published a story about pornographic images being transmitted within the organisation.

Disciplinary procedures [11.9]

A disciplinary procedure should be structured so as to allow managers to deal fairly, consistently and lawfully with employees who breach the company's rules. The procedure should always have as its principle aim improvement in employees' conduct, rather than punishment. Nevertheless it is important to set out clearly the penalties that will apply in the event that an employee breaches the rules.

Matters that should be incorporated in the disciplinary procedure include:

- a clear picture of the types of disciplinary action that may be taken following certain types of misconduct;

- who is authorised to take the various forms of disciplinary action;

- the need for management to investigate any alleged infringement of the rules before taking any action against the employee;

- a statement that any employee known or suspected to have breached company rules will be informed in writing of the complaint against them;

- an opportunity for the employee to put forward their version of events at an interview before any decision is taken as to whether to impose a disciplinary penalty, and what level of penalty to impose;

- the opportunity for the employee to be accompanied at the interview (if they wish) by a fellow worker or trade union official of their choice (as required by the Employment Relations Act 1999, s 10 – see **11.18** below);

- a statement that employees will be given an explanation for any penalty imposed;

- the opportunity for the employee to appeal against any disciplinary decision, including a decision to dismiss, and an indication of how appeals should be raised.

Other elements inherent in fair disciplinary procedures include the need for confidentiality, consistency and, above all, adherence to the terms of the organisation's own disciplinary procedure. Confidential records should always be kept of disciplinary interviews held, warnings issued and any other matters concerned with the formal discipline of an employee.

Forthcoming changes to the law on disciplinary procedures [11.9a]

At the time of writing, proposals are in the pipeline (under the *Employment Act 2002*) to impose a new duty on all employers (including small employers) to introduce and operate minimum statutory dispute resolution procedures.

The minimum procedures will be a statutory dismissal and disciplinary procedure (DDP) and a statutory grievance procedure (GP). It is expected that these provisions will come into force in October 2004. Under the proposed DDP, all employers will be obliged (as a minimum set of standards) to:

- set out the employee's alleged misconduct in writing and give or send a copy to the employee, inviting the employee to attend a meeting to discuss the matter;

- hold a meeting to enable both parties to explain their cases prior to any disciplinary action being taken. The employee in turn will be under a duty to take all reasonable steps to attend the meeting;

- allow a right of appeal against any decision to impose disciplinary action or dismissal.

Any dismissal implemented without the correct application of the DDP will be automatically unfair (provided of course that the non-application is the employer's fault). For example, if an employee has not been invited to attend a meeting, or has not been given written details of any alleged misconduct prior to the meeting, this will render a subsequent dismissal automatically unfair. However, compliance with aspects of the employer's in-house disciplinary procedure that go beyond what is required in the DDP will no longer be an absolute requirement for a dismissal to be fair – provided the employer can show that the application of their own more detailed procedure would have made no difference to the decision to dismiss, and provided the employer can show that they acted fairly and reasonably in an overall sense.

The ACAS Code of Practice on Disciplinary and Grievance Procedures [11.10]

The advice and guidance contained in the ACAS Code of Practice on Disciplinary and Grievance Procedures, published in September 2000, is invaluable as an aid to the fair and lawful handling of disciplinary matters. The Code emphasises that disciplinary procedures should not be viewed primarily as a means of imposing penalties, but instead as a way of encouraging employees whose conduct is unsatisfactory to improve.

Although the ACAS Code (like other Codes of Practice) is not legally binding, a failure to follow the principles it contains can be taken into account by an employment tribunal in assessing whether an employee has been dismissed unfairly. The practical effect of this is that if the employer has acted in a way that is contrary to the provisions in the Code, it is likely that they will lose the case.

Investigating Alleged Breaches [11.11]

It is inherent in the notion of fairness that, before an employee is disciplined (or dismissed), a fair and thorough investigation should be carried out into their alleged misconduct. Unless and until all the facts relevant to the case are established, the manager dealing with the employee will not be in a position to judge whether the employee's behaviour potentially constitutes a breach of the rules justifying disciplinary action.

The likely outcome of dismissal without a proper investigation [11.12]

Furthermore, if an employee is dismissed without a proper investigation having first been carried out, this will almost certainly have the effect of rendering the dismissal unfair (see **11.45** below) as occurred in the following case:

Case Study [11.13]

Parr v Derwentside District Council [1998] Case No 2501507/98

Facts

Mr Parr was dismissed following his employer's discovery that he had used the company's internet facility to access sexually explicit material. There was evidence that he had visited a particular site to view pictures and moving images on more than one occasion. At a disciplinary interview, Mr Parr claimed that he had accessed the website by mistake, and had returned to it only because he was concerned about the ease with which it was possible for children to get to the site.

Mr Parr's employer did not, however, believe his version of events and chose to dismiss him for gross misconduct. In making this decision, they took into account that, as a local authority, they had a duty to provide a high standard of public service and this in turn required a high level of moral integrity amongst its employees. Mr Parr brought a claim for unfair dismissal to an employment tribunal.

Findings

The employment tribunal dismissed Mr Parr's claim. One of the key reasons for the finding of fair dismissal was that there was evidence that the employer had investigated Mr Parr's conduct thoroughly, efficiently and

---

329

objectively. Following the investigation, they had formed the view on reasonable grounds that he was guilty of breaching an established code of conduct, and was also in breach of his duty of trust and confidence towards the employer. This was despite Mr Parr's version of events which the employer was entitled to disbelieve, given the evidence against him.

Implications

The importance of a proper investigation was evident in this case and was one of the key factors leading to the tribunal's finding of fair dismissal.

Guidelines for investigating misuse of email or the internet [11.14]

In investigating an employee's alleged misuse of email or internet facilities, the employer should do the following:

- check on whether the employee has received previous warnings for similar misconduct (or other types of misconduct), and if so whether any earlier warnings are still in date;

- talk to any employees who may have evidence relating to the employee's alleged misuse of the employer's communications systems in order to gain more detailed information;

- endeavour to persuade any employees who may have been witness to the employee's alleged misconduct, or who may have knowledge of it, to give a written statement to that effect;

- assess objectively whether the employee's conduct appears to have been in breach of a company policy or rule;

- adopt an objective and balanced approach to the information gained as a result of the investigation;

- avoid allowing personal views about the employee generally to influence the overall assessment of the conduct under review.

Methods of investigation [11.15]

One difficulty that may arise for an employee who wishes to investigate an employee's alleged misuse of email or internet facilities is the extent to which the employer's policies allow them to monitor the employee's use of their communications systems.

Under the *Telecommunications (Lawful Business Practice) (Interception of Communications) Regulations 2000 (SI 2000 No 2699)*, it is legitimate for an employer to intercept employee's emails in certain defined circumstances provided that the purpose of the interception is relevant to the business and all reasonable steps have been taken to inform employees in advance that such interception may take place. One of the specific permitted purposes for interception is to investigate or detect unauthorised use of the employer's communications systems. It follows that an employer would be able, as part of a disciplinary investigation, to lawfully review and read the employee's emails or monitor which internet sites they have accessed through their workplace computer provided that:

- a policy is in place allowing monitoring to be carried out;

- employees have been properly informed about monitoring;

- the purpose of the monitoring is one of those defined as permissible in the Regulations.

If the above conditions are not all met, the employer's only recourse would be to obtain the employee's express permission before carrying out such investigations. Otherwise, reading an employee's emails or monitoring their internet activities may be unlawful because such action could be in breach of the *RIP Act 2000* (see **CHAPTER 6**) and/or the employee's right to privacy of correspondence under *Article 8* of the *Human Rights Act 1998* (see **CHAPTER 7**).

Fairness and reasonableness [11.16]

There is, however, one possible complication. If the employee is dismissed following an investigation into alleged misconduct, the employer may later have to demonstrate to an employment tribunal that the dismissal was carried out fairly and reasonably. Even though the *Telecommunications (Lawful Business Practice) (Interception of Communications) Regulations 2000 (SI 2000 No 2699)* make interception of employees' communications for the purpose of investigating unauthorised use of the employer's communications systems *lawful* (provided the employee has been informed about the possibility of such interception), this does not necessarily make such interception *fair and reasonable* in relation to the dismissal process. To be fair and reasonable, the employee's express consent should be obtained before any emails are intercepted or read. Monitoring without consent as a means of gathering evidence against the employee would create a serious risk that an employment tribunal could find any subsequent dismissal unfair on procedural grounds on the basis that such a course of action was unreasonable.

A further conundrum is that, if an employer obtains information about an employee's email and internet activities in a way that is contrary to the right to respect to privacy contained in the *Human Rights Act 1998*, and subsequently dismisses the employee on the basis of the findings of such investigations, an employment tribunal assessing a complaint of unfair dismissal may conclude that, because the employer breached one of the employee's fundamental rights as defined in the *Human Rights Act*, the procedure leading to dismissal was flawed and unreasonable. Unreasonableness of procedure will generally render a dismissal unfair (see **11.45** below).

Disciplinary Interviewing – How to Get it Right [11.17]

Whenever an employee is thought to have breached any of their employer's rules, however fundamentally, it is essential that they should be interviewed and afforded a proper opportunity to present their version of events and any mitigating factors. A fair hearing is an essential ingredient of fair procedure. Furthermore, a dismissal without a fair hearing having first taken place will inevitably mean that the employee will be able succeed in a claim for unfair dismissal at an employment tribunal (see **11.45** below).

Disciplinary interviewing should therefore not be carried out in haste, nor in the heat of the moment. It should be arranged in advance, with a reasonable period of notice being given to the employee (there is no minimum or maximum period of notice in law, but the notice should in any event be long enough for the employee to prepare thoroughly). The employee should be informed (in advance of the interview) of the nature of the allegations against them, and the fact that the interview is to be held under the banner of the organisation's disciplinary procedure. Future changes to the *Employment Rights Act 1996* (expected to be implemented in October 2004) will mean that it will be a legal requirement for employers to set out employees' alleged misconduct in writing prior to holding a disciplinary interview to discuss the matter.

The right for the employee to be accompanied [11.18]

All workers (including those engaged indirectly by the organisation) have a statutory entitlement, under the *Employment Relations Act 1999*, to be accompanied at any formal disciplinary (or grievance) interview that they are required or invited to attend. The ACAS Code of Practice on Disciplinary and Grievance Procedures confirms that the statutory right to be accompanied applies whenever the worker makes a reasonable request to be accompanied, and whenever the disciplinary interview is one that could result in a formal warning.

This raises the tricky question of where the borderline lies between informal warnings and formal warnings, an issue that was addressed by the EAT in the two conjoined cases of *London Underground Ltd v Ferenc-Batchelor and Harding v London Underground Ltd [2002] 1039/01 and 0045/02*, in which the employees each claimed that they had been denied the right to be accompanied at a formal disciplinary hearing. The employer argued that, since the warnings in both cases were informal oral warnings, the statutory right to be accompanied at the preceding disciplinary hearing did not kick in.

In the *Ferenc-Batchelor* case, the employee had attended a disciplinary hearing that was designated informal by the employer. Following the hearing, he received an oral warning which was subsequently confirmed in writing and placed on file. The warning specified a time limit during which it would remain live on the employee's file, and that it could be taken into account in the event of further disciplinary proceedings against the employee. The EAT ruled that these features meant that the disciplinary action was formal in nature and the employee should thus have been granted the right to be accompanied at the disciplinary hearing.

The circumstances were similar in the Harding case. The warning was headed 'informal oral warning' but had been confirmed in writing and placed on the employee's file for a defined period of time. The EAT took the view that this was the first stage in a formal disciplinary process and consequently formed part of that process. The employee had therefore been unlawfully denied the statutory right to be accompanied.

The EAT went on to give some helpful guidance as to the factors that will help to determine the question of whether a disciplinary interview constitutes a formal hearing. Relevant factors will include (but not be limited to) the form and substance of what takes place at the hearing, the process of decision-making that the hearing entails and the consequences or possible consequences of the hearing.

Choice of companion [11.19]

Specifically, employees and other workers have the right under s.10 of the *Employment Relations Act 1999* to bring a 'companion' to a disciplinary interview. The worker is entitled to choose their own companion provided the person selected is either a fellow worker or a trade union official. A trade union official for this purpose need not belong to a union recognised by the employer.

Employees have no statutory right to select a companion who is not a fellow-worker or trade union official, unless their contract of employment or the disciplinary procedure itself states otherwise. Thus an employee's request to bring a solicitor or relative to the interview can legitimately be refused. The matter is one between the employer and the employee, and there is no automatic right to bring an outsider (other than a trade union official) into what is essentially an internal matter.

The role of the companion [11.20]

At the interview itself, the manager conducting it must allow the companion to present the employee's case (if the employee so wishes), although the manager is entitled to require the employee (and not the companion) to answer any questions put. Additionally, however, the employee has the right to confer with the companion during the hearing.

No obligation to act as a companion [11.21]

There is no obligation on any individual to agree to act as someone else's companion at a disciplinary interview. It is up to the employee to persuade their preferred companion to agree to accompany them to the interview, and to inform the employer accordingly. It is worth noting also that if the chosen companion is a fellow employee, the employer must grant the accompanying employee paid time off work for this purpose.

Refusal to allow an employee to bring a companion to a disciplinary interview [11.22]

Refusal to agree to allow an employee to bring a companion to a disciplinary interview can lead to a complaint to tribunal at which the employee whose rights have been breached could be awarded up to two weeks pay (subject to the statutory ceiling on a week's pay, set by the Government from time to time. At the time of writing, this is £270 per week).

Guidelines for managers [11.23]

At the time a disciplinary interview is being arranged therefore, the manager who is to conduct it should:

- consider whether the interview is one that could result in a formal warning being issued to the employee (although no final decision on whether to issue a warning should be taken until after the interview);

- if the interview could lead to a formal warning, inform the employee of their statutory right to be accompanied and that their choice may be a fellow worker or trade union official;

- make sure the chosen companion is granted time off work for the purpose of the disciplinary interview, and not penalised in any way for acting on behalf of the employee.

If the purpose of an interview is investigatory, or if the interview is no more than an informal discussion or counselling session, then there is technically no right for the employee to bring a companion. Indeed, the ACAS Code of

Practice of Disciplinary and Grievance Procedures recommends that it is not generally good practice for a worker to be accompanied at such sessions and that informal matters are best settled directly between the employee and their manager. The Code also states however, that if it becomes clear during an informal or investigatory interview that formal disciplinary action may be needed, then the interview should be terminated and a formal hearing convened so that the worker can be granted their right to be accompanied.

Conducting the interview [11.24]

The key purpose of any disciplinary interview is to establish the facts and review objectively whether the employee's conduct is sufficient to merit disciplinary action, and if so what level of action. The manager conducting the interview should approach the matter with an open mind, and be willing to listen actively to the employee's version of events, the reasons given for their behaviour and any mitigating factors. The rules of natural justice dictate that the employee should be given a full and fair hearing, no matter how deficient or deleterious their behaviour appears to have been.

The manager's role should therefore be to:

- inform the employee of the case against them, and any evidence, for example statements made by other employees, or information gleaned from monitoring;

- seek to establish all the facts through open questioning of the employee, and active listening;

- review objectively whether the employee's conduct is genuinely unacceptable as measured against company standards, policy statements and/or the company's rules;

- take into account any mitigating factors;

- refrain from adopting a blaming or critical attitude;

- be prepared to adjourn in order to carry out further investigation if new information comes to light;

- inform the employee clearly (if the matter is one that is likely to lead to a warning, rather than to dismissal) that if there is any further instance of misuse of email or the internet, then further formal disciplinary action will be taken and the employee could be dismissed eventually;

- make an objective and impartial decision on whether or not disciplinary action is appropriate, and if so what type or level of action.

The decision as to what disciplinary action, if any, to take against an employee who has misused email or internet facilities should not be made until after the disciplinary interview has been completed. The principles of natural justice demand that the interview should be conducted without bias. If there is the smallest piece of evidence that the manager conducting the interview had decided in advance that the employee was to be dismissed, this could be fatal to the employer's case in consequent unfair dismissal proceedings. It is therefore advisable, once the interview has been completed, to adjourn, even for a short time, to review all the facts and the employee's case before making a decision. This approach is more likely to be fair, and be seen to be fair.

Consistency [11.26]

It is important to apply disciplinary rules and procedures consistently, whilst at the same time taking into account any mitigating factors relevant to the individual case. This does not mean, however, that the manager should automatically apply a particular disciplinary penalty to an employee who is found to have misused email or the internet. Each case should be carefully considered on its own merits before a decision is reached. It is not advisable to dismiss an employee for misuse of email or the internet only for the purpose of setting an example to others, especially if the misdemeanour in question has occurred very soon after the introduction of a new policy or rules. This may be viewed as unreasonably harsh by a tribunal.

On the other hand treating two (or more) employees who have committed the same offence differently as regards disciplinary sanctions could also create problems. If the outcome of disciplinary interviewing is that different disciplinary sanctions are applied to two employees, then there should be clear reasons justifying the different treatment. These reasons should be recorded. There may be a specific factor justifying treating a particular employee leniently, for example a young employee whose behaviour in misusing email was heavily influenced by another employee. Alternatively, although two employees may have committed the same type of offence, one individual may have had previous warnings, whilst for the other, it may be a first offence.

At the other extreme, a decision not to dismiss an employee who had committed a serious breach of the organisation's email or internet policy could be viewed as unfair to others. Such leniency may also inadvertently send out the wrong message, i.e. irrespective of any policies or rules on the matter, such conduct is in reality condoned by the organisation. Employees could quite reasonably form the view that, because a particular employee 'got away with it', it must be acceptable for them to ignore or 'bend' the rules in the future.

This does not mean that the manager tasked with judging an employee's misconduct should evade taking the responsibility for making what could be a difficult decision, but rather than all factors should be carefully weighed up first.

Records of interviews [11.27]

It is very important to maintain a confidential record of the key points that were discussed at the disciplinary interview, and of course, a record of the outcome, for example a verbal warning. Without such documentary evidence, an employer will find it very difficult to defend a subsequent claim for unfair dismissal at an employment tribunal. Although the manager dealing with the disciplinary matter should be seeking primarily to encourage the employee to improve their behaviour, or refrain from inappropriate activities in the future, if this aim is not achieved and the employee is later dismissed, lack of documentary evidence could seriously damage the employer's version of events at tribunal.

There is no length of time laid down in law for which employers should retain records of disciplinary action taken against employees. However, under the *Data Protection Act 1998*, employers are required not to keep data for longer than is necessary in relation to its stated purpose. Retaining copies of disciplinary warnings indefinitely would not therefore be appropriate. Furthermore, the Data Protection Code of Practice on Employment Records, published in 2003, recommends that employers should have clear procedures on what happens to disciplinary warnings once they expire. It should be explicitly stated, for example, whether a spent warning will be removed or deleted from the employee's file, or whether the warning will remain on the file but no longer be considered 'live', i.e. it will not be taken into account in the event of further misconduct. The Code recommends that a diary system should be set up to alert management when a disciplinary warning is about to expire, so that the appropriate action can be taken.

Warnings [11.28]

Contrary to popular myth, there is no legal obligation on employers to give a minimum number of warnings to an employee prior to dismissal. The ACAS Code of Practice on Disciplinary and Grievance Procedures recommends a four-stage procedure, and this would normally be appropriate in the event that an employee repeatedly misused their employer's email and internet facilities in relatively minor ways. Thus a series of warnings can be given, beginning with a verbal warning, followed by a written warning and finishing with a final written warning. If there is another instance of similar misconduct whilst the final written warning is still in date, then the employee can be dismissed, or alternatively some other sanction imposed such as demotion, loss of increment or transfer (provided these sanctions are allowed for in the employee's contract or in the disciplinary procedure itself).

Although this approach is to be recommended in a general sense, it is possible to enter the disciplinary procedure at any stage, depending on the seriousness of the employee's misconduct. The important point is that the nature of the penalty (i.e. the stage of the procedure which is implemented) should be proportionate to the seriousness of the employee's misconduct. If, for example, an employee with no previous disciplinary record is found to have been spending an excessive amount of time surfing the net for personal purposes, it may be appropriate to enter the disciplinary procedure at the written warning, or even the final written warning stage, depending on the existence of any policy or rules on this subject, and on an objective assessment of the degree of seriousness of the individual's misconduct following an interview.

Managers should take care, when dealing with cases of email or internet misuse, not to over-react and impose over-severe sanctions where misconduct has been relatively minor, or where there are mitigating circumstances. The case of *Stanley Cold (Wainfleet) Ltd v Sheridan [2003] IRLR 52* demonstrates this point. In this case, the EAT held that a final written warning issued to an employee with five years of unblemished service for a first offence that was relatively minor represented a breach of trust and confidence, and hence a fundamental breach of contract. The employee had taken an extra hour off work at lunchtime following a heated argument with a colleague which had upset her. The EAT held that the penalty of a written warning in these circumstances was disproportionate and unjustified. The employee, who subsequently resigned, succeeded in her claim for constructive dismissal.

The content of a written warning [11.29]

Where the outcome of disciplinary proceedings is that the employee is given a written warning, the warning should:

- state the nature and extent of the employee's misconduct;

- re-state any rules and indicate clearly that these rules should not be broken in the future;

- stipulate the length of time the warning will remain 'active' on the employee's file in accordance with the provisions laid down in the organisation's disciplinary procedure and what will happen to the warning once it expires;

- state that if there is any further instance of misconduct of a similar kind, or any other type of misconduct, within a stated time-frame further disciplinary action will be taken. It is particularly important to state this unambiguously if the warning given is a final written warning in which case the employee should be told unequivocally that any further instance of misconduct will lead to dismissal;

- inform the employee that they may appeal against the warning, how they should appeal and specify the timescale within which they may appeal.

The shelf-life of a warning [11.30]

There is no legal provision governing the length of time a disciplinary warning should remain active. It is therefore up to each employer to decide, as part of their disciplinary procedure, what time periods should be applied. Typically, a verbal warning may remain active on an employee's file for six months, a written warning for 12 months and a final written warning for 18 or 24 months. There time periods are guidelines, however, and not mandatory. Once a warning has 'expired', then the employer should no longer have regard to it in determining what disciplinary action to take against an employee in the event of further misconduct. This does not necessarily mean that the warning must be destroyed (unless the disciplinary procedure states that this will happen). The employer should, however, have a clear and consistent procedure in relation to what happens to disciplinary warnings that have expired (see also **11.26** above) and should not retain them indefinitely unless there is a specific reason to do so.

Example of a written warning for email misuse [11.31]

The following could be adapted to form the basis of a written warning to an employee following on from a disciplinary interview. Items in square brackets indicate alternative clauses or information to be inserted.

Dear ....

The purpose of this letter is to inform you of the outcome of the disciplinary interview held on [date].

Having considered all the evidence, I have decided to issue you with a first written warning for misconduct. This is because [you have admitted that you breached the company's rules on email/internet usage] [I have reached the conclusion that your conduct constitutes a clear breach of the company's policy and rules governing email and internet access] [you have used email and/or the internet for personal purposes contrary to the company's rules] [you have been found to have been viewing and/or downloading inappropriate non work-related material from the internet].

This warning will be placed in your personnel file. However, it will be disregarded (but retained on file for a reasonable period thereafter) [destroyed] after a period of [12 / 18] months, provided that your conduct is satisfactory throughout that period.

If there is any repetition of this type of misconduct, if you commit any further breach of the company's policy or rules on email use and internet access, or if there should be an occurrence of any other type of misconduct during the period defined above, you will be subject to further formal disciplinary action.

If you wish to appeal against this decision, you should do so within [three / five] working days. Your appeal should be made in writing to [name].

Please sign and return the enclosed copy of this letter to acknowledge receipt of this warning.

Yours sincerely

[Name of manager]

For and on behalf of [company name]

I acknowledge receipt of this warning.

I *do/do not wish to appeal against this decision.

(*please delete as applicable)

Signed:

Date:

Appeals [11.32]

It is standard practice for disciplinary procedures to include a right for employees to appeal against any formal disciplinary sanction, including dismissal. The ACAS Code of Practice on Disciplinary and Grievance Procedures suggests that the opportunity to appeal against a disciplinary decision is essential to natural justice, and recommends that appeals should be dealt with as promptly as possible. New statutory provisions governing disciplinary and dismissal procedures, set to be implemented in October 2004, will make it compulsory for employers to offer the right of appeal to all employees who have been subject to formal disciplinary action or dismissal.

It is important that any appeal against a disciplinary sanction is not heard by a person who was involved in the original disciplinary proceedings, and especially not by the person who took the decision to discipline (or dismiss) the employee. The employee has the right have the appeal heard by someone whose view of events is likely to be objective and unbiased. Normally the person hearing an appeal would be in a more senior position than the person who took the original disciplinary decision.

This can present a problem for small organisations, and the ACAS Code of Practice suggests that if it is not possible to identify someone who was not involved in the earlier proceedings, then the person dealing with the appeal should act as impartially as possible. The main points for the employer are to take all reasonable steps to identify someone to lead the appeal who has had minimum involvement in the case and, at the very least, make sure that the appeal is conducted fairly and without bias so that the principles of natural justice can be seen to be upheld.

Although access to an internal appeal is not at present a statutory requirement, the *Employment Rights (Dispute Resolution) Act 1998, s 13* decrees that if a dismissed employee is refused a right of appeal, and if they subsequently succeed in a claim for unfair dismissal at tribunal, the tribunal can order the employer to pay additional compensation of up to two weeks' pay. Conversely, an employee's compensation can be similarly reduced if they were notified in writing that they had the right to appeal, but failed to make use of the appeal facility.

Gross Misconduct and Summary Dismissal [11.33]

Gross misconduct is a single very serious act of misconduct which is sufficient on its own to justify the employee's immediate dismissal (known as 'summary dismissal' – see **11.33** below). This is because the employee's misconduct is viewed as sufficient to destroy the trust and confidence that is implied into every employment relationship, making it impossible for the employer to entertain the thought of the person's employment continuing. It should be noted, however, that an immediate dismissal does not mean an over-hasty or on-the-spot dismissal. It is vital, as in all misconduct dismissals, to follow proper disciplinary procedures as detailed earlier in this chapter. This must include a proper investigation into the employee's behaviour and a proper opportunity for the employee to respond to the case against them at a properly convened interview.

Summary dismissal [11.34]

Dismissal on account of gross misconduct is know as summary dismissal, which means dismissal without notice, or pay in lieu of notice. It is worth noting that gross misconduct on the part of the employee is the only circumstance that can justify dismissal without notice. Summary dismissal thus brings employment to an end on the date the decision to dismiss is communicated to the employee, and all pay and benefits under the contract terminate that day. The letter to the employee informing them of the employer's decision to dismiss should, of course, make this clear.

It is irrelevant in a case of gross misconduct whether or not the employee has received previous warnings for misconduct or whether any warnings are still in date, because the underpinning notion is that the employee's behaviour is serious enough *on its own* to justify dismissal.

The type of conduct that can be regarded as gross misconduct [11.35]

Whilst there is no law that sets down what type of misconduct is to be regarded as gross misconduct, certain types of misconduct would in most instances be viewed as gross misconduct, such as (for example) serious fraud or stealing from the employer. It is strongly advisable, however, for every employer to specify in writing the types of misconduct that will lead to summary dismissal, otherwise a dismissed employee could argue later that they were unaware that their conduct could lead to dismissal and that their dismissal was thus unfair on account of the employer's failure to act reasonably.

Where, however, an employee's conduct at work involved serious dishonesty or deliberate and flagrant breach of company rules, this would normally justify summary dismissal as such conduct would, arguably, constitute a fundamental breach of the duty of trust and confidence. Similarly, misconduct which involved breaking the law, or the misuse of confidential information, whether held manually or stored on a computer, would normally justify summary dismissal, since such conduct could have serious repercussions for the employer's business and could be in breach of the *Data Protection Act 1998* and other legislation.

In devising a list of the types of behaviour that are to be viewed as gross misconduct, it is advisable for the employer to include a clause stating that the list of examples is illustrative rather than exhaustive. It may also be useful to include a statement that the organisation has the right to exercise discretion in its approach to employees' misuse of email and the internet depending on all the circumstances of the particular case. A reasonable degree of flexibility and discretion, provided the discretion is applied fairly (and not irrationally or perversely) will allow the employer to take into account the individual circumstances of each case.

Suggested list of offences that could be regarded as gross misconduct [11.36]

The list of offences relating to email and internet misuse that would constitute gross misconduct could include some or all of the following:

- deliberate or serious abuse of the company's email and internet policy;

- unauthorised use of, or access to, company computers;

- obtaining or using another employee's password, or disclosing one's own password to another person without management authority;

- unauthorised disclosure of confidential information by email;

- harassment or bullying of another employee by email;

- excessive use of email and the internet for personal or private purposes; *or alternatively*, any use of email and the internet for personal or private purposes without prior permission from management;

- unauthorised access to the internet through a company computer or inappropriate use of internet access;

- viewing pornography on the internet, whether or not any material is downloaded;

- using material downloaded from the internet in a way that could constitute a breach of copyright;

- playing computer games during working time.

The above list is illustrative and not exhaustive. Whether a particular offence will justify summary dismissal will depend on all the circumstances. One key factor will be whether it can be shown that the employee deliberately breached the employer's rules, as opposed to making a mistake, for example, accessing an internet site by accident.

Warning or dismissal? [11.37]

In a case where an employee has simply failed to comply with the company's email policy, normally a warning would be appropriate rather than summary dismissal. If, however, the employee continues to breach the employer's policy on email and internet usage despite having received warnings, then dismissal could be the eventual outcome.

Viewing such conduct as dishonesty could lead to a dismissal being unfair, as the following case demonstrates:

Case Study [11.38]

John Lewis plc v Coyne [2001] IRLR 139

Facts

Ms Coyne had worked as a clerk in one of the John Lewis stores for over 13 years and had a clean disciplinary record. The company had introduced a policy prohibiting employees from using workplace telephones for personal calls and it had been made clear that any breaches of this would be viewed very seriously and might lead to dismissal. Following a complaint, an investigation was carried out by the general manager into some of the calls made from Ms Coyne's telephone. These included regular calls made to a colleague about work matters, short calls made to her husband following a miscarriage and calls to a letting agency in relation to a rented house with which she was experiencing some difficulties. Work-related calls had also been made to Ms Coyne on her mobile by some of her colleagues using the phone on her desk. Following the investigation, it was revealed that in the previous year, a total of 111 calls had been made to Ms Coyne's mobile telephone, to her colleague and to the letting agency. The majority of the calls were to her colleague, and the estimated total cost was £37.76.

Having established these facts, the general manager made the assumption that Ms Coyne's conduct amounted to stealing, and following a brief interview carried out without any warning, she was suspended. She was later summoned to a further meeting at which she was summarily dismissed in accordance with the general manager's view that even one unauthorised call was an act of dishonesty. She claimed unfair dismissal at an employment tribunal.

Findings

The tribunal and the EAT upheld the employee's claim ruling that the dismissal had been unfair. Although it was quite proper that the employee should be subjected to disciplinary action for breaching the company's policy on use of the telephone system, it was not reasonable to treat the matter automatically as one of dishonesty justifying summary dismissal. It was not obvious by ordinary standards that the conduct in question amounted to dishonesty and there was no evidence to suggest that the employee would have realised that her personal use of the telephone system would be so regarded. The company had not investigated the employee's conduct sufficiently in order to establish whether it in fact amounted to dishonesty and had acted unfairly in treating the conduct as tantamount to stealing. Ms Coyne had not had a fair hearing and the decision to dismiss her was not fair or reasonable in all the circumstances.

Implications

A decision to dismiss an employee for breach of a company policy governing use of company telephones (or use of email or the internet) should be taken according to all the circumstances of the case, and not as an automatic response to the policy. The fairness of a such a dismissal will depend not only on the number of calls made, but also, for example, on the purpose of the calls, whether the calls were made on account of a personal crisis and whether the employee's conduct was persistent. The circumstances of this case could be applied equally to cases of misuse of email or the internet.

Suspension from work pending investigation into the employee's misconduct [11.39]

If, following the exposure of possible misconduct on the part of an employee, there are grounds to believe that the employee's behaviour (if proven) would constitute gross misconduct, it is often advisable to suspend the employee from work until a full investigation can be carried out. Such suspension should only be for as long as is required to investigate the employee's conduct.

The company's disciplinary procedure should expressly authorise suspension from work in these circumstances, otherwise suspension may be viewed as a breach of contract. For the same reason, suspension from work pending investigation into an employee's conduct should be on full pay. A further problem that could arise if an employee is suspended without pay, or on reduced pay, could be the perception that the manager responsible for suspending the employee had already formed the view that the employee was guilty. This in turn could give an employee who is later dismissed grounds to assert at an employment tribunal that the manager was biased, that their conduct had been pre-judged and that their treatment had thus been unfair.

The ACAS Code of Practice on Disciplinary and Grievance Procedures recommends that:

- suspension should only be imposed after careful consideration;
- suspension should not be unnecessarily protracted;
- it should be made clear to an employee who is suspended that the suspension is not considered a disciplinary action.

Model Disciplinary Procedure [11.40]

The following is an example of a disciplinary procedure.

1. *Purpose and scope*

The aim of this procedure is to allow management to deal fairly and consistently with employees whose individual conduct, attendance or job performance falls below acceptable standards, and to encourage and support improvement. This procedure sets out the key principles and stages of the disciplinary process. A key aim of the procedure is to achieve consistent and fair treatment for all the organisation's workers.

2. Principles

A thorough investigation will be carried out into any unsatisfactory conduct, attendance or performance prior to any disciplinary action being taken. If time is needed to complete relevant investigations, the employee under investigation may be suspended on full pay for a period of time (normally up to three working days) to allow completion of the investigation. Such suspension is not in itself a disciplinary action.

At every stage of the procedure, employees will have the right to be informed in writing of the case against them, including any evidence provided by witnesses. They will also be afforded the opportunity to state their case at an interview before any decision is reached.

Employees have the statutory right to be accompanied at any formal disciplinary interview, if they wish, by a companion who may be a fellow worker or trade union official. Where the employee does not wish to be accompanied, this fact will be recorded.

No employee will be dismissed for a first breach of discipline except in circumstances where the employee's conduct amounts to gross misconduct. Gross misconduct is covered below.

The company reserves the right to invoke any stage of the disciplinary procedure, depending on the nature and seriousness of the employee's misconduct, unsatisfactory attendance or unacceptable job performance. The level of any penalty imposed will be in line with the seriousness of the offence.

3. Responsibilities

It is the responsibility of management to keep their employees properly informed about the rules applicable in the organisation. Employees must for their part familiarise themselves with these documents and abide by them.

It is the responsibility of an employee's immediate line manager to bring any unacceptable conduct, attendance or job performance to the employee's attention as soon as any problems come to light. First instances of misconduct or unsatisfactory job performance that are minor in nature will be dealt with initially by means of an informal discussion with the line manager. Such informal discussions do not form part of the formal disciplinary procedure, although a record will be kept of them.

Depending on the perceived level of seriousness of the employee's conduct, attendance or performance, the matter may be dealt with by the line manager or by a more senior manager. This will be at the company's discretion. Where the outcome of disciplinary proceedings is dismissal, the final decision to dismiss must be approved by the managing director.

Before taking any disciplinary action, the employee's line manager must, by means of thorough investigation, be satisfied that an offence (including any breach of rules or a failure to meet defined standards) has actually been committed. In cases of conflicting or insufficient evidence, the employee should, where appropriate, be given the benefit of the doubt.

4. Stages of the Procedure

Stage one – Formal oral warning

If conduct or performance is unsatisfactory, the employee will normally be given a formal oral warning, which will be recorded. The employee will be informed of the reason for the warning and that it constitutes the first stage of the formal disciplinary procedure. A written summary of the warning will be prepared and a copy held on the employee's file. A copy will also be given to the employee.

Stage two – First written warning

If the offence is more serious, if there is no improvement in standards, or if a further offence occurs of the same or a different nature, a first written warning may be given. This will include the reason for the warning, any improvement in conduct, attendance or performance required, and a note that, if there is no improvement within an agreed time period, a final written warning will be given. The warning should be signed by the employee and the line manager, and a copy given to the employee. A copy will also be held on file.

Stage three – Final written warning

If a first offence is serious, if conduct or performance remains unsatisfactory, or if a further offence occurs, a final written warning may be given. Once again this will include the reason for the warning and any improvement in conduct, attendance or performance required. A final written warning will specify clearly that any recurrence of the offence or other serious misconduct within a defined time period will result in the employee's dismissal. The warning should be signed by the employee and the line manager, and a copy given to the employee. A copy will also be held on file.

Stage four – Dismissal

If there is no satisfactory improvement within the defined time-scale or if (further) serious misconduct, or unsatisfactory job performance occurs, the employee will be dismissed. A letter confirming the dismissal and the reason for it will be issued to the employee.

5. *Appeals*

An employee who believes that a formal disciplinary warning or dismissal has been imposed unfairly has the right to appeal. The appeal should be made in writing, stating the ground for the appeal, and should be sent within five working days of the disciplinary warning/dismissal to the manager who took the disciplinary action. The appeal will, wherever possible, be heard by someone who was not involved in the original disciplinary decision, and the case will be decided as impartially as possible. The appeal will normally be dealt with within five working days.

6. *Offences*

The following lists of offences are given as a guide and should not be taken to cover all the offences which will justify resort to disciplinary action.

Misconduct

The following are examples of the types of misconduct that may lead to a disciplinary warning. It is for the employee's line manager to decide the appropriate level of action (i.e. formal oral warning, first written warning or final written warning). The list below is illustrative and not exhaustive:

- repeated absenteeism or lateness without just cause;
- failure to follow the company's rules and procedure regarding sickness absence;
- minor breaches of safety rules;
- producing work which is unsatisfactory without good cause;
- refusing without good reason to carry out a lawful and reasonable instruction given by a superior, or negligence in carrying it out;
- insolence or abusive language incompatible with the continuance of good working relationships;
- carelessly or negligently causing minor damage to the property or equipment of the company;

- a first instance of inappropriate or excessive use of company telephones, email or internet access for personal or private purposes;

- minor breaches of the company's policy on email and internet use.

Gross misconduct

If, after investigation and an interview with the employee, it is confirmed that an employee has committed a serious offence amounting to gross misconduct, the normal consequence will be summary dismissal, i.e. dismissal with immediate effect without notice or pay in lieu of notice. This will be irrespective of whether the employee has received previous warnings, or whether these warnings are still in date. The list below is illustrative of the types of conduct the company regards as gross misconduct, and is not exhaustive:

- serious breach or deliberate non-compliance with statutory safety regulations or the company's in-house safety rules;

- carelessly or negligently causing serious damage to the property or equipment belonging to the Company or to a fellow worker;

- gross negligence in carrying out duties;

- flagrant and wilful disobedience of a lawful and reasonable instruction issued by a superior;

- deliberate rudeness, abusive language or offensive behaviour towards colleagues, customers or contractors;

- stealing money, tools or equipment from the company or from a colleague;

- any type of fraud, e.g. falsely claiming expenses, or falsification of records, whether intended to benefit the individual or any other person;

- any involvement whatsoever in the offer, payment, soliciting or taking of any form of bribe or inducement, whether monetary or otherwise;

- fighting during the course of employment, or physical assault on another employee or visitor to the company whether on company premises or elsewhere;

- harassment or bullying of another employee, or any type of intimidating behaviour, whether verbal, non-verbal, written or in electronic format;

- smoking in areas of the company where smoking is banned;

- being under the influence of alcohol or illegal drugs whilst at work;

- unauthorised use of confidential information, including the disclosure of confidential information or trade secrets to an unauthorised person;

- serious misuse or excessive use of company telephones, email or internet access for personal or private purposes;

- serious breaches of the company's policy on email and internet use;

- unauthorised use of, or access to, computers.

7. *The shelf-life of disciplinary warnings*

Completion of the following periods of satisfactory conduct, attendance or performance will in normal circumstances be sufficient to merit formal cancellation of the warning. This means that after the given time period, the warning will be disregarded when considering the penalty for any further instances of misconduct, poor attendance or unsatisfactory job performance. The shelf-life of a warning may, however, be extended at management discretion, in which case the employee will be informed of the period of the extension.

Formal oral warning – 6 months

First written warning – 12 months

Final written warning – 18 months

A period of satisfactory conduct will lead to cancellation of only one category of warning at a time. For example, after a period of 12 months' satisfactory conduct, a first written warning will normally lapse and revert to the status of an oral warning. Thereafter, a further 6 months' satisfactory conduct will be required to cancel the oral warning.

Spent warnings will normally be deleted or removed from the employee's file immediately after they have lapsed, unless management considers that there is a proper reason to retain the warning on file for a longer period. If this is the case, the employee will be notified.

Avoiding Unfair Dismissal [11.41]

Under the *Employment Rights Act 1996, s 94(1)*, all employees have the statutory right not to be unfairly dismissed by their employer. This right is subject to the employee having a minimum of one year's continuous service. Only employees (i.e. those engaged on a contract of employment) have this right, and not other workers. It is nevertheless important that employers deal fairly with anyone who breaches the rules on use of email and internet facilities so that morale and motivation will not be damaged. Equally importantly, if a fair approach is taken and despite this a complaint of unfair dismissal is nevertheless taken to tribunal, the employer will be in a strong position to defend the case.

Potentially fair reasons for dismissal [11.42]

At tribunal, the burden of proof is on the employer to establish the reason, or principal reason, for the employee's dismissal and that this reason falls within one of the potentially fair reasons defined in the *Employment Rights Act 1996, s 98(1)*. Four potentially fair reasons for dismissal are listed in s 98(2) of the Act although it is also possible under s 98(1)(b) for an employer to dismiss fairly if the reason for dismissal is 'some other substantial reason of a kind such as to justify the dismissal of an employee holding the position which the employee held'.

The four specific potentially fair reasons for dismissal listed in the Act are:

- capability or qualifications for the performance of the job the employee is employed to do. Capability is further defined in s.98(3) as having reference to 'skill, aptitude, health or any other physical or mental quality';

- conduct;

- redundancy;

- legal restriction, i.e. where it would be illegal for the employee to continue to work in their job.

Where dismissal is on account of an employee's misuse of email or internet facilities, the appropriate heading under which dismissal could be justifiable would be 'conduct', or, as an alternative, 'some other substantial reason'.

If an employer cannot demonstrate the reason for the employee's dismissal to the tribunal's satisfaction, the dismissal will be unfair. Equally if the employer cannot provide any evidence to substantiate the reason given for the employee's dismissal, or if the tribunal does not find the employer's evidence credible, the dismissal will be held to be unfair.

Proving the reason for dismissal [11.43]

There is, however, no need for the employer to prove the reason for an employee's dismissal beyond reasonable doubt. Employment tribunals operate according to the 'balance of probabilities' principle. Instead, if an employer can show that they genuinely believed on reasonable grounds that the dismissed employee was guilty of misconduct, that is enough to show the reason for dismissal provided the tribunal finds the evidence credible. However, the tribunal will take into account only factors known to the employer (or genuinely believed by the employer) at the time the decision to dismiss was taken in determining the reason for the dismissal. It is not therefore open to an employer to dismiss an employee and concoct a reason for the dismissal at a later date, nor to attempt to justify a dismissal for a reason that did not exist at the time.

For example, if an employee was dismissed on account of a whimsical allegation of minor misuse of the internet at work, the dismissal would be unfair. This would be the case even if the employer later discovered absolute proof that the employee was guilty of serious abuse of the internet, for example viewing and downloading pornographic material. Even though the employee's conduct, had it been known to the employer at the time of the dismissal, could have amounted to a fair reason for dismissal on the grounds of gross misconduct (depending on the employer's rules on internet use), the fact remains that at the time the decision to dismiss was taken, there were insufficient grounds for the employer to form a genuine belief that the employee's conduct justified dismissal.

Despite these provisions, facts uncovered after a dismissal may be relevant for the tribunal when they are assessing any compensation to be paid to the employee on account of an unfair dismissal.

Another point to note is that it is not open to an employer to substitute a different reason for an employee's dismissal on account of information coming to light at an internal appeal hearing.

The 'sufficiency test' [11.44]

Having established the reason for the dismissal and that it is one of the potentially fair reasons, the employment tribunal will go on to assess whether the employer acted reasonably in treating the reason as sufficient to justify the penalty of dismissal (the *Employment Rights Act 1996, s 98(4)*). Whether the reason for dismissal was sufficient will depend on all the circumstances of the particular case including the size and administrative resources of the employer's business, and of course the degree of severity of the employee's misconduct. *Section 98(4)* requires the tribunal to consider the 'equity and the substantial merits of the case.'

However, the employer does not have to prove that the reason did in fact justify the dismissal, since that is a matter the tribunal is entitled to judge for itself. This approach was succinctly summarised in the case of *Gilham & ors v Kent County Council (No 2) [1985] ICR 233:*

> 'The hurdle over which the employer has to jump at this stage of an enquiry into an unfair dismissal complaint is designed to deter

employers from dismissing employees for some trivial or unworthy reason. If he does so, the dismissal is deemed unfair without the need to look further into its merits. But if on the face of it the reason could justify the dismissal, then it passes as a substantial reason, and the enquiry moves on ....'

Procedural fairness [11.45]

In order to succeed in defending a case of unfair dismissal, the employer has to do more than just show the reason for dismissal and that it was substantial. There is also the overall test of reasonableness in procedure, which has evolved as a result of case law and which links in with the question of whether the employer has followed proper disciplinary (or other) procedures prior to taking the decision to dismiss the employee.

The principles of the Polkey decision [11.46]

The test of reasonableness in procedure was firmly established following the case of *Polkey v A E Dayton Services Ltd* [*1987*] *IRLR 503*. The House of Lords ruled in the *Polkey* case that any procedural shortfall in the manner of carrying out a dismissal would make the dismissal unfair, except in rare cases where it could be shown that it would have been utterly futile to follow procedures. The *Polkey* case concerned a driver who had been summarily dismissed on account of redundancy having been afforded no warning nor consultation, and without proper consideration having been given to whether he might be offered suitable alternative employment. Although *Polkey* was a case of dismissal by reason of redundancy, the principles of procedural fairness emanating from it are relevant to all dismissals.

The House of Lords provided guidance in the *Polkey* case as to the procedural steps which would be necessary for a dismissal to be fair:

- in cases of incapacity, the employee should be given fair warning and a reasonable chance to improve;

- in cases of misconduct, the matter should be fully and fairly investigated and the employee allowed a proper opportunity to explain their conduct;

- in cases of redundancy, any employees affected should be warned and consulted, selection should be on a fair basis and reasonable steps should be taken to re-deploy affected employees.

Guidelines from the Whitbread case [11.47]

In the case of *Whitbread & Co plc v Knowles* [*1988*] *IRLR 501* the following further criteria for procedural fairness were established by the EAT:

- whether the employer complied with the procedures that a reasonable employer would have applied in the circumstances;

- whether the employer carried out the essentials of a contractual appeal process (where one existed);

- whether the employer dealt fairly with the employee during the disciplinary interview and the appeal process.

The importance of following fair procedures [11.48]

Procedural fairness is therefore an integral part of the overall test of reasonableness in determining a case of unfair dismissal. It is far more common in practice for managers to go astray in the adherence to procedures that it is for them to dismiss an employee without a proper reason. This may not be of much comfort to employers, however, as a dismissal may be unfair regardless of the manager's motive or ignorance. The only consolation is that, in the event that a dismissal is unfair purely on procedural grounds (i.e. the reason for the dismissal was a proper and sufficient reason), the tribunal may at its discretion reduce any compensation otherwise payable to the employee on account of their contributory conduct.

Essentially therefore, if a dismissed employee can show that their employer did not follow proper procedures relating to their dismissal, then the outcome of the case, following the *Polkey* principle, will be that the tribunal will rule the dismissal unfair. Following 'proper procedures' in this context means broadly adhering to the stages and principles inherent in the employer's own disciplinary procedure, treating any breach of company rules according to the procedure and taking rational decisions based on facts.

The burden of proof in relation to reasonableness [11.49]

The burden of proof in relation to the responsibility for showing whether the employer acted reasonably is neutral as between the employer and the dismissed employee. The tribunal will consider all the evidence presented to them by both parties and their witnesses and make an objective assessment as to whether the employer acted reasonably in dismissing the employee for the reason given, and whether proper and fair procedures were followed.

The band of reasonable responses [11.50]

In hearing cases of unfair dismissal, tribunals work to what is known as the 'band of reasonable responses' test which was approved in the case of *Iceland Frozen Foods Ltd v Jones EAT [1982] IRLR 439*. Under this test, the tribunal is not entitled to substitute their own view of the circumstances of the case for that of the employer, but instead will assess whether the employer's actions were within the overall band of reasonableness. This ensures an objective approach is taken.

Guidelines from the Iceland case [11.51]

In the *Iceland* case, the EAT stated:

'We consider that the authorities establish that in law the correct approach for the ... tribunal to adopt in answering the [reasonableness] question ... is as follows:

(1) the starting point should always be the words of [*s 98(4)*] themselves;

(2) in applying the section [the] tribunal must consider the reasonableness of the employer's conduct, not simply whether they (the members of the ... tribunal) consider the dismissal to be fair;

(3) in judging the reasonableness of the employer's conduct [the] tribunal must not substitute its decision as to what was the right course to adopt for that of the employer;

(4) in many (though not all) cases there is a band of reasonable responses to the employee's conduct within which one employer might reasonably take one view, another quite reasonably take another;

(5) the function of the ... tribunal, as an industrial jury, is to determine whether in the particular circumstances of each case the decision to dismiss the employee fell within the band of reasonable responses which a reasonable employer might have adopted. If the dismissal falls within the band the dismissal is fair: if the dismissal falls outside the band it is unfair'.

Options open to the employer [11.52]

Clearly there may be occasions where the employee's conduct is such that it is open to the employer either to dismiss, or impose a lesser disciplinary sanction, for example a final written warning. It is inevitable that different employers will choose different courses of action. Thus an employer will not be penalised for deciding to dismiss an employee just because one or more of the tribunal members would have taken a different view if they had been in the manager's position. Instead the tribunal has to consider whether the employer's actions fell within the band (or range) of reasonable responses open to the employer.

Compensation [11.53]

Most successful cases of unfair dismissal result in compensation being paid to the applicant. Compensation in most cases comprises a basic award, which is calculated according to a fixed formula, and a compensatory award based on what the tribunal judges to be just and equitable under all the circumstances of the case.

The basic award [11.54]

The basic award is calculated according to the same formula as statutory redundancy pay and the maximum payable at the time of writing is £8,100. The amount payable is based on the individual's number of years' service, their age and their weekly earnings.

The basic award can be reduced (by a percentage or even to zero, where appropriate) in certain circumstances:

- if the dismissed employee refuses a reasonable offer of re-instatement;

- where, in the tribunal's judgement, the employee's conduct prior to dismissal caused or contributed to the dismissal. For example, if the reason for the employee's dismissal was that they had acted in serious breach of the employer's email and internet policy, and the dismissal was unfair purely on procedural grounds, a reduction could be made;

- where the employee has already been paid a sum of money by the employer that is in excess of the total of the maximum basic and compensatory awards;

- where the employee has already received a statutory redundancy payment from the employer.

The compensatory award [11.55]

The compensatory award, which is paid over and above the basic award, does not follow a fixed formula. Instead, the tribunal will assess what is just and equitable in all the circumstances of the case, taking into account the financial loss suffered by the dismissed employee. The maximum payable at the time of writing is £55,000.

Financial loss for the purpose of calculating the compensatory award may include:

- loss of wages and company benefits from the date of dismissal up to the date of the tribunal hearing;

- estimated future loss of earnings resulting from the dismissal;

- expenses incurred in seeking new employment;

- loss of statutory rights;

- loss of pension rights.

At present, however, it is not customary for the compensatory award to include an amount to cover injury to feelings.

The employment tribunal may reduce the amount of any compensatory award in any of the following circumstances:

- where the employee has received income from new employment;

- where the employee has been paid money by the ex-employer in lieu of notice, or as an ex-gratia payment;

- where the employee's actions caused or contributed to their dismissal;

- where the employee has failed or refused to seek new employment (i.e. failed to mitigate their loss).

Cases Where Misuse of Email or the Internet is Suspected but not Proven [11.56]

Managers may face particular difficulties if there are grounds to suspect that an employee has abused the employer's facilities for use of email and access to the internet, but no proof.

The Burchell case [11.57]

Guidelines for dealing with this conundrum emerged from the case of *British Home Stores Ltd v. Burchell [1980] ICR 303*, a case involving suspected dishonesty. In this case it was held that a dismissal for conduct which is suspected but not proven may be fair provided:

- the employer genuinely believed that the employee was guilty of misconduct or dishonesty;

- the employer had reasonable grounds for their belief;

- the employer had carried out as much investigation as was reasonably possible under the circumstances of the case.

Although the *Burchell* case concerned suspected dishonesty, the principles emerging from it have become well established as a means of judging the sufficiency of the reason for dismissal and procedural fairness in cases involving other types of misconduct where no clear proof of an employee's misconduct is available.

Thus the fairness of a dismissal for serious abuse of email or the internet is not dependent on the employer having absolute proof that the employee has committed the misdemeanour in question. However, the manager dealing with the employee must act reasonably, investigate as thoroughly as possible, and make a rational decision based on the facts insofar as they are known.

Burden of proof [11.58]

In the event that an employee is dismissed on suspicion of email or internet abuse, the burden of proof is on the employer is to show that they held a genuine belief that the employee's conduct was sufficient to merit dismissal based on all the circumstances of the case. The concept of reasonable and genuine belief is paramount to the case. It should be borne in mind also that the function of an employment tribunal is to assess whether the employer acted reasonably in taking a decision to dismiss the employee, and not to judge the employee's guilt or innocence.

Case Study [11.59]

The following case is an example of an employer who got it wrong:

Gale v. Parknotts Ltd [1996] Case No 72487/95

Facts

Mr Gale had received a warning about misuse of the company's computer facilities after a routine check showed he had loaded unauthorised material on to his computer's hard disk. The material, although unauthorised, was inoffensive. Following the installation of new software two years later, the employer began to experience serious problems with their computer network. It was subsequently established that the entire computer system was infected by a computer virus and was in imminent danger of collapse.

On further investigation, it appeared that the virus could be traced back to a computer game programme that Mr Gale had installed on his computer some time before he received the warning. The investigation also revealed that Mr Gale had CV's, job applications and lottery ticket permutations on his computer's hard drive. The employer thus decided that Mr Gale was the person responsible for the introduction of the virus, and that his conduct amounted to a serious breach of trust. He was dismissed.

Findings

An employment tribunal hearing Mr Gale's claim for unfair dismissal held that the suspicion that Mr Gale was responsible for the introduction of the computer virus was not backed up by any evidence. The employer had formed a view that was not based on reasonable grounds. Furthermore the tribunal held that the kind of information Mr Gale had put on to his computer was innocent and its installation could not therefore be regarded as a breach of trust justifying dismissal. The dismissal was held to be unfair.

Implications

Although it is possible to dismiss an employee fairly on account of a suspicion of serious misconduct, dismissal will be unfair unless the employer can show not only that they held a genuine belief that the employee was guilty of the misconduct in question, but also that their belief was backed up by evidence that amounts to reasonable grounds justifying the belief. Otherwise the dismissal is likely to be held to be unfair.

Accidental infringement of the policy or rules [11.60]

Another point to consider in dealing with cases of suspected internet abuse is that it is all too easy to access an internet site accidentally. Managers should be open-minded to the possibility that an employee who alleges that offensive material on an internet site was accessed by accident may be telling the truth. If, on the other hand, the evidence shows that the amount of time the employee has spent accessing the site in question was (for example) half an hour or more, the employee's version of events may be viewed with suspicion.

This leads to another possibility that, even though offensive material is found on an employee's computer, it may not be the employee who was responsible for putting it there. Depending on how carefully employees guard their passwords, and how common-place it is for employees to use their colleagues' computers for work-related purposes, it may be easy for one employee to use someone else's computer for illegitimate purposes, including sending private emails, surfing the net, playing computer games or viewing pornography on the internet. Managers should take all these factors into account when assessing an employee's suspected misconduct. Unless there is some tangible evidence to suggest that the employee has committed the offence of which they are suspected, the employee should not be dismissed. Although tribunals do not require proof of an employee's guilt for a dismissal to be fair, they do require the manager making the decision to have acted out of a genuine belief formed on reasonable grounds, and not just on a vague suspicion that is not backed up by any evidence at all.

Cases where more than one employee is suspected [11.61]

The picture becomes even more complicated if an employer has concrete evidence that abuse of email or internet facilities is taking place, but cannot identify which employees are guilty of the abuse.

In this situation, all the employees suspected of the abuse should be interviewed and the matter investigated as far as is reasonably practicable. If, at the conclusion of this process, it is not possible to identify the individual who was responsible for the abuse, then the employer has the option of dismissing **all** the employees who are reasonably suspected. Although this seems a draconian step to take, and such measures should of course not be taken lightly, it is possible for such dismissals to be fair in law. This follows principles established in the case of *Monie v Coral Racing [1981] ICR 109* in which two employees suspected of misconduct were dismissed fairly even though the employer could not prove which of the two was to blame.

Case Study [11.62]

These principles were also followed in the later case of *Parr v Whitbread plc [1990] IRLR 39*, described below:

Parr v Whitbread plc [1990] IRLR 39

Facts

Mr Parr was the manager of an off-licence in Brighton. One day he discovered that the safe had been robbed of money, cheques and credit card vouchers. He reported this to the police immediately. The police, on investigating, found that the alarm system had been switched off, doors were unlocked, and nothing was broken. They concluded therefore that the robbery had been an 'inside job' as there was no sign of a break-in.

To obtain access to the safe, it was necessary to have a door key, a safe key and a knowledge of the alarm code. Four people were under suspicion. These were two of Mr Parr's staff who were key-holders and who knew the alarm code, another employee who was with one of the key-holders the evening before the theft was discovered, and Mr Parr himself.

The company conducted a full investigation and concluded that all four employees had had the opportunity to commit the crime, but they were unable to determine which of the four was the guilty party. They therefore dismissed all four. Mr Parr brought a complaint of unfair dismissal to a tribunal.

Findings

The dismissal was held to be fair because the company had acted reasonably in believing, after a proper investigation, that it was an inside job, and that any one or more of the four employees could have committed the act. The employer had formed their beliefs on solid and sensible grounds at the time of the dismissals.

In the *Parr* case (above), the EAT set out useful criteria for tribunals (and hence useful guidelines for employers dealing with cases where more than one employee is suspected of serious misconduct). These were:

- whether the act of misconduct would justify dismissal if it had been committed by an individual;

- whether a reasonable investigation has been carried out with appropriate procedures being followed;

- whether, following the investigation, the employer believes that more than one employee could have committed the act of misconduct;

- whether the employer has acted reasonably in identifying the employee(s) who could have committed the act of misconduct;

- whether the employer has established that each employee in the group suspected was individually capable of carrying out the act;

- whether the employer was genuinely unable to identify the individual perpetrator.

Case study   [11.63]

Barry, Garry and Larry are three workers in the IT department of a medium-sized company. The manager of the department, Harry, has been carrying out routine monitoring of the internet sites accessed by his staff. In the course of this monitoring, Harry has discovered that a number of internet sites containing pornography have been accessed on several occasions from a particular computer in the department. Due to the nature of their work and the password restrictions in force, all three employees (but no others) have access to the internet through the computer in question. Harry has therefore been able to conclude that one or more of the three is guilty, but is not in a position to identify for certain which of them has been accessing the unacceptable sites.

The company has a policy in place that expressly states that the accessing of pornography or other similarly inappropriate material on the internet will be regarded as gross misconduct leading to summary dismissal. Harry's problem is that he has been unable to identify which of the three employees is guilty of the offence, or whether all three of them have been involved.

Would Harry be able lawfully to dismiss all three employees in these circumstances?

If, at the conclusion of a fair disciplinary procedure, it is possible to establish that one or more of a defined group of employees is guilty of an offence that amounts to gross misconduct, they may all be lawfully dismissed. This conclusion derives from the case of *Monie v Coral Racing [1981] ICR 109*, in which the Court of Appeal held that where two employees are suspected of misconduct and the employer, despite a thorough investigation, has been unable to establish which of them is responsible, it may be fair to dismiss both of them on reasonable suspicion. The principles established in the case of *Parr v Whitbread [1990] IRLR 39* (see **11.62** above) are also relevant.

If, as a result of his investigations, Harry can establish reasonable grounds on which to form the view that one of the three, for example Barry, was not guilty of the offence, it would then be possible to dismiss only Garry and Larry, provided Harry could show solid and sensible grounds for differentiating between them. Without concrete grounds justifying different treatment, however, there would be the risk that claims for unfair dismissal from Garry and Larry would succeed.

Conclusion [11.64]

Where an employee is found to have been misusing their employer's telephones, email facilities or internet access, the matter should be dealt with through the employer's disciplinary procedure. In some cases, misuse will justify dismissal, but unless the employee's conduct is of a very serious nature, a first offence would not normally justify such a severe penalty and would be more appropriately dealt with by means of a warning.

In light of the many complex issues surrounding employees' use of email and the internet at work, it is advisable for employers to develop and implement a special sub-section to form part of their disciplinary procedure setting out the kinds of activity that are not permitted and the disciplinary penalties that will be imposed following a breach of the rules.

Whether or not an employee's misuse of email and the internet constitutes misconduct (or gross misconduct) will depend on a number of factors and managers should review each case on its own merits rather than applying the disciplinary code rigidly.

When applying disciplinary procedures, managers should act fairly, and great care should be taken to follow correct procedures prior to dismissal, otherwise the dismissal may be found unfair by an employment tribunal.

Questions and Answers [11.65]

Question

How should a company's disciplinary procedure be used in relation to employee misconduct involving abuse of email or internet facilities?

Answer

Provided employers make it clear to employees what their rules are regarding use of email and the internet, and any limitations to be imposed on the extent and purpose for which they may use these facilities, the normal principles inherent in disciplinary procedures and fair dismissal can be applied.

Question

What is the purpose of having disciplinary rules governing employees' use of email and the internet?

Answer

The key purposes of any disciplinary rules should be to set down a framework defining and (where appropriate) limiting employees' conduct at work, and specifying the types of conduct that will be regarded as misconduct leading to disciplinary action. The consequences of different forms of misconduct should be stated, i.e. the disciplinary penalties that are likely to be imposed following a breach of the rules. In this way every employee understands fully what is, and is not, acceptable conduct in the workplace.

Question

What sorts of rules should employers introduce to govern employees' use of the employer's communications systems?

Answer

Every employer's business needs are different, and it is therefore up to each individual employer to devise and implement their own rules, which should be in writing. Rules governing the use of telephones, email and the internet should cover not only the purposes for which these facilities may be used, but also the extent to which they may be used. When devising disciplinary rules, it is particularly important to make sure that employees understand clearly what types of offences are regarded by the employer as sufficiently serious to constitute gross misconduct, leading potentially to summary dismissal.

Question

To what extent is it reasonable to regard an employee's negligent misuse of email as a disciplinary offence?

Answer

Negligent misuse of any facilities provided by the employer could legitimately be regarded as a disciplinary matter by the employer, provided the employee had been made aware (as a result of written policies and rules) that the type of conduct in question could amount to a disciplinary offence. However, much will depend on the seriousness of the employee's offence, the reasons or explanations put forward for their conduct and any other relevant factors. The employer should act objectively and refrain from jumping to a hasty conclusion that the employee has committed a disciplinary offence.

Question

If it appears obvious to a manager that an employee has blatantly breached the employer's policy on email and internet usage, why would it be necessary to carry out an investigation into the employee's conduct?

Answer

It is inherent in the notion of fairness that, before an employee is disciplined (or dismissed) for misconduct, a fair and thorough investigation should be carried out into the alleged misconduct. Unless and until all the facts relevant to the case are established, the manager will not be in a position to judge whether the employee's behaviour is enough to justify disciplinary action, and if so what level of action. Furthermore, if an employee is dismissed without a proper investigation having first been carried out, this will almost certainly have the effect of rendering the dismissal unfair.

Question

If there are grounds to believe that an employee has been seriously misusing the employer's email system, can the employer review and read the emails on the employee's computer as part of the investigation process?

Answer

The employer cannot insist on doing this unless the employee has been previously informed that interception of their email messages may take place (i.e. if a policy on monitoring has been properly implemented). Whilst it is permitted under the *Telecommunications (Lawful Business Practice) (Interception of Communications) Regulations 2000 (SI 2000 No 2699)* for an employer to intercept employee's emails if the purpose of so doing is to investigate or detect unauthorised use of the system, this is only permissible if employees have been informed about such interception in advance. If no such policy is in place, then the only course of action open to the employer would be to obtain the employee's express permission before reading their emails. Otherwise interception may be in breach of the *RIP Act 2000* and the employee's right to privacy of correspondence under *Article 8 of the Human Rights Act 1998*.

Question

If a manager wishes to interview an employee who is thought to be guilty of misconduct involving misuse of email or the internet, must the employee be given the option of bringing a representative to the interview?

Answer

Under the *Employment Relations Act 1999*, all workers have a statutory entitlement to be accompanied at any formal disciplinary interview that they are required or invited to attend, if the interview is one that could lead to a formal warning being issued to the employee. The employee is entitled to select their own companion who may be a fellow worker or a trade union official. If, however, the purpose of an interview is investigatory, or if the interview is no more than an informal discussion or counselling session, then there is technically no right for the employee to bring a companion.

Question

What is the main purpose of a disciplinary interview where an employee has clearly acted in breach of the employer's policy on email and internet use?

Answer

The key purpose of any disciplinary interview is to establish the facts and review objectively whether the employee's conduct is sufficient to merit disciplinary action, and if so what level of action. No decision on this can properly be made until after the interview is complete. It is important, no matter how serious the employee's conduct appears to have been, that the person should be given a full and fair hearing. A failure to do this will almost always render any subsequent dismissal unfair in law.

Question

How many warnings is it necessary to give an employee on account of internet abuse before they can be lawfully dismissed for misconduct?

Answer

There is no legal obligation on employers to give a minimum number of warnings to an employee prior to dismissal. The important point is that the nature of the penalty (i.e. the stage of the disciplinary procedure which is implemented) should be proportionate to the seriousness of the employee's misconduct. Clearly this will depend also on whether the employee has had previous warnings and whether these warnings are still in date. The employer should aim to be objective, reasonable and fair towards the employee and should make sure they follow the terms of their own disciplinary procedure.

Question

In the event that a decision to dismiss an employee on account of internet abuse has been taken by the most senior manager in the organisation, who can realistically hear an internal appeal if the employee chooses to appeal?

Answer

The main point is to take all reasonable steps to identify someone to lead the appeal who has had minimum involvement in the case. If there is no other manager in the organisation who was not involved in the disciplinary proceedings against the employee, then the person dealing with the appeal should act as impartially as possible. In this way the principles of natural justice can be seen to be upheld. Tribunals understand that this issue can be a problem, especially for small employers.

Question

Under what circumstances can an employer summarily dismiss an employee once it has been clearly established that they have committed a serious breach of the employer's rules on email and internet use, and what does this mean in practice?

Answer

Summary dismissal is only lawful if the employee's conduct amounts to gross misconduct as specified in the employer's disciplinary procedure. This means that the employee's conduct must be a fundamental breach of contract which then allows the employer to dismiss the employee without notice, or pay in lieu of notice. It is irrelevant in a case of gross misconduct whether or not the employee has received previous warnings for misconduct or whether any warnings are still in date, because the underpinning notion is that the employee's behaviour is serious enough *on its own* to justify dismissal.

Question

What sorts of email and internet activities can an employer regard as gross misconduct?

Answer

It is up to each employer to define their own rules and specify clearly what types of email and internet abuse would constitute gross misconduct leading to summary dismissal. These might include any conduct involving dishonesty or flagrant breach of the company's email/internet policy, or specific conduct such as viewing or downloading pornography from the internet, unauthorised disclosure of confidential information by email, unauthorised access to company computers, harassment or bullying of another employee by email, and excessive use of email and the internet for personal or private purposes. Any list of conduct regarded as gross misconduct should be stated to be illustrative rather than exhaustive.

Question

If an employee is dismissed following the discovery that they have been spending an inordinate amount of time surfing the net and using email for personal purposes, what are employer's chances of convincing an employment tribunal that the dismissal was fair?

Answer

Provided the employer can show that they genuinely believed on reasonable grounds that the dismissed employee was guilty of gross misconduct, that will be enough to show a proper reason for dismissal (provided the tribunal finds the employer's evidence credible). This will depend also on how the employee's conduct relates to any company policies and rules. Thereafter the fairness of an employee's dismissal will depend on whether or not the employer followed fair procedures in carrying out the dismissal. The key criteria for procedural fairness in cases of misconduct are a full and fair investigation and a proper opportunity for the employee to explain their conduct at a properly convened interview.

Question
What can a manager do if there are solid grounds to suspect that an employee has abused the employer's facilities for use of email and access to the internet, but no proof is available?

Answer
A dismissal for conduct which is suspected but not proven may be fair provided the employer genuinely believed that the employee was guilty of misconduct, this belief was based on reasonable grounds, and as much investigation as possible was carried out. The fairness of a dismissal for abuse of email or the internet is not dependent on the employer having absolute proof that the employee has committed the misdemeanour in question. In order to ensure fairness, however, the manager dealing with the employee must act reasonably, investigate as thoroughly as possible, and make a rational decision based on the facts insofar as they are known.

Index